THE COMPUTERLAND GUIDE TO

Local Area Networks

Edited by Alan Rinzler and David Gancher

CB
ComputerLand Books
Pleasanton, California

ComputerLand

Design by Marianne Ackerman; illustrations created in Adobe Illustrator 88 by Winston Sin; type, graphics, and page layout created with PageMaker 4.0 on an AppleTalk/TOPS LAN of Macintosh computers by Desktop World, Inc. Set in Adobe Utopia and Utopia Expert fonts.

ComputerLand Books, Pleasanton, California 94566

First published 1990.
Printed in the United States of America.

ISBN 0-9627212-0-4

Foreword

At ComputerLand, networking is a familiar subject. No other computer dealer in the world comes close to ComputerLand in networking excellence. ComputerLand installed about 13,000 networks in 1989—about twice as many as our nearest competitor. ComputerLand has installed more than 40,000 networks in all—about as many as our next four competitors combined.

Though networking is not new technology, it is currently in an explosive phase of growth. More and more companies are getting involved in networking—and with good reason. Local Area Networks (LANs) offer tremendous advantages in productivity and economics. First, networks allow companies to connect their personal computers, achieving new levels of computing power, information management, and cost savings. Now, networks are leading a computing revolution. Here's how *The Wall Street Journal* put it in a recent story: "As PCs get ever faster and remain astonishingly cheap, more and more companies are concluding that their mainframes are dinosaurs."

Some companies and computer users find networking a perplexing subject. And to tell the truth, networking is complex and technically challenging. But it need not be confusing! When we looked around, we found that there was a definite shortage of general information on LANs. It's easy to find tons of technical material, but it's almost impossible to find a readable introduction to LAN technology. Existing books seem to have all been written either for experts or for total novices.

So we decided to publish our own. The book you are holding is the first ever ComputerLand Book. It isn't a comprehensive encyclopedia; no single book could ever completely cover networks. This book is a guide to the most important issues involved in LANs.

Our readers are interested in results, so we've included a complete Buyer's Guide to LAN hardware and software. It was accurate as of June 14, 1990. But LAN technology changes rapidly, and prices and models may be different when you're reading this book. So call your local ComputerLand for the latest in up-to-date information.

If you're serious about computers, the chances are good that you'll be getting involved in the world of networks. We may be prejudiced, but we consider ourselves the optimal networking resource for any business. So, we hope that when you're ready to get involved, you'll call us.

David Gancher
ComputerLand Books

Contents

Introduction

THERE COMES A TIME in the natural evolution of every business when standalone PC's aren't enough. Smart managers everywhere—whether they're running a specific department in a larger company or in charge of the entire operation itself—have been quick to realize that with growth and success there is an increased need for communication between people, for trading data and special software, and for using the same super-storage disks, printers, telecommunications, and other peripherals.

That's why so many executives and managers approach us here at ComputerLand to find out more about Local Area Network systems. A LAN, they've heard, is a cost-effective way to improve efficiency and increase productivity. A LAN can save you money, they've been told, because instead of investing in several standalone mega-workstations with their own software libraries and laser printers, a LAN makes it possible to upgrade existing equipment into one interconnected network. This way everyone working on the same task can communicate, share information, and use the same specialized software and hardware.

ComputerLand is the leading source of personal computer networks in the United States. We've installed nearly three times as many networks as our nearest competitor, and have acquired valuable first-hand experience in designing all kinds of systems for thousands of different businesses. Consequently, we appreciate the need among executives, managers and other decision makers for information about LANs. What can it do for me? How does it work? What are the choices?

That's why we've published this ComputerLand Guide to Local Area Networks. We understand the need for a basic introduction to LANs—a book that provides both a straightforward, understandable approach, and the necessary detail to back up an intelligent decision.

When Local Area Networks first appeared on the market a few years ago, they were limited in function and tied users into a single-vendor solution. Luckily, however, tremendous energies have been focused on perfecting these systems and applications. Today, the art of Local Area Networks has reached a point where a great variety of reliable, hard-working and versatile LAN products and systems are run under defined industry standards. The pioneering phase of experimentation and working through obstacles is over and the Age of LAN has truly arrived.

We hope this book will help you understand how a LAN works and how it can be applied to your particular situation. The first thing to keep in mind is that there is no one simple LAN that you can go out and buy; no kit, no single piece of beautiful hardware that you can just plug in. All of today's manufacturers follow industry standards, but virtually every Local Area Network is a custom design based on many factors, which are special for you, including:

[1] The business you're in; the specific needs of your unique operation, whether it be mail-order catalogue fulfillment, magazine publishing, or a doctor's office.

[2] How your staff works together; where the people sit geographically and the way your space is designed; the flow of work and the daily process of your office.

[3] What equipment you have right now. Even if your equipment is old, there's probably no need to discard all of it. What's needed, rather, is an upgrade and a new way to hook it all together.

[4] How much money you want to spend. There are a lot of choices to make when you're putting in a LAN. And you don't need to do it all at once. You can start putting a system together that has the potential to grow bigger and better.

So before you rush out and start trying to put together a LAN, you do need to analyze your own operation and carefully examine the many choices there are to make. It can be confusing and you can make mistakes if you don't know what you're doing.

That's why you need this ComputerLand Guide to LANs. It's focused on the subject of Local Area Networks only and not on other multiuser technologies or on any larger mainframe system or Wide Area Network (WAN). It's written and designed to provide you with the basic information you need to:

[1] Take a good look at your own business needs and understand what a LAN can do for you.

[2] Understand the basic ingredients of a LAN: How it works; how one will fit into your particular operation; how to keep it going.

But let's take this one step at a time, from the top.

Getting Started

What is a Local Area Network and why should you buy one? How can a LAN work in your operation, and how do you choose the right one for your particular business?

Getting Started

What is a LAN?

A LAN IS A DATA COMMUNICATIONS network spanning a limited geographical area, a few miles at most. It allows users to share information and computer resources, including mass data storage, backup facilities, software, printers, plotters, and processors.

Typically, a LAN is made up of network interface cards (circuit boards) that fit inside the connected computers; cable to connect these computers; protocol software to move data from computer to computer; user interface software to connect user and network; and operating-system software to actually service users' needs for things like files and printers.

Through a LAN, an individual personal computer can link up with other workstations in a department. Additional types of networks broaden the possible interconnections between computers. Large-scale networks can connect computers located in different buildings or cities; they can even connect personal computers with mid-range computers and mainframes. Often, the Local Area Network serves as a "gateway" to larger computer networks that are interlinked to form a company-wide information system.

Why buy a LAN?

As personal computers appear on more and more desks, the prospect of linking them together in a Local Area Network becomes increasingly appealing. One of the major advantages is financial; it makes economic sense for computer users to share certain kinds of sophisticated and expensive equipment, such as laser printers, high-performance hard disks, tape backup devices, and mainframe computer linkages. Furthermore, software designed for LAN users costs less per user than individual copies.

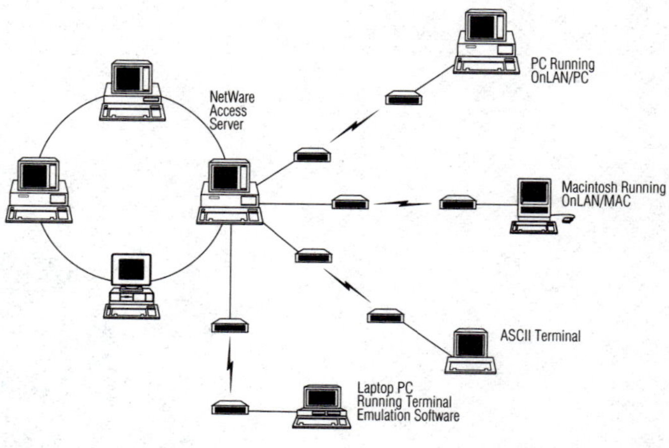

Connecting remote workstations to a LAN via modem

A second benefit of linking standalone computers with a LAN is that previously impossible jobs come within reach. A network gives multiple computer users concurrent access to data. This would, for example, allow a group of employees to fill customer orders, place orders with suppliers, and prepare invoices, all at the same time. Without a LAN, tasks that involve several steps or related operations can be unmanageably cumbersome. Either they must be done sequentially, one step after another, on a single computer, or else information must be transferred among computers via floppy diskettes. A network is a more efficient solution—and the only workable one, if the information is to be completely up to date.

Even where passing diskettes from user to user is possible, it is often less than ideal. One example: A newsletter editor who needs to track successive revisions of articles can attempt to enforce strict diskette labeling and file-naming conventions on all authors and editors. Inevitably, under the pressure of deadlines, something falls through the cracks. A systematic tracking mechanism would be painless and simple on a LAN, saving time and providing common access to such resources as customized spelling dictionaries and style sheets.

"With a LAN, previously impossible jobs come within reach."

LANs require a certain mindset, something different from traditional MIS (Management of Information Services) thinking. Once a LAN is installed, things like initiative, democracy, participation, communication, and independence take over. Hierarchy, dependence, regulation, and isolation are thrown out the window.

If you have the right mindset, the best reasons to buy a LAN are:

Shared Equipment

Networks can help your company save money. For example, LANs enable workgroups to share expensive peripheral equipment, such as high-performance hard disks, laser printers, fax servers, and tape backups with the flick of a switch.

Communication

A LAN connects the people in your company. Once connected, every possible form of discourse is possible, from electronic "yellow sticky notes" to formal legal briefs. People like to communicate. Messages and files can be exchanged electronically on the network quickly and easily, whether the other users are at the next desk or on another continent. Most network users say the benefits of electronic mail alone justify the investment.

Democracy
A LAN distributes your company's computer resources to everyone connected. Once the LAN is installed, everyone from mail clerk to CEO will want, and should have, access.

Productivity
A LAN's ability to share computer resources and information easily helps people do their jobs quickly, efficiently, and with less hassle. The LAN will quickly become the heart of your business.

Shared Information
The concept is simple: Networks connect all individual personal computers so that everyone can share the same data—and update each other's data simultaneously. Networks are especially useful when many users are constantly updating the same files.

Connectivity
Networks can be linked in a variety of ways to each other and to much larger systems that include mid-range computers and mainframes. Through sophisticated "gateways," networks can provide users with ready access to vast information resources—still using the familiar software that PC users are accustomed to.

Economical Software
In most cases, software designed for networks costs less per user than buying individual copies. More importantly, everyone connected by the network can use exactly the same software, reducing problems of compatibility and upgrading. Also, network users can get the benefits of multiuser systems without having to change software. So there's no need to lose your company's investment in OS/2, or Macintosh-based software.

Security
Networks offer your data a new level of security. Even though a network connects many users, it has security safeguards built in. Passwords and access codes make sure that only authorized people can read or write to sensitive files. Networks offer another type of security, too. Single-user systems can lose valuable data when a hard disk malfunctions. But some

network software protects against data loss by using more than one hard disk drive on the network for data storage. Since duplicate records are being kept, data integrity is virtually assured.

Room to Grow

Networks can start out small and be expanded to meet almost infinite demands. There is virtually no limit to the number of users that can be linked with networks. A LAN can be used to link just a few users, while a complex network can connect an entire company in several locations.

Can a LAN work in my operation?

Different people have different concerns about what a LAN can do for them, depending on the specific job needed to do. Here are some typical questions chosen at random from a broad variety of potential LAN users.

What can a network do for me—a telemarketing department head?

You can have online access to customer account and inventory information. Now, the phone sales staff won't promise items that are out of stock, and customers won't exceed their credit limits by placing multiple orders before they are posted.

For the project leader of a regularly revised training manual?

You can make orderly revisions, and ensure that each team member works on the most current version.

For a regional sales manager?

Electronic mail can be used to communicate with salespeople who are always on the phone, and to collect information you must assemble and report.

For a lead programmer?

You can give each team member access to common library modules and control the proliferation of multiple versions.

For a publisher?

You can standardize style specifications, spelling, and hyphenation dictionaries to ensure consistency in the company's publications.

How hard is it to link my computers together?

It depends. How many computers? What kind? How will the wiring run between computers? Three **Macintoshes** and a **LaserWriter** with

AppleTalk cables draped over the partitions wouldn't challenge even an average user. But linking 30 PCs on four floors of a rented office building would probably require the help of experienced installers.

A few rules of thumb: Macs are easier to connect than IBM-compatibles. Getting wires from desktop to desktop is usually the toughest installation job. If high performance is necessary—because there are many computers, because they are situated far apart, or because an application uses the network intensively—a specialist will probably be needed.

Can I install a network myself?

Can you read reference manuals? You'll probably end up rummaging through more instruction books than you ever thought possible. Networks can be highly intricate systems, requiring careful planning and setup. In addition to the wiring, you have to install PC boards (unless you have Macs), file servers (the central store for shared information), and special network operating system software. Your existing software may not work properly with the network installed.

That sounds like a lot of work. Can someone set it up for me?

"ComputerLand is an excellent resource for almost all networking services, including consulting, installation, upgrades and maintenance."

There are several ways to get help. If you want someone to handle all of the details of choosing the network, buying and installing the cable, and setting up the whole system, consider contacting a qualified consultant. ComputerLand is an excellent resource for almost all networking services, including consulting, installation, upgrades and maintenance.

For help with running network cabling throughout your building, contact a phone installer, or someone with experience installing the thick cable required. Again, your ComputerLand store or a consultant can help put you in touch with one.

What are the options for linking my IBM-compatible PCs together?

For the latest generation of DOS machines, Novell and 3Com are the principal suppliers of network operating software and dedicated file servers. Both companies' systems work with a range of network boards and cabling systems. Some widely adopted choices are IBM's **Token-Ring**, 3Com's **Ethernet**, and AT&T's **Star-LAN**. Major software packages, including ***1-2-3, dBASE III Plus, Paradox, Word, WordPerfect***, and a good selection of well-known accounting products, have been adapted to work fully on networks.

In comparison to the Macintosh world, the PC-compatible world has loosely defined standards. You may find that certain hard disks, multi-function boards, communications hardware, and even some purportedly compatible computers will not work with a network. Some

RAM-resident utility programs are inconsistent with networks too.

Can I network IBM's new PS/2 computers?

IBM delivered **Token-Ring Network** boards and **PC Network** boards for the PS/2 line when it first came out. Since that time, **Micro Channel boards** for most of the other network systems have been released. Today, the options for connecting PS/2 systems are still not quite as abundant as those for other PCs, but the situation is changing quickly.

My business uses Macs. What about linking them together?

Networking Macs is much easier and less expensive than networking PCs. Even the first Macintoshes were designed with networking hardware built into the machine. Connecting a group of Macintosh users requires only the cabling to reach from one machine to another and a network file sharing program.

"Connecting a group of Macintosh users requires only the cabling to reach from one machine to another and a network file sharing program."

LocalTalk and **AppleTalk**, the networking hardware built into the Macintosh and the LaserWriter, are designed to let small or medium-size work groups communicate with each other or with shared printers. But LocalTalk by itself does not provide Macintosh users with the ability to share files. For that, Apple provides ***AppleShare***, software that handles the details of networking, like retrieving files from the Macintosh file server and routing them to the right place.

To use AppleShare, you need to set aside one Macintosh as a file server. (Although giving up one computer makes the system more expensive, it allows the network to work much faster.) Setting up an AppleShare/AppleTalk network is easy; it simply involves installing the cabling to connect the computers and printers, then installing the network software. Once that is done, users see additional hard disk icons on their Macintosh desktops. Up to 16 users can use the file server's hard disks as if they were their own.

What if I can't run cables through my office?

If installing additional cabling in your office is a problem, you can use your phone wires to run an AppleTalk network; Farallon Computing, Inc., makes ***PhoneNet***, which allows you to use existing phone wiring to connect AppleTalk devices. Most phone wiring in offices today has excess capacity built-in: unconnected wires bundled with those that carry voices. Since phone cable is cheap and generally easy to install, even offices without excess phone capacity should consider using phone-based networks. In addition, PhoneNet allows an AppleTalk network to span greater distances—a 3,000-foot limit on total length, versus Apple's 1,000 feet. (In the PC realm, phone lines can be employed similarly by networking hardware from AT&T, Hewlett-Packard, and IBM.)

My application may be too big for LocalTalk. Are there alternatives?

If you need to move mountains of data between users on your network, the LocalTalk hardware may well be too slow. For people who need to transfer data faster, Apple, in conjunction with 3Com, has introduced **EtherTalk**, which performs LocalTalk's job faster. It can handle data at the rate of 10 megabits per second (versus 230 kilobits per second for AppleTalk). You can use the network just like AppleTalk; AppleShare will work with it, as will any network file-sharing program designed to work with AppleTalk.

Everyone on our network needs to share the information on their hard disks with everyone else. A dedicated file server will be too costly. What else can I do?

The **TOPS** network allows each person to share files and hard disks with everyone else. Each machine can act as both a file server and a workstation. This approach to networking can work well for companies that share spreadsheets, word processing documents, or small, individually managed databases.

How hard is it to link my combination of PCs and Macs?

If you need to share data between different kinds of systems, one of the key factors is whether the application software on one type of machine can accept files from the other type. For example, trying to read Macintosh ***MacWrite*** files with ***WordStar*** on the PC may present a challenge. On the other hand, Microsoft Word files are easily shared between PCs and Macintoshes. Even so, you will probably still have to convert most files on the Macintosh; many applications on that machine are able to format files for the PC, while PC programs often ignore Macintosh file formats.

What do I need to set up a combination network?

Apple's AppleShare PC is probably the simplest network for hooking PCs into a Macintosh AppleTalk network. PC users can use AppleTalk PC cards to connect to the network. In return, they can access the file server's hard disk.

The TOPS network can integrate Macintoshes and PCs (and Sun's line of workstations, too). It uses AppleTalk; PC users will need to buy AppleTalk interface cards, available from TOPS, Apple, and Hercules. To Macintosh users, files on shared PC hard disks show up as the familiar icons, just like any other Macintosh file. To PC users, Macintosh files look just like PC files.

If you need a larger, more capable network than AppleTalk, you should consider one of Novell's or 3Com's network systems. All of 3Com's networks for the Macintosh use a fast dedicated file server. Able to integrate several different types of networking protocols (including those for AppleTalk, Token-Ring, and Ethernet), the Novell and 3Com systems provide enormous flexibility in designing a network system. For example, you could put together a Macintosh system with 3Com's ***3+Share*** software and a dedicated file server. As you expand to include PCs on the network, you might purchase a supplemental file server, Ethernet cabling and interface boards, and 3+ software for the PCs. Alternatively, 3+ software for the Macintosh supports direct access to Ethernet from each Macintosh or PC, allowing high-speed data access.

What problems should I watch out for once the network is installed?

Networked life is different. You're suddenly dependent on equipment not on your desktop. Someone has to be responsible for the shared system. The responsibilities include helping new or forgetful users; troubleshooting; backing up central files; administration of passwords and access privileges if such a system is implemented; and updating software consistently so stragglers can't disrupt the network by running old versions of a program.

Even when the computer manufacturer has made it easy to connect PCs, a network adds complexity to users' lives. But if it's important to share data, a little extra complexity is a small price to pay.

How to choose the right LAN for your particular business

As you decide how to network your business computers, you'll need to take a close look at how your company does things now, and what you want the LAN to do. To help guide you through the decision-making process, we've assembled some questions you can ask yourself about your networking needs.

What tasks do I need to perform on the network?

List your objectives for the networked system—do you need to keep extensive records in a database manager, build complex spreadsheets with information from several people, or do you primarily need to share word processing files?

The tasks you list may be somewhat different from what your office currently does; networked computing may allow you to do things that aren't feasible with your current system. For example, a networked system can give several people instant access to live database information, so more people throughout the company can have up-to-date information without requiring one person to print reports for everyone.

How does the company do those tasks now? What's wrong with (or inefficient about) how I do them now?

Is your correspondence getting lost in the filing process? If the people in your company keep spreadsheets (manual or electronic), do they need to incorporate information from other people's spreadsheets? Do desktop publishers incorporate documents that are being updated by others, right up to the last minute?

How do I want the network to improve what we do now?

Here's where you can get creative—think about what works smoothly, as well as what takes too long or is simply impossible with your present system. Some aspects of your business may not benefit from computerizing yet (the baseball pool, for example).

What style of network will work best for me—a peer-to-peer network or a central file server?

"A centralized file server tends to provide a more easily controlled environment."

Some workgroups function best with decentralized file resources; certain employees take responsibility for their own portion of the company's data, sharing their data in turn with other employees. This approach enables individuals to intimately control and modify their own specialized data files, but also requires them to perform routine administrative tasks that could more easily be handled centrally from a single file server. On the other hand, a centralized file server tends to provide a more easily controlled environment—a "mainframe-like" approach, in which users don't need to worry as much about tasks like backing up or making sure that other users have the most current version of their files.

These two styles of networking don't have to be mutually exclusive; you can combine the features you find most useful for your business. For example, users on a centralized file server can take full responsibility for certain databases or collections of files, while taking advantage of the central file server's file backup and printing capabilities.

How much time do I want to spend administering the network?

Depending on the number of users you plan to include on the network, you may want to designate one or more LAN administrators. The amount of time spent administering the network depends heavily on the type of network you choose. Peer-to-peer networks tend to distribute the tasks among individual users, while networks built around a central file server are easier to administrate centrally. Either way, you'll need to

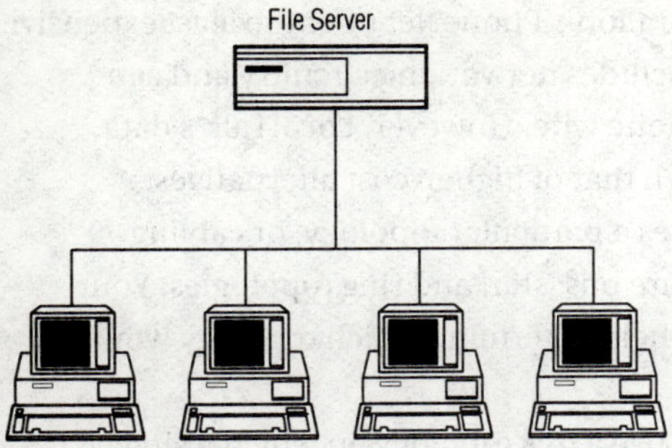

A Bus Network Topology

think about who will perform critical housekeeping tasks, such as backing up data or clearing unused files, and how often those tasks will need to be performed.

What network configuration makes sense for my company?

Where your employees are located can make a big difference in how you set up the network. If all of the PCs in a workgroup are close together (within the same building or on the same floor), you can choose from several types of cabling, such as thin Ethernet, twisted-pair, or **ARCnet**. Networks spanning longer distances or multiple buildings need to use more expensive cabling, such as thick Ethernet or fiber-optic cabling. However, you're not limited to one type for your entire network; networks can combine different types of cabling (and the appropriate adapter cards) to provide the most appropriate configuration for different areas within a company. For example, you might link different buildings with fiber-optic cabling, while departments within a building would use Ethernet cabling.

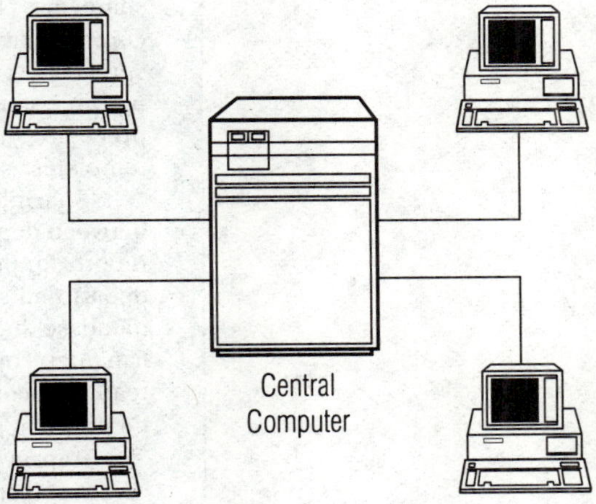

A Star Network Topology

Other important considerations are data transmission speed, the ease with which you can change the network's configuration when employees move or change offices, and installation expense. While Ethernet offers exceptional transmission speed, it requires relatively expensive and hard-to-install coaxial cabling. IBM's Token-Ring networking products provide similar performance and can use less expensive, four-conductor twisted-pair cabling (many buildings already have this wiring installed), but require more expensive adapter cards and multistation access units (**MAUs**). At the other end of the spectrum, Macintoshes

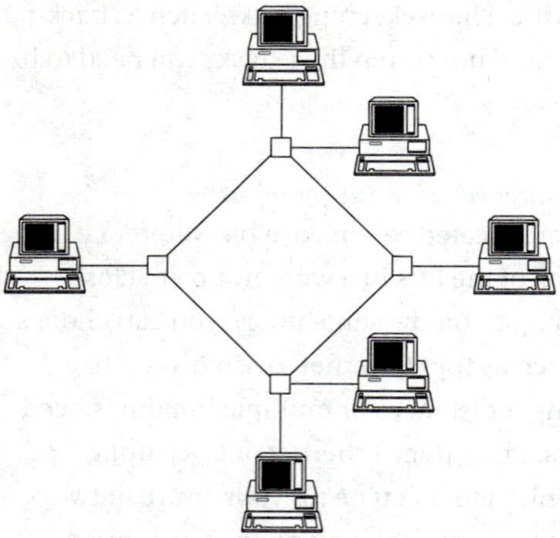

A Ring Network Topology

connected with LocalTalk or Farallon's PhoneNet offer the least expensive alternative—each Macintosh includes networking circuitry and can communicate over standard phone wire. However, LocalTalk's data transmission rate can't approach that of higher-cost alternatives.

Each type of network uses a particular topology, or cabling scheme—some common ones are bus, star, and ring topologies. Your company's building layout can help determine which topology would be best for your situation.

Ethernet and AppleTalk use a bus topology, in which a single stretch of cabling runs the length of the network, with each node connecting to the main cable directly. This topology works well when all workstations are located relatively close to one another and the workstations

Networking Objectives

Sharing information within workgroups or departments: Employees within a department share files, each updating a common database, combining spreadsheet information from multiple sources, or word processing from common templates.

Sharing information between departments: Produce reports for people in other departments, maintaining a database that other departments can query, or, conversely, reading records from another department's database.

Improving corporate communications: Electronic mail enables employees throughout a company to easily send or receive messages, regardless of whether the recipient or sender is currently on the network. Users can attach any type of file to the message, including word processing documents, graphics files, or spreadsheets.

Improving customer service: Disseminate information to people outside the company or gather information from them—customer ordering information or account status, vendor parts lists and availability information.

Improving departmental productivity: Reduce the amount of time employees spend searching for the most up-to-date information by giving each user access to the same files. Network safety features prevent more than one user from simultaneously updating the same record or file.

Improving security: Limit access to sensitive data, so that only qualified employees can examine or change private files. Diskless workstations can prevent unauthorized users from copying files to diskettes.

Sharing expensive peripherals, such as laser printers, plotters, fax servers, and modems: A network gives each user the ability to use any network device, reducing the need to buy each workstation a printer or modem.

Accessing host computer files: Access minicomputer or mainframe computers by emulating terminals, thus reducing the need to buy terminals in addition to the PC workstations.

don't often need to be moved. While Ethernet uses coaxial cabling, AppleTalk uses twisted-pair cabling. Thus, installers can use telephone wiring closets to connect each workstation to its neighbors on the bus.

ARCnet uses coaxial cabling, and is most often arranged in a star topology, making it easy to route through central wiring closets.

Electrically, IBM's Token-Ring cabling looks like a ring—the cable passes through each workstation, looping back on itself to form a ring.

Financial Considerations

Unfortunately, networks still cost money, so budgeting for hardware, software, and installation and arranging the most favorable payment terms should be a part of your network planning. Prices range from $200 or $300 (to connect existing Macs over Farallon's PhoneNet with TOPS) up to thousands of dollars (for a dedicated file server, high-speed network interfaces, and cabling). For example, Novell's ***Advanced NetWare*** retails for $3,295, and each 3Com **EtherLink II Ethernet board** retails for $345 (include one for each file server and workstation)-and don't forget to include the price of cabling and a dedicated PC for use as a file server.

If you're lucky, you'll be able to plan the ideal network first and then get budget approval for the proposed network. However, you may not be so lucky (or rich); you'll have to plan your network around a more limited budget. Either way, you should leave enough time to obtain all the necessary approvals and allow all the paperwork to flow through whatever channels your company requires.

Make sure that you have an approved budget for the network or at least an estimate of what you will be able to spend for the network. Take note of when the funding budget amounts are available—some accounts must be used by their target dates or they are lost.

In addition to the initial cost of the equipment, you should estimate the continuing costs of the network system. Include such items as printer supplies, cabling and installation costs (for new users or those relocating their desks), and service contracts or repair costs.

To make sure that you leave enough time for all approvals, write down a list of all people who need to approve your plans, estimating the time each step will take.

You may also want to consider alternatives to purchasing, such as leasing the equipment for your LAN.

Lastly, you may need to justify the costs of the LAN and be able to measure its effectiveness. To do that, you can choose a financial criterion for gauging the success of the implementation, such as the reduction in data entry costs, improvement in customer response time, increased sales for the computerized department, or any other measure appropriate to your business.

However, IBM designed the cabling so that it can be installed in a star configuration. Each cable leading from the MAU (multistation access unit) to a workstation contains a pair of wires leading to the node and another pair of wires leading back to the MAU. With this cabling design, users can install the MAU in a central wiring closet, making reconfiguration and workstation relocation easy.

Is wiring in place already?

Often, companies have exsisting cabling left over from previous terminal installations or unused pairs of wire in exsisting phone installations. These exsisting cables and wires can often be used to save on cabling costs—often a major part of a network's cost.

Major network vendors offer a variety of tools and adapters to enable you to use exsisting cabling—even if the cabling is different than the cabling you will use for the rest of the network.

What types of computers do we need to network?

Most of the popular networking products support both IBM-compatible PC's and Apple Macintoshes. However, most network operating systems have a definite preference for their native environments. For example, Novell's NetWare only recently introduced support for the Macintosh, requiring PCs for the file server and at least one workstation.

Putting It Together

What is the specific hardware that you need to assemble? How do you connect into one network? And how does LAN equipment work in a unified system?

Putting It Together

What equipment do I need?

WHAT ARE THE BASIC ingredients of a Local Area Network system? How do they work? What are some of the choices you have in reconfiguring your existing equipment and in upgrading with new components?

Some of the basic ingredients are devices with which you may already be familiar. Others may be new to you. Let's go through the main elements of a Local Area Network, one at a time, beginning with the basic engines of our system, the servers.

A server is a computer providing a service to LAN users. Servers provide shared access to a file system, a printer, a modem or an electronic mail system. Servers can be PCs, minicomputers, mainframes, or specialized computers designed to do nothing but dole out services to multiple users. One machine often can be used to handle many such tasks, if lightly loaded. There are several main ways that one or more servers can be configured, including:

[1] A File Server contains files shared by everyone connected to the LAN. In some LANs the file server is an ordinary PC, in others it's a special computer with lots of memory, a huge disk drive and specialized software. In still other LANs, any PC in the system can be a file server, depending on the software it runs.

Many networks are built around *dedicated* file servers, which can either be high performance PCs or specialized devices designed for optimal file-serving speed and flexibility. The file server's hard disk contains the network operating system software, along with most of the applications programs and user data. Network operating system software permitting, a high-performance, general-purpose microcomputer can usually operate as both a workstation and a file server.

[2] A Print Server is a computer and/or program providing LAN users with access to a centralized printer or a workstation's shared printer. LAN users can send their printer output to the print server, which then temporarily stores each print job until it is printed.

With a print server, users can send output to the printer any time and their jobs are usually handled in the order received. But "big jobs" can be given priority and bumped to the head of the line.

Print servers allow fewer printers to satisfy more users and are also especially useful for expensive, laser or high speed printers since they spread the cost of these machines over many users, thus making them more affordable.

[3] A Database Server may consist of hardware, software, or both, depending on your LAN's design. Any machine that stores your company's database on disk so that it's accessible to multiple users may be considered a *hardware* database server. But you will get the best results

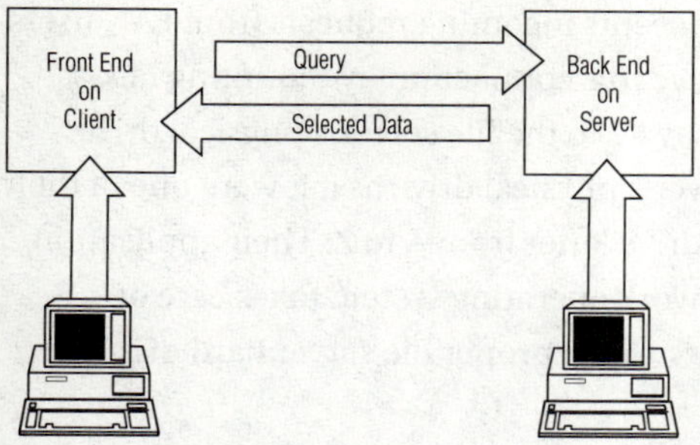

The Database Server Model: *With this configuration, the database program is broken into two parts. The back end resides on a powerful machine and manipulates the data, searches files, and secures information. The front end resides on the user's workstation and displays and reports data. With the file server approach, the entire database is sent to the workstation, where it is searched for the needed records. Thus, a database server greatly reduces network traffic.*

from that hardware by installing specialized database *software* using "client/server" architecture.

The *client* component of this software, which runs on one or more LAN workstations, provides the user interface and allows people to ask for information or modify records in the database. The *server* component, running on a central machine, actually stores and controls the data—protecting it, granting access to multiple users, updating and deleting records on disk, and perhaps communicating with other servers holding data elsewhere.

The advantages of client/server design include a substantial reduction in network traffic; faster response time; greater data security; and more modest hardware requirements for client PCs. In addition, because it separates the database function into two different segments, client/server design means workstations can run a variety of different "front ends"—customized spreadsheets, query languages, etc.—and still retrieve information from the common database.

[4] A Fax Server combines a fax board in one PC on the LAN with software allowing access by all users in the system. This way, any workstation on the LAN can send faxes. Some fax servers are self-contained—they connect directly to the network without requiring a PC.

That may be enough information for some readers. But here and throughout the rest of this book we will follow a basic brief introduction to the material with a series of more detailed expert tutorials about each aspect of our subject.

File servers

A file server is a computer that doles out files to users on a network. It is a combination of hardware and software that allows LAN users to share computer programs and data. Often, though not always, a file server will have significantly more data storage capacity than other computers on the network. It might also have more memory, several printers and modems attached and tape backup capacity.

File servers come in all shapes and sizes. In almost all cases, it is the software that distinguishes a file server from a regular LAN workstation computer. For example, a regular PC may be a LAN file server if it runs software that allows other network users to communicate with it and use its resources, i.e., its hard disks, its printers, its modems, etc. More often, users will install faster, more powerful machines for file servers because they are better able to serve many users at the same time.

Hardware File server software is the part of the network operating system that serves up a computer's hardware resources to other users on

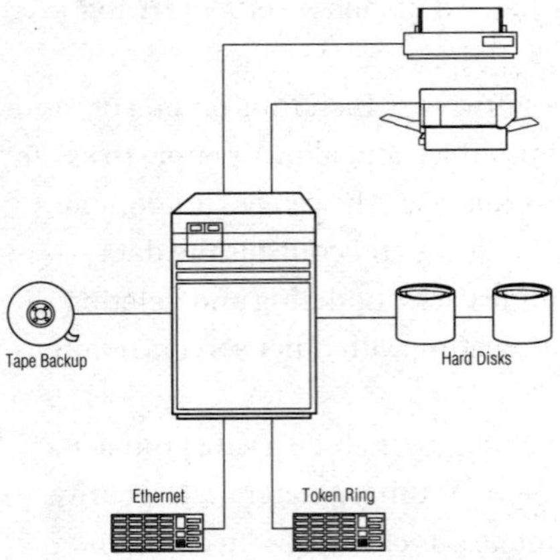

File Server Architecture:
The ideal file server is an 80386-based PC running at 20 MHz with six expansion slots, a parrallel port, a serial port and 8M bytes of RAM. The expansion slots hold two network interface cards connected via a bridge software, an ESDI disk controller with 2G bytes of storage, and a tape backup controller with software that backs up automatically at specified times.
Two printers are attached: one draft, one laser.

the LAN. It is the software that accepts incoming requests from LAN users and gives back files. Users achieve this connection by mounting (a.k.a. mapping) a local logical drive, say F:, to the file server's physical drive. That is, users access the file server's physical drive as if it were one of their local drives using a designated drive letter from A to Z. Their application programs do the same. The network operating system takes care of routing traffic across the network to the proper file server hard disk and back.

Crucial to the workings of a file server is its ability to find data quickly and get it back to the requesting workstation without delay. Many factors affect the performance of a file server. These include the speed of the network interface card, the type and length of cable, the efficiency of the network software, the type of application being run, the number of users on the network, and the amount of RAM available. Probably the most important factor in file server performance is the speed of the hard disk.

Most high performance file servers include a very fast, and usually very large, hard disk. In general, an access speed of less than 30 milliseconds is very good for a server hard disk. Under 20 milliseconds is even better. The access time is the time required to get data off the disk. Access times are broken down into two parts: seek and rotation. Average seek time is the time taken by the heads of the disk drive to move to the correct track on the platter. This is most of the access time. The average time of rotation is the time taken for the platter to turn to the correct sector where the data is stored. Most of the time, the average access time is all you need to know when buying a server hard disk. Usually, larger hard disks are faster than smaller ones.

One often overlooked aspect of the file server hard disk drive is its controller. Debates rage over which controller is better: standard ST controllers, ESDI (Enhanced Small Device Interface) or SCSI (Small Computer System Interface). Each has different advantages, price, speed and expandability, respectively. The tradeoff you make depends on your application and financial situation. An "intelligent" hard disk controller can unload much of the work involved in handling a hard disk from the file server's central processor. Though it adds costs, the disk upgraded controller provides enormous performance improvements.

Performance is not the only question to think about when installing a file server hard disk. Capacity is crucial. A general rule is to take the amount you think you need and double it. It's hard to get too much data storage on a file server. Plus, since LANs always grow, expandability is important. Your file server should accommodate more disk drives as needed.

Processor and Clock Most file servers are larger and faster than most network workstations. Almost all vendors now recommend at least an 80286-based file server and several sell file servers based on the 80386 chip. In addition, system clock speeds up into the 33 MHz range are becoming popular. File servers with this type of hardware are faster than normal AT-type machines running at 10 or 12 MHz. Though they are also more expensive, the performance advantages usually justify the added cost.

The 32-bit 80386-and 80486-based machines can use LAN operating software, such as Novell's ***NetWare 386*** specifically adapted to take advantage of their processors. This can increase performance even further.

Not all networks require these "monster" file servers. In networks with nondedicated file servers lightly sharing data, normal AT-type machines may work well and PCs may do the job in a pinch. Once data sharing passes beyond a handful of users or light word processing, more powerful file servers become a necessity.

> *"Once data sharing passes beyond a handful of users or light word processing, more powerful file servers become a necessity."*

Fault Tolerance While performance is probably the most important factor when buying a file server, reliability is also crucial. Here is where fault tolerance comes in. Fault tolerance is the general name given to any scheme designed to prevent data corruption or loss. Events that cause data to be lost or corrupted include power failures, disk crashes, electromagnetic interference and disk controller failure.

One form of fault tolerance is to read behind every write to the disk, verifying that what was placed on the disk was correct. Some file servers do this.

Another form of fault tolerance is to protect the file allocation table (FAT). This is usually done by keeping an extra copy of the FAT somewhere else on the hard disk. If the original FAT is corrupted for some reason, the extra copy can be used to regenerate the original. Several vendors have this type of fault tolerance. Novell's System Fault Tolerance is the most popular.

Transaction tracking, also from Novell, goes a bit farther than this. It divides operations on the network into transactions and remembers each one. All operations within a transaction must be complete or none of them are completed. If the file server is interrupted for some reason during a transaction, transaction tracking will return the file server back to the previous point of consistency. This is especially useful if a database is being updated when something happens. It can also increase performance by grouping updates together, thereby putting all disk accesses together so they may be done at the same time.

Two more types of fault tolerance are disk mirroring and disk duplexing. In disk mirroring one hard disk controller writes to and reads from two hard disks. If one hard disk should fail the other can be used since it is an exact replica. However, if the controller fails, both disks will be corrupted. Disk duplexing takes care of this by using two disk controllers and two hard disks. Disk duplexing has several advantages, though it is more expensive. First, a controller problem does not corrupt all data. Second, though the two controllers ultimately have the same data, they need not do the same thing at the same time. While one is writing data another may be reading it, thereby speeding overall performance.

An extension of disk duplexing is called shadowing. Here, a second file server, also attached to the network, receives all the data of the first. Should, the first file server fail for any reason, the second file server may take over. This is one of the most expensive forms of fault tolerance but it will help LAN users recover from a broken file server more quickly than any other method. Shadowing is used in downtime-sensitive situations, where loss of the file server for more than a few minutes can be devastating.

Print servers

One of the best reasons to get a LAN is to share computer peripherals, including hard disks and printers. Sharing printers means only one PC need have printers attached. Other users send their print jobs, documents, spreadsheets, reports, etc., to this *print server.* The print server machine handles all the printing requirements for the group of users. This can save money on printers and can even make printing easier and faster. In order for a print server to handle many jobs coming in at the same time, it must have something called a *spool.* Spool is an acronym for Simultaneous Peripheral Operation On Line, but nobody ever says that. A spool is a piece of hardware or software or a combination of both that controls a *buffer.* The buffer holds data before it is sent to a printer. This way, one or more print jobs can sit in the buffer while the printer is working on another job. Most of the time, print jobs are spooled to a hard disk at the print server. Once at the print server, the spooled jobs join a *queue,* waiting to print in a first-in, first-out order as the printer becomes ready. Queues are just what they sound like, waiting lines for access to the printer. Most print servers allow users to assign priorities to their print jobs so they can move up or skip to the head of the queue.

LAN Printing In general, LAN printing works as follows. Software in the user's machine captures the printed information and sends it over the network. The application that is running, say a word processor, believes it is printing a document out the local printer port, but the print software steps in to redirect the output over the network.

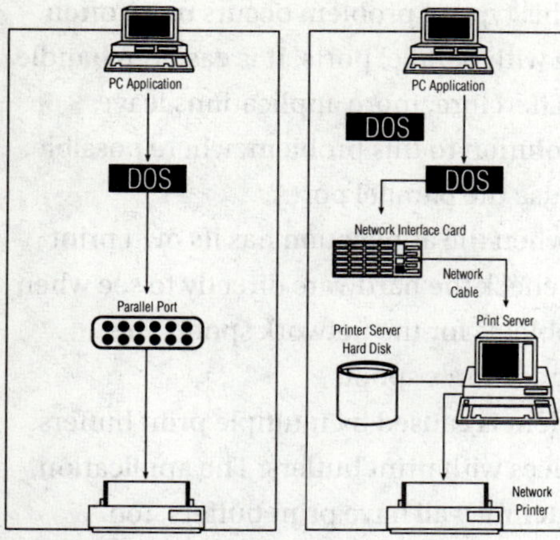

LAN Printing:
A standalone application (left) sends data to DOS, which then sends it to the parallel port to the printer. On a network (right), the print job is redirected over the network by the network operating system, bypassing DOS. At the print server the file is spooled to the disk before it prints. Since the disk can take the data faster than the printer, this prevents the user from having to wait while the file is printed. If the printer is busy with another print job, the file is stored until the printer is free. The process may seem simple, but many things can go wrong, especially if the application is a little out of the ordinary.

At the print server, software awaits to handle the incoming print job. If the printer is free, the document may be printed out immediately. If the printer is not free, the document will be stored in a print file on the print server's hard disk. That is, it will be spooled. The file will also join the queue, waiting its turn to be sent to the printer.

Key to the whole process is printer *redirection.* Printer redirection is a common occurrence, locally as well as over a network. For example, a serial printer requires that output bound for the parallel port (LPT1), be redirected out the serial port (COM1). DOS allows you to do this with the MODE command. What is sent to LPT1 then goes out COM1.

Over the network, the same redirection takes place. The difference is that DOS is not doing the redirection. The network operating system is. The user tells the network operating system to redirect all output headed for the local LPT1 port over the network to, say, the print server's LPT3 port. This way, any output destined for local LPT1 will print out LPT3 at the print server. The network operating system takes care of getting the print job to the print server.

At the print server, the file is spooled to disk. Spooling may be done for two reasons. First, the printer is busy, so the print server must store the file until the printer can take it. Second, the printer is not fast enough to take the whole file at once, so the print server stores the last parts of the file while the first parts print.

The print server also has a buffer. The buffer, a chunk of memory, is used to feed print jobs to the printer at the correct pace. Data waiting to be printed is stored in the buffer right before it is sent. The larger the buffer, the faster the printing, since fewer accesses to disk are necessary to pick up the file. More can be stored in memory while being sent to the printer.

This points out the difference between a spool and a buffer. The spool is the software/hardware combination that stores the files for printing and then sends them when ready. The buffer is the chunk of memory that holds the data while the printer and PC communicate. Both improve the performance of LAN printing.

In principle, that's all there is. LAN printing should be easy. Redirection, spooling, and buffering should all work well. However, there are a number of problems that almost always occur.

That's why there are special programs for printing on a LAN.

Print Problems There are a number of common problems that crop up when trying to print on a network. One of the most common is conflict between the application and the network. Many times, the application will talk to the printer port directly, bypassing DOS. If this is the case, the network operating system will not have the opportunity to step in and redirect the output. This type of problem occurs more often when printing to serial ports than with parallel ports. It is easier to handle a serial port than a parallel port. Therefore, more applications leave parallel operations to DOS. The solution to this problem, where possible, is to configure the application to use the parallel port.

Another problem occurs when the application has its own print spool. Again, the application will check the hardware directly to see when to send data, thereby causing problems for the network spool. The solution here is to disable the application's spool.

"The solution to printing disruptions is to use only one of the buffers."

A third LAN printing problem is caused by multiple print buffers. Print servers are not the only devices with print buffers. The application, the PC, the network, and the printer may all have print buffers, too. Usually, all these buffers will work together. Sometimes, disruptions happen while one buffer waits for another. The solution is to use only one of these buffers. Performance will not be hurt significantly and memory resources may be conserved.

A fourth LAN printing problem comes with multiple users sharing one printer. Each user sets the printer differently, different fonts, character widths, line spacing, etc. Once a user is finished, the printer may be stuck with that user's settings. Some applications allow users to send printer control codes. Others don't. The same is true for some network operating systems and some LAN printing utilities (see below). These codes can be used to reset a printer after every print job. This way, all users know the printer is starting with particular settings, no matter who has used it previously.

Unfortunately, in some cases, the printer control codes used by an application may interfere with network operations or network printer control codes. For example, a printer control code from the application may be misinterpreted by the network operating system as a release printer code, leaving the user disconnected from the printer. Another symptom of such conflicts is garbled printing. Only trial and error can eliminate these problems. Most likely the application will have to be reconfigured not to use the printer control code commands. Those of the network operating system or a printer utility will have to be used.

The last set of LAN printing problems is unavoidable. Multiple users have multiple requirements for paper, but most printers can only hold one type of paper at a time. To use more than one type of paper some kind of procedure has to be developed. One way to do this is to have more than one shared printer. Each printer will use different paper. If this is too expensive or inappropriate, some type of notification needs to be implemented when users switch paper. Electronic mail is probably the best tool for this. With E-mail notification, users will not send print jobs to printers with the wrong paper installed. Some network operating systems handle forms automatically, notifying operators when paper changes are needed. Some printer utilities can also serve this purpose.

"When any PC can act as a print server, printers may be placed conveniently throughout a LAN."

Utilities Virtually all network operating systems support some kind of LAN printing. However, the variation in features is great. Some network operating systems require the user to leave the application before setting up the print process. The user must explicitly tell the network operating system to be on the lookout for a print job and then tell it when the job is over. This can be very annoying. Other network operating systems require that all shared printers be attached to a file server. This, too, is inconvenient, especially when file servers are locked up for security purposes. Finally, many network operating systems will not allow network users to send printer control codes to network printers. Again, more inconvenience.

Luckily, several LAN printing utilities exist to solve these problems. They are usually pop-up programs that may be called up on the screen no matter what application is being used. Such printing utilities allow users to control the printer and print server from their own PCs, without quitting what they are doing. Users may manipulate the print queue, check on which files have been spooled, choose printing codes, send jobs, reconfigure the printer and perform many other tasks, all without leaving their application.

One particularly nice feature many printing utilities have is the ability to automate printer configuration. For example, a printing utility will send printer control codes to reset the printer to default configuration after every print job. This way, every user knows how the printer is set before using it.

Many LAN printing utilities also allow any PC on the network to act as a printer server. These utilities are really additions to the network operating system, since they are fundamentally enhancing its operation. When any PC can act as a print server, printers may be placed conveniently throughout a LAN.

A very nice feature of many printing utilities is print notification. Users are notified when their print jobs have finished printing, a terrific convenience if the printer is out of earshot. Another nice feature is the ability to standardize line feeds and form feeds so users don't have to do this manually. This reduces the chance that users will go to the printer and change it, or leave it off line.

Small Advice Printing on a network should be easy. It's not. Most problems arise because printing in general is not as easy as it should be.

There are no printer standards. Pinouts, cables, and ports create an endless stream of problems. Add the network and printers become even more of a hassle.

The best advice we can offer is the following: Use parallel ports where possible, since serial ports are less predictable, more difficult to manipulate, and slower. Avoid exotic printers where possible, since they use different cables, different handshaking protocols, and different interfaces. The biggest source of printing problems is PC-printer communications. Set standard printing procedures. For example, hang signs explaining printer operation above the printer. Remind people to leave the printer online, with paper loaded. Remind them to download printer default settings when they are finished. Use printer utilities. There are many. Almost all of them help. Finally, have patience. You'll need it.

"Use parallel ports where possible, since serial ports are less predictable, more difficult to manipulate, and slower."

Server Hard Disks

These mass storage devices are called hard disks by most normal people but don't be alarmed if you see ads for **Winchester** or **Whitney** or fixed drives. The term Winchester merely refers to the fact that the first hard disks had a head assembly that was developed at IBM's Winchester lab. Whitney refers to another type of head. IBM itself refers to them as fixed disks to distinguish them from removable floppy disks. Some people also call them rigid drives to further distinguish them from the lowly floppy.

Briefly, a hard disk works like this: Data is read off the disk surface and stored in a buffer on a controller card. The card then processes the data and sends it to the computer, which stores it in its own RAM buffers. When data is written the user tells the computer what data is to be written. The data is then moved to the RAM buffers, transferred to the controller buffer, then written onto the disk.

A hard disk isn't so very different from a floppy in its basic technology. Both store data on a magnetic surface in thin lines called *tracks* arranged in concentric circles. These tracks are each divided into an equal number of *sectors*. Data is read off both disks by a read/write head. The head moves out over the surface of the disk until it's positioned over the track it needs, and then the disk spins until the sector needed is under the head. That's where the similarities end.

A floppy disk is some flexible material covered with an iron oxide coating, the same kind of coating used on audio and video tapes. A hard disk is a rigid, aluminum disk that is often coated with the same oxide material as a floppy. The speed at which hard disks are read makes it imperative that the disks be inflexible, so as not to come into contact with the read/write head. Hard disks also come

continued on page 27

❦ *"Performance should be the least of your worries."*

Server Hard Disks

covered with a much harder magnetic material, commonly called *thin film.* It's basically a mixture of metals applied to the surface of the disk through a technique called *sputtering.*

To further increase storage capacity, hard disk drives actually contain two or more hard disks. Each individual disk is called a platter. These platters are all joined on a common spindle, one above the other, like a stack of record albums on a turntable. The platters spin in unison, and data is written onto both surfaces of each platter.

It's actually deceptive to compare the architecture of a hard disk drive to a record player. The stylus on the turntable arm actually comes into contact with the record album. The head in a hard disk is never supposed to touch down onto the surface of the disk. Instead, the head flies over the surface of the disk on a cushion of air created by the spinning of the disks.

Since it would take forever for one head to be responsible for reading all the surfaces (not to mention being mechanically impractical) each surface has its own head. These heads are also joined together and move in tandem across their respective surfaces. While it would be more efficient for the heads to move independently of one another, the technology is at this point prohibitively expensive.

While examining the guts of a hard disk may give you a clue as to how to get the highest performance hard disk drive, performance should be the least of your worries. Access times and data transfer rates are measured in *milliseconds.* That's just the tiniest fraction of a second, and the difference between 15 and 150 milliseconds is not enough for a puny human to notice. Even if it took a full second or five seconds for a disk to access information, you're probably halfway to an ulcer if you can't wait that long for your data. Far more important than speed is capacity. A rule of thumb for a hard disk subsystem on a file server is to allot 5OM byte for each user, double it and you'll still run out in a week. "They're like closets," says Andrew Silberstein, executive vice president at Morton Management (Silver Spring, MD). "Fill up every inch and you'll still never have enough."

Since you'll almost definitely be needing more storage than you thought, try opting for an easily expandable system. Plus Development (Milpitas, CA) is one among many companies that sell hard disk subsystems. These are cabinets that hold two or more disk drives and provide all the cabling and interfaces necessary. They can be purchased with or without the drives, although, again, it's better to use them with the products they were intended for.

Optical Disks

Magnetic disks aren't the only mass storage devices out there. *Optical disks* are enjoying increasing popularity. Optical disks use reflected light instead of magnetic pulses to store data. They also use a controller, but where a hard disk drive has several disks, an optical disk only has one. They're also removable and interchangeable.

Optical disks are a little slower than regular magnetic disks. However, what you sacrifice in time you more than make up for in durability. Optical disks are made of an extremely hard, resilient plastic. They can withstand all sorts of physical abuse. Furthermore, the information is chemically sealed onto the plastic and the optical beam never touches the surface, so you don't risk head crashes.

Most optical disks used on LANs are write-once, read-many, or WORM drives. Files cannot be erased from WORM drives, so a complete trail of up dates is kept. There's no such thing as accidentally erasing a file.

The newer type of optical disk is rewriteable. Just like magnetic disks, files can be erased from these disks and the space can be used again. Since multiple platter technology isn't yet feasible for rewriteable optical disks your storage capacity is limited from the outset. The big advantage to optical disks is that they are far more reliable than regular magnetic disks.

Fax servers

The fax is hot. Very hot. Facsimile machines have become as essential as the telephone. The question is not " Do you have a fax?" but " What is your fax number?" Faxes are wonderful, but frankly, we're all tired of waiting for the fax machine to free up. And we're tired of that ear-piercing screech when the paper jams.

Fax boards are the next stage. Fax boards drop into a slot in a PC, and enable that PC's users to send faxes to any other fax machine or fax board. If you are sending a computer file, fax boards eliminate the need to print out the file and fax it. On the receiving end, it saves fax paper.

Fanning the fax fire is the fax server. The fax board still only resides in one PC on the LAN, but the fax server software lets all users access the services of the fax board. Giving your LAN fax capability has two advantages: accessibility and speed.

One reason for sharing a peripheral is making it accessible to many users. Faxes are no different. Both fax machines and fax boards are limited to a single location. That's a real pain if you happen to be on the other side of the building from the fax machine. Fax servers change that, since any workstation on the LAN can send a fax. The fax server effectively places a *virtual* fax machine on every desktop.

The fax server's second justification is speed. Quite simply, a fax server is faster than either a fax board or fax machine. The speed doesn't come from a higher transmission rate, that's standardized, but because there's less involved with a fax server. There's no printing out the file, no walking to the fax machines, no waiting on line. Just type the fax and it's off. The software takes care of the rest.

There's one major drawback to fax boards and fax servers. Using them assumes that the document you want to send is already in your computer. Unless you are willing to type in the paper document, or buy a costly scanner, fax servers are useless to transmit documents that are already on paper.

"Quite simply, a fax server is faster either than a fax board or fax machine."

Faxing Methods There are three ways to implement a fax server. The first is with communication software. With communication software, such as Brightwork's ***NETremote*** or Norton-Lambert's ***Close-up/LAN***, a node on the network temporarily takes control of the PC housing the fax board. It's as if the node were actually the fax server. With control of the fax PC, all operations at the host become available at the remote workstation. When a fax is not being transmitted, that PC can be used as a normal workstation.

You will want to use an intelligent fax board, so the user doesn't have to stop working every time someone on the LAN sends a fax. The communications software approach has its drawbacks. People like things simple. Electronic mail has proven that. Successful E-mail packages are a cinch to use. People don't want to be bothered with learning a whole new software package just to send a fax. Moreover, with a communications package, only one PC can control the server at a time. To send a fax, the server must be available. Anyone working at the server must switch into fax mode. What a pain. And once the server is in use, nobody else can send a fax. To their credit, communications packages take control of the PC for a very short period of time. Still, it's precisely these potential bottlenecks you want to avoid.

A second method is setting up a fax server. Fax servers are dedicated machines devoted to the sending and receiving of faxes. Often a fax server doubles as a file server or print server on the LAN. In other instances, they are distinct machines dedicated as a communication or facsimile gateway.

Fax servers are a solid approach to integrating fax machines into a LAN. They enable multiple users to send faxes simultaneously, avoiding the major drawback of communications software. They can use a dedicated PC or their own hardware. The nice feature about the ones using their own hardware is simplicity. According to both Castelle and Interpreter, their dedicated fax servers are "plug-and-play" units. Pop 'em onto the network and you're off. No configuring, no messing around.

"The only problem with fax servers is notification of sent messages," says Jeff Harrison, executive vice president of Alcom. "The fax server mimics the idea of a print server. The problem is print servers only send messages one way from user to the printer. Fax servers, though, have to handle messages being sent two ways.

"Once a user sends his message to be faxed he should be able to forget about it," Harrison continues. "If there are any problems with the transmission, the computer should let him know. With a fax server that is not what happens. The user must check a list to see if the fax was sent. There is no automatic notification."

"Users familiar with the E-mail will have virtually nothing to learn."

The third method calls for using the existing E-mail system. With this approach faxes are sent using E-mail as if they were a regular E-mail message. However, instead of being sent to a user's computer, they are sent to the fax gateway. The address includes the phone number to be dialed. The fax gateway strips away the E-mail codes and sends the fax on its way.

This approach is great if you already have an E-mail system installed. Users familiar with the E-mail will have virtually nothing to learn. They send the fax to the fax computer and the software handles the rest. Once the document is sent the user is notified through the E-mail system. Simple, convenient, and efficient. Just the way we like it. Of course, this approach assumes you have an E-mail system.

It's the software which gives the fax server its character. Virtually every manufacturer we spoke to pointed out the importance of software. Harrison says, "In terms of hardware there generally isn't much of a difference between the different fax boards. It's like comparing modems. Once you separate 9600 baud from 4800 baud and dumb boards from intelligent boards they are all pretty much alike. The big difference is the software."

"Software, software, software," is how Bob Stevans, vice president of communications development at Dest, sees it. It's the software that the user sees. It's the software that manages incoming and outgoing messages. It's the software that will determine how well a fax server will function. The software is what makes or breaks a fax server.

In the past, software has tended to be a bit clumsy, adding an additional layer of difficulty to sending faxes. Clumsy user interfaces will discourage users from using the fax server.

What To Look For Here are seven points to consider in your quest for the perfect fax server.

"Be sure the software you purchase works with your fax board."

Does it operate with the LAN's operating system?

Be sure the fax server works with your LAN's network operating system. Like any other add-in board, the fax board needs a driver to operate. The driver is a software program sitting between the network operating system and the fax board. It enables the card to run with the operating system. Poorly written drivers will slow up the board's performance and it can crash the LAN.

What fax board does the software use?

Not all fax software will function with every fax board. Be sure the software you purchase works with your fax board. Better yet, purchase the software and then the hardware. You'll avoid all sorts of potential problems.

What file formats are accepted?

Different packages convert different file formats. All handle ASCII but many will also handle database and word processing formats. More importantly, the software should handle graphics formats. There are a number of different types of formats out there: DR Halo, PCX, and DCX, to name a few. Check your software to see which formats are being used.

It should keep you informed.

Does the software notify the user when the fax was sent? Or do you have to keep looking at a log? Interpreter claims to be able to notify a user when a fax arrives. Great, eh? There only two problems. First, the message needs to be typed, still a rarity. However, this will change if the product catches on. Second, a special fax form must be used. The form contains a space for the particular ID. Using optical character recognition (OCR), Interpreter's package interprets the ID and routes the fax to the user's "fax box." But will people use the special fax forms? Maybe.

It should be simple to use.

Make sure users don't find sending a fax painful. People shouldn't have to learn a new software package just to operate the fax board. Using the existing E-mail system is good if you have the E-mail or if you're planning on installing it. "Keep It Simple, Stupid" is a good motto.

Does it operate in the background?

Make sure the communications functions of the fax software on the workstations operate in the background. Memory-resident software has a knack for hogging up the keyboard buffer. Conflicts between different applications software abound. But keep in mind total background operations become total bottlenecks.

Can users send a fax from within an application?

Some RAM-residency is critical. If users have to exit their applications to send a fax, they will be discouraged from using the fax server. On the other hand, RAM-residency can create compatibility problems.

Fax Wrap Up Fax servers can be a boon to your office. They expand the capabilities of your fax machine. Like a print spooler, a fax server allows many people to access the capabilities of the fax machine, without giving each one a dedicated machine on his or her desk.

Fax servers are not without drawbacks. Fax servers solve the problem of having to print out your computer files to fax them. But if the document you want to fax is already on paper, a fax server is of no use unless you have a scanner to put that paper document into electronic form. A scanner will set you back about $2,200. Still, as we move further towards electronic media, fax servers will become more relevant.

Workstations

The most common type of LAN workstation is the standard **PC, XT, AT, PS/2**, or compatible machine, in many cases because those machines were already installed as single-user systems before the network was installed. With these PCs, users retain control over their own machines, using network storage and printing resources as they become necessary.

Standalone PCs and compatibles used as workstations also provide flexibility in case of changes in the network (and during emergencies in which the network file server is temporarily unavailable). Their expandability, power, and independence—the same characteristics that have made general-purpose microcomputers so popular—make PC workstations well-suited for networking in companies where users' computing needs vary greatly. While some users might use their network workstations for word processing only (and could get by with inexpensive 8088- or 8086-based PCs), other users might need high-powered, 80386-

or '486-based workstations for CAD applications, complex spreadsheets, or graphical operating environments.

In choosing PC workstations, you will also want to keep ease of installation and maintenance in mind; the more different types of machines you have on the network, the more different software configurations the network will require, and the higher the chance of incompatible combinations of CPUs and expansion cards. Try to strike a balance between standardizing network installations and installing customized hardware designed for individual users' needs.

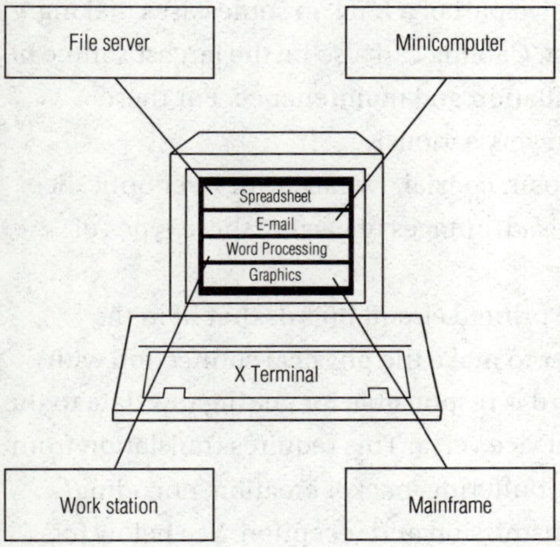

An X Terminal:
An inexpensive machine which does not have the full power of a desktop computer but provides the use of a mouse and windows which can display graphics, spreadsheets, electronic mail, word processing and other applications from other computers within the Local Area Network.

Low-Cost Workstations A popular alternative to buying complete, standalone PCs for use as network workstations is buying specialized network nodes. Typically, a low-cost workstation resembles a standard DOS-based PC, except that it lacks disk drives and is limited in its expansion capabilities. Often called diskless workstations, these inexpensive PC nodes don't need bays for disk drives, and so can be built smaller and lighter than their standalone cousins. They can range from 8088-based machines, suitable for word processing or simple database or spreadsheet processing, to powerful, 80286-based workstations with high-resolution graphics capabilities built in. 3Com's **3Station/2E** ($2,195) is just such a machine, lacking disk drives but including an 80286 processor, Ethernet interface, and a built-in VGA controller.

An important advantage of diskless workstations is their added security in a networked environment. Because the workstations have no floppy disk drives, copying sensitive data from the network to a floppy disk is impossible, so the network administrator can control who copies files to or from the network. Some "diskless" workstations include a hard disk controller but not a floppy drive, enabling users to operate locally on the PC—without relying completely on the network file server—but preventing users from copying data to floppy disks without permission. AST's **Bravo/86, Model 1** ($1,095) fits into this category; it includes a hard disk controller and room to accept an internal hard disk. Diskless (or hard-disk-only) workstations usually have network interfaces that can start up the PC directly from the network file server, without requiring "boot diskettes."

Making the connections

Now that we're beginning to understand the main ingredients in a Local Area Network, it's time to consider how it's all hooked together. A lot of this information is pretty technical and may be more than some of us really need to know. So before we go on to a more detailed discussion, let's preview the basic elements required to connect up all the parts in your system.

Here are some of the things we may need to assemble a LAN:

Cabling connects workstations on a LAN. Though it may seem to be the simplest component on a LAN, it is not necessarily the cheapest. Cabling can be the most expensive part of a LAN, in some cases making up to 50 percent of the total cost. Cabling can also be the largest source of network problems both in installation and maintenance. For these reasons cabling should be taken very seriously.

Cabling can be twisted-pair, coaxial, twinaxial, or fiber optic. See below for the advantages and disadvantages of each of these types of cables.

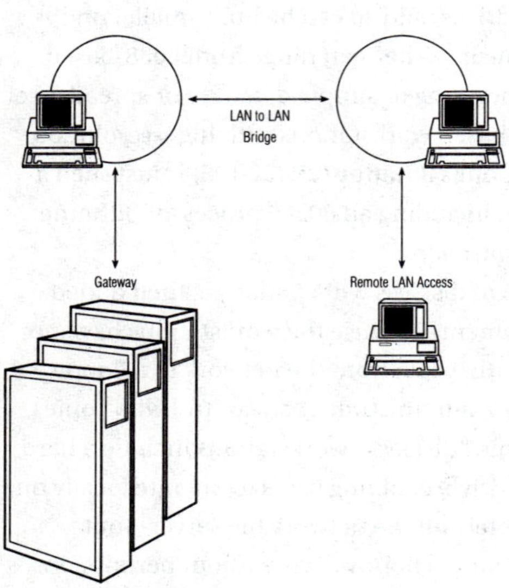

Network Connections

Interface Cards are the printed circuit boards that fit in the expansion chassis of a computer to make the physical connection with the LAN cable. The interface card is responsible for getting raw data to the computer onto the network and vice versa. This requires translation from parallel to serial form and back, buffering, packet creation, encoding/decoding, cable access, and transmission and reception. See below for details on each of these functions.

Bridges are devices that connect different LANs, allowing communication between devices on separate cabling systems. Bridges will connect LANs with different hardware and different protocols. They keep networks manageable by allowing a department to connect several small networks, rather than create one large, unwieldy network. This reduces traffic for individual computers and improves network performance.

Bridges are related to but differ from other devices like routers, which determine the best way to forward data toward its correct destination, connecting LANs with the same protocols but different hardware; and gateways, which connect two LANs with different protocols by translating between them.

Enough said for now. Here are expert tutorials for some of these components:

Cabling

Cable is the medium used in most networks to connect devices. It is cable's ability to transmit encoded signals of some kind that allow it to carry data from one place to another. These signals might be electrical in the form of moving electrons as in copper cable, or they might be optical signals in the form of flashing lights, as in fiber optic cable.

A few networks don't even use cable. They use air and microwave or infrared signals to transmit and receive data. These rare networks are usually more expensive, less reliable, and operate where cable is inappropriate, say, across a river or freeway.

Most networks use cable because it has certain properties that may be used to transmit information. These properties differ from cable type to cable type. Understanding these differences helps the user choose the right cable.

"There are three basic cable types to choose from—coaxial, twisted-pair and fiber optic."

Three Choices For LAN users today there are three basic cable types to choose from—coaxial, twisted-pair and fiber optic. Each has certain advantages and disadvantages. While the majority of installed LANs use coaxial cable, twisted-pair cable has become very popular and fiber optic cable's use is growing.

Originally, access protocols were tied to cable type. Ethernet and ARCnet only ran on coaxial cable. These protocols have been around the longest, explaining why the majority of installed LANs use coaxial cable. Recently, however, these protocols have been modified to run on twisted-pair and fiber optic cable. The same is true for other protocols, including Token-Ring. The result is that access method no longer determines cable type. LAN users who once used Ethernet or ARCnet and coaxial cable may now use twisted-pair or fiber optic cable. Same holds for Token-Ring and other access protocols.

One common rule to remember about cable is there is often a trade off between speed and distance. This is especially the case with copper cables. It is possible to push the speed of data transmission on a cable but in doing so the distance that data can travel is usually reduced. Devices like repeaters and amplifiers can help here, but the physical properties of the cable impose certain limits.

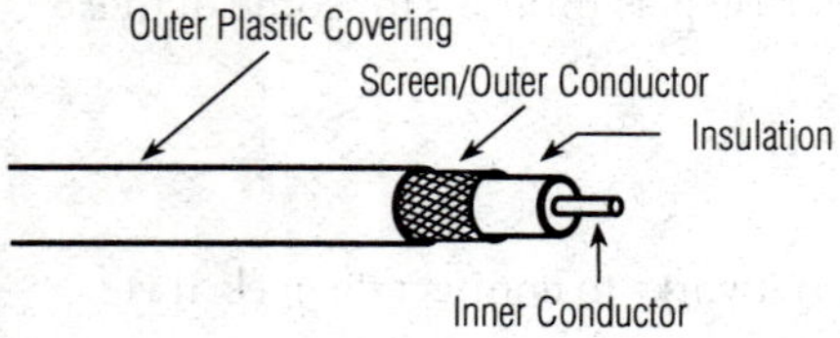

Coaxial Cable:
The grandaddy of data cable, coaxial cable is proven, easy to use, and has large capacity and distance. It's also versatile, carrying voice, video and camera.

Coaxial Cable has been around the longest of any data transmission cable and has a long, glorious history. Coaxial cable has four parts. The first is the inner conductor, a solid metal wire. It is surrounded by the second part, insulation. The third part, a thin, tubular piece of metal screen, surrounds the insulation. Its axis of curvature coincides with that of the inner conductor (hence the term coaxial). The fourth part is an outer plastic cover that surrounds the rest.

If you have cable TV, you have coaxial cable. In fact, broadband transmission, a type of LAN transmission, uses the same principles as cable TV and runs on coaxial cable. The main property of coaxial cable that both cable TV and broadband LANs take advantage of is the ability to transmit many signals at the same time. In both cases, each signal is called a channel. Each channel travels along the cable at a different frequency so it doesn't bump into another channel.

Coaxial cable has high bandwidth. This is another way of saying it can handle plenty of traffic, which is probably its biggest advantage. High bandwidth is also another way of saying high speed. If the cable can carry more traffic it can carry data faster. That is, coaxial cable supports high-speed networking. Other advantages of coaxial cable include its relatively low immunity to interference, its ability to carry signals over significant distances and its familiarity to many LAN installers.

There are several sizes of coaxial cable. Standard Ethernet cable, also called thick Ethernet, is as thick as your index finger. Newer Ethernet cable, often called **Cheapernet** or **Thinnet**, resembles cable TV/(CATV) coaxial cabling. The thicker cable is more robust, harder to damage, and transmits over longer distances. It's also harder to connect.

Standard Ethernet coaxial cable requires something called a vampire tap and drop cable to connect to a LAN device. This combination is bulky and expensive. Thinnet uses something called a **BNC connector** to attach to computers. It's easy to use. Thinnet with BNC connectors has become the standard office coaxial cable.

The experience of coaxial cable should not be underestimated. It is a proven technology, handling just about every type of transmission, including video, voice, and data. Twisted-pair cable cannot come close to this versatility. Fiber is only beginning to.

Twisted-Pair Cable Twisted-pair cable has been around longer than coaxial cable, but it has not been carrying data. Instead, it has been carrying voice. It is used extensively in the nationwide telephone system. Practically every building has twisted-pair cable installed in its walls.

In the past few years, however, vendors have been able to transmit data over twisted-pair cable at reasonable speeds. Some of the first proprietary networks to use twisted-pair cable, like ***Omninet*** and ***10Net***,

Twisted-Pair Cable:
Simple in design, twisted-pair's advantages include flexibility, price, and ease of use. You may be able to use the twisted-pair cable already installed in your building for your LAN.

sent data at 1M bits per second. While only one-tenth the speed of Ethernet on coaxial cable, it was much faster than the asynchronous transmission speeds used over the voice-grade cable before.

Token-Ring networks, introduced in 1984, raised twisted-pair speed to 4M bits per second. In 1987, several vendors introduced Ethernet on twisted-pair cable, raising the speed to lOM bits per second. The distance between computers for these types of networks, however, is much shorter than Ethernet on coaxial cable, about 300 feet compared to approximately 2,000.

Nevertheless, twisted-pair cable offers some significant benefits. It's lighter, thinner and more flexible than either coaxial or fiber optic cable. These characteristics make it easier to install. It's also cheaper, usually. The most significant advantage of twisted-pair is its ubiquity. It is everywhere. It's familiar. The dumbest people can install it, move it, use it. Look at the telephone industry.

The most important result of the telephone industry's use of twisted-pair cable is modular cabling. While modular cabling is being developed in coaxial and fiber optic environments, it grew up in the telephone industry's twisted-pair world. A modular cabling system, built with patch panels, wiring closets, and common connector jacks, makes it easier to move computers from one place to another without rewiring the LAN.

There are many types of twisted-pair. The most important distinction is between shielded and unshielded. The former has an insulating material wrapped around the two twisted wires and the latter doesn't. Shielded is more immune to interference, which usually translates into higher speeds and longer distances. It is more expensive, however. There are many types of both shielded and unshielded twisted-pair cable.

Twisted-pair makes sense in many installations. Its low cost, ease of use, and flexibility make it ideal in offices or workgroups without heavy traffic or electromagnetic interference.

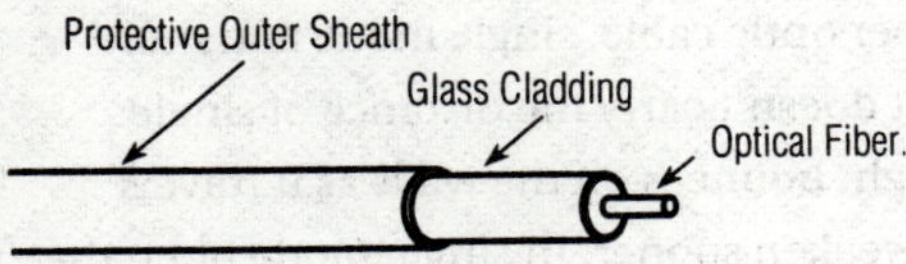

Fiber Optic Cable:
Since the potential is enormous, the fiber optic should be the cable of choice, if you can find the right installer.

Fiber Optic Cable Fiber optic cable has been touted as the answer to all the problems of copper cable. It is immune to electromagnetic interference, has enormous bandwidth, sends data over huge distances and can carry voice, video, and data. But it has not been embraced by many LAN users yet.

The biggest reason fiber optic cable is not the cable of choice is experience. There are not enough experienced cable installers familiar with it. Fiber optic connectors, though much easier to put on the cable than previously, are still more difficult to install than coaxial cable. The same is true with splicing fiber optic cable, the most difficult part of fiber optic installation.

Another problem is the lack of diagnostic tools for fiber optic cable. Time domain reflectometers, ohmmeters, voltmeters, and oscilloscopes can all be used to find copper cable faults and generally diagnose cable conditions. Only a few of these types of tools exist for fiber optic cable, making maintenance more difficult and more expensive. It is this lack, combined with the lack of knowledge, that makes LAN users wary of fiber optic cable.

"Fiber optic cable has enormous potential. Its capacities are tremendous."

In the LAN arena, fiber has enjoyed its greatest success as a backbone medium connecting LANs in different buildings together. All its properties make it ideal for the heavy traffic, rough environment and great distances these backbones support. These properties have also proven fiber optic cable to be appropriate in factory environments, especially its immunity to interference.

Slowly, fiber optic cable is migrating into office LAN environments. Standards are being developed that will allow fiber to interface with other media. The two most important of these standards are Fiber Optic Distributed Data Interface (FDDI), a 100M-bits-per-second token passing ring, and the IEEE's FOSTAR attempt to put Ethernet on fiber optic cable. Both these standards should help the installation of fiber.

Fiber optic cable is simple in design. There is a hollow core fiber of standard diameter, measured in microns. Surrounding this is a solid "cladding." Outside the whole thing is a protective covering. Originally, fiber optic cable was made of glass. Plastic fibers have been introduced recently.

LEDs, or light emitting diodes, are used to send signals down a fiber optic cable. A detector receives the signals and converts them back to electrical impulses. Signals are encoded into light in many ways. The most popular way is to vary the intensity.

There are two types of fiber optic cable, single mode and multimode. Multimode is cheaper but doesn't carry the distance of single mode. In multimode fiber, the light bounces off the walls as it travels down. This causes the signal to weaken sooner. In single mode fiber, the light travels straight down the fiber. Single mode has a smaller diameter than multimode, making it harder to manufacture.

Fiber optic cable has enormous potential. Its capacities are tremendous. With an experienced fiber optic installer it makes sense to put in as much fiber as possible since it prepares the LAN for the future when data rates and capacities will be orders of magnitude higher than today.

Connectors and Costs When trying to choose between the three types of cable there are a few items to keep in mind. First, all three have problems with connectors. Twisted-pair cable is the easiest to "connectorize." A couple of hand-held tools put modular phone jacks directly onto twisted-pair with just a snap of the wrist. Nevertheless, some types of twisted-pair cable, like some IBM cables, are more difficult to put connectors on. Coaxial and fiber optic cable is extremely difficult to connectorize. There is a way around this, though. Buy cable that is already connectorized and buy more length than you need.

Price is also a difficult problem when it comes to cable. Each type of cable varies widely in price. Each type can cost less than a dollar a foot or more than five. It is possible to find fiber optic cable that is less expensive than twisted-pair cable, especially shielded twisted-pair. If price is a large factor in the decision, use twisted-pair.

Each type of cable connects different end devices. While many network interface cards, for example, use coaxial and twisted-pair, few have connectors to fiber optic cable.

"Cable is by far the largest source of network problems."

Finally, your application, especially the speed, distance, and capacity desired both now and in the future, should guide your choice of cable. Twisted-pair might be fine for a medium sized LAN with light traffic. Connect it to another building or add more processing power and you might need fiber.

Contrary to expectations, cable can be the most expensive part of a LAN, in some cases making up to 50 percent of the total cost. True, cable itself can be inexpensive. Twisted pair cable can run as little as two cents a foot. On the other hand, installation expenses— buying, pulling, connectorizing, etc.—can run the price per foot into the tens of dollars. That can run cable costs into the thousands of dollars for even a small office and into the tens of thousands of dollars for a building.

On top of this, cable is by far the largest source of network problems. It is the largest source of troubleshooting , installation and maintenance problems.

Nevertheless, few LAN users take cabling very seriously. "They take months agonizing over LAN hardware and software decisions and then demand the cable be delivered and installed the next day," says Charles McGovern, director of marketing at Vertex Cable and Computer Products in Farmingdale, NY.

Cable should get more respect.

There are literally thousands of different cables, connectors and interfaces to choose from and almost as many vendors. Choosing cable is not automatic. Virtually every network type can run on virtually any cable type. Plus, it is possible to combine cable types in the same network, making the decision even more complicated.

Bridges

A Data Link *bridge* is a device that connects two similar networks. It takes packets from one network and puts them on the other, and vice versa. While it does this, it regenerates the signal strength of the packets, allowing data to travel further. In this sense, a Data Link bridge is just like a *repeater* which also regenerates packets to extend a LAN. But a bridge does more than a repeater.

A bridge is intelligent. It can look at each packet and decide on which of the two networks it belongs. Repeaters simply forward every packet from one network to the other, without looking at them. A bridge looks at each packet as it passes, checking the source and destination addresses. If a packet coming from Station 1 on LAN A is destined for Station 5 on LAN B, the bridge will pass the packet onto LAN B. If a packet coming from Station 1 on LAN A is destined for Station 3 on LAN A, the bridge will let it go on its merry way.

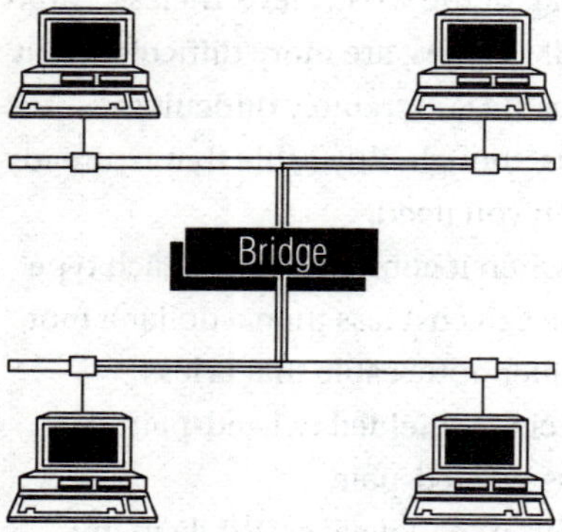

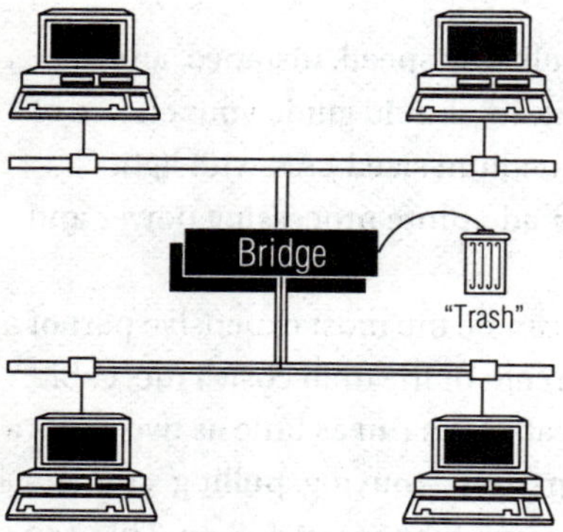

Moving Packets:
Above, the bridge allows a packet destined for node 2 to pass through based on the packet's source and destination address. Below, the bridge does not copy the packet onto the upper segment because the packet is destined for node 3. Instead the bridge ignores the packet.

Bridges know which packets belong where by looking at the Media Access Control (MAC) layer information carried in the packet. The MAC layer is part of the second layer of the Open Systems Interconnection (OSI) model. The MAC layer defines how packets get on the network without bumping into each other. It also contains information about where the packet came from and where it should go. As we will see, because bridges use this level of information, they have several advantages over other forms of interconnecting LANs.

Why Bridge? The most common reason to use a bridge is to improve performance. A bridge improves performance by reducing traffic. It reduces traffic by dividing one large LAN into two smaller parts. This reduces the amount of traffic on each, while still allowing workstations on both segments to talk to each other.

It is possible that a poorly placed bridge can reduce performance by creating a bottleneck. However, it doesn't take too much effort to discover the best place to put a bridge. For example, it doesn't make sense to split up a workgroup of five or ten people if they work closely together. A bridge between this workgroup and another workgroup, however, could improve performance dramatically. With the bridge, the two workgroups may still communicate transparently. Only communication between groups, not communication within groups moves through the bridge.

Another reason to use a bridge is to change from one type of cable to another. For example, you may run twisted-pair cable in the offices and fiber optic cable between buildings. Segments can be connected with a bridge, so "long distance" traffic can flow freely from one segment to another while local traffic stays local. Broadband and baseband Ethernet networks may be connected this way, too. Same goes for Starlan and Ethernet. Or, a 16M-bits-per-second Token-Ring backbone may use bridges to connect to a number of local 4M-bits-per-second Token-Rings.

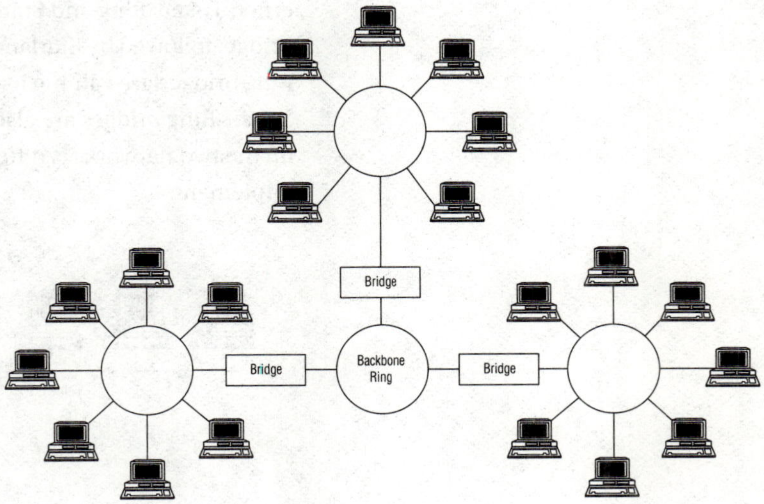

A Backbone Ring Connecting Three LANs' Token-Ring Networks: *This backbone doesn't have to be a ring, since LANs can be virtually any topology.*

The MAC Layer Bridges work at the MAC layer. This means they will interconnect LANs that use many different protocols. That is, bridges are *protocol-independent.* For example, the same bridge may connect networks running TCP/IP, DECnet, OSI, IPX, and XNS protocols. All these higher-layer protocols are "encapsulated" within the MAC layer, so to speak. That is, the MAC layer is below the network layer where the upper-layer protocol information is kept. The bridges use the MAC layer so it will work with them all, too.

Don't get us wrong. A bridge will not allow a user "speaking" TCP/IP to talk to a user "speaking" IPX or OSI. A device which will allow this is called a *gateway.* A gateway actually translates between protocols. A bridge simply passes packets back and forth, regardless of the protocols. A bridge will let any two users "speaking" the same protocol talk to each other.

Many networks have more than one protocol running on them. For example, two groups of Sun workstation users may use TCP/IP most of the time and OSI some of the time. A bridge between the groups will pass both TCP/IP and OSI packets. In fact, the bridge won't even know which protocol it is passing. It doesn't care. The key thing to remember about the bridge is that the two machines on either side must use the same protocols.

The most common standardized MAC-layer protocols are Ethernet, Token-Ring and Starlan. Ethernet-to-Ethernet is the most common bridge, followed by Starlan-to-Starlan and Ethernet-to-Starlan. Token-Ring bridges are gaining in popularity as Token-Ring grows. Ethernet-to-Token-Ring bridges are also just appearing. Because the packet size used on the two networks is different, this is a more difficult bridge to implement.

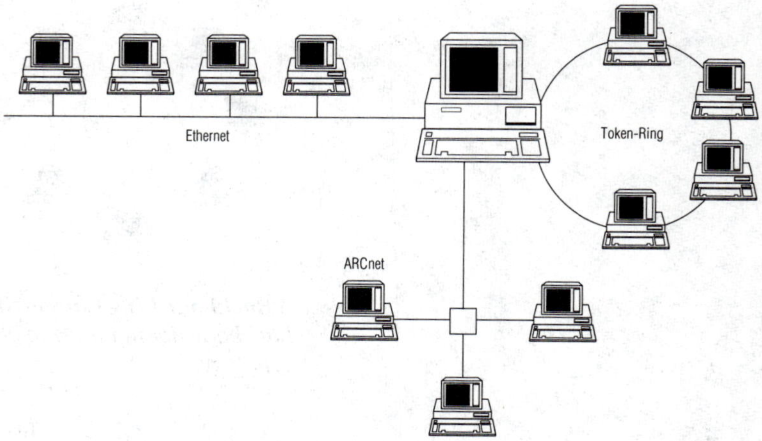

Network Computing: *An internal bridge.*

Learning and Filtering A bridge works with something called an *address table.* When a bridge is attached and plugged in, it begins to send out broadcasts asking for all the stations on the local segment of the network. As the stations return the broadcast, the bridge builds a table of local addresses. This process is called *learning.* Most bridges are learning bridges, though one or two still force the LAN manager to enter all the local addresses. These are called *static* bridges.

Once the bridge has the local address table, it is ready to operate. When it receives a packet, it examines the source address. If the packet's address is local, the bridge ignores it. If it is for another LAN, the bridge copies the packet onto the second LAN. Looking at the packet's address is called *filtering.* Actually copying the packet to the other side is called *forwarding.*

The most basic type of filtering is keeping local packets local, and sending remote packets to the other subnetwork. The next type is filtering based on specific source and destination addresses. For example, a bridge might stop one station from sending packets outside of its local LAN. Or a bridge might stop all "outside" packets destined for a particular station, thereby restricting the other stations with which it can communicate. Both types of filtering provide more control over internetwork traffic and better security.

Some bridges will filter broadcast and multicast packets. This can help prevent traffic overloads called broadcast storms since these types of packets rarely go beyond the local LAN. In a broadcast storm, a broadcast message is repeatedly copied across bridges until the network screeches to a halt.

Source Routing Some Token-Ring bridges, notably those from IBM, use a routing scheme called source routing to get packets between networks. The bridges we've talked about so far use transparent routing, which all Ethernet and Starlan, and some Token-Ring, bridges use. With transparent routing, the packet does not know the route it will travel, nor do the bridges it passes over. Each bridge will forward a packet that is not local, until it finally reaches its destination LAN.

"With source routing, the packet itself contains its routing information."

With source routing, the packet itself contains its routing information. This information specifies the LANs and the bridge through which the packet will travel to get to its destination. The sending machine is responsible for putting this information into the MAC-layer packet header, the part of the packet which contains the source and destination addresses along with some other information about the packet.

In order for sending stations to know the route their packets will take, they must learn the layout of the entire network. This is done dynamically through a process called route discovery. During route discovery, packets are passed around the network. As they are passed from LAN to LAN, they are filled with information about the network. Each bridge a packet passes through puts three numbers into the packet: the number of the two LANs to which it is connected and its own bridge number. This information is then passed back to sending stations. Using this information, sending stations can then create a map of the network and appropriately route their packets.

Source routing is used primarily by IBM on its Token-Ring LANs. Other vendors are just beginning to use it, too. Source routing does impose some small amount of extra overhead on the network which might diminish performance ever so slightly. However, this is more than offset by the advantages of the routing scheme. Because the sending machine knows the route its packets will take, it can always choose the optimal (i.e., fastest or cheapest) path at the time of transmission, which is not possible with transparent routing. With transparent routing, the optimal path remains "optimal" until a bridge or a link fails. Also, source routing provides better management since the path of a packet is immediately accessible from the packet itself. Finally, source routing bridges can be faster than transparent bridges since they do not have to "look up" each packet to see if it must be bridged. The packet tells them immediately.

Remote vs. Local So far, we have been discussing local bridges. Remote bridges connect two geographically separate LANs. Most of the time this is done with some type of telecommunications link, like a telephone line, a public data network, microwave or a T-1 line. A bridge at one end of the link puts packets destined for the other LAN out over the link. A bridge at the other end of the link receives these and passes them to its local LAN. The process works in both directions.

"Once bridges begin to connect LANs over a longer distance, reliability and fault tolerance become more important."

Telecommunications links are not the only way to connect two LANs via a remote bridge. Broadband networks and fiber optic links can also bridge two networks. For example, bridges might be used to pass traffic over a fiber optic backbone between the buildings of a university or business campus. This is one of the most common uses of a bridge. Technically, this might not be called a remote bridge since it is connecting two LANs that are local, the building LAN and the backbone LAN.

Either way, once bridges begin to connect LANs over a longer distance, reliability and fault tolerance become more important. Bridges at both ends must take precautions against data corruption over the remote link.

Spanning the Globe An IEEE 802.1 algorithm or procedure called *spanning tree* makes it possible for a bridged network to include loops, which are illegal with Ethernet. Spanning tree makes it possible to have parallel bridges so a back-up bridge can take over in case the primary bridge fails. Such a layout is usually impossible with Ethernet. Without a backup bridge using spanning tree, a failed bridge causes the network to be partitioned until the broken bridge can be found and fixed.

According to the spanning tree algorithm, one bridge is designated the primary bridge. This bridge is the only bridge to pass traffic. If it fails, the traffic is automatically shunted to a parallel bridge. Nearly all bridges which support a backup bridge use the 802.1 spanning tree algorithm, although some have made nonstandard "improvements."

Spanning tree overcomes a major obstacle in bridging, but the back-up bridge is idle as it waits for a failure. This is costly. If the back-up link could carry traffic, the cost of the second link would be better justified. Here's where load *balancing* comes in. Using load balancing, traffic can be evenly divided over the two remote parallel bridges. This provides much better performance since not all traffic is going over one remote link. Since the spanning tree technology is still in place, loops are not an issue. If one bridge happens to fail, the other can carry all the traffic.

Bridges should have network management capabilities. These include providing information to the LAN manager on how much traffic is passing through, what type of traffic it is, how many errors occur, etc. With this information, the LAN manager can configure and manage the network.

How does LAN equipment work together?

Now that we understand the basic components of a Local Area Network and how it's connected, let's take a look at what makes it run, at the special software which makes it possible for everyone in the system to communicate, share peripherals, and accomplish other tasks.

The working controller of any Local Area Network is called a network operating system.

What is a network operating system?

A network operating system is the software used to connect devices, share resources, transfer files, and perform network activity.

There are usually two main parts to network operating system software: workstation software and server software. The workstation software puts the PC on the network. It reroutes data over the network when needed. The server software makes disks, software, and ports available to other PCs on the network.

LAN system software is the controlling brain of the operation. Among the many crucial functions it performs are:

[1] Controlling the operation of the network-who uses it when, what they have access to, which network resources are available,

[2] Moving data around, redirecting it to whatever workstation, server, or other resource in the system you have commanded,

[3] Providing other crucial administrative tools which add, change, and remove users and equipment from the network,

[4] Supporting file and record locking and providing other security features such as different passwords and privilege levels for each user.

See next page for more functions and new features.

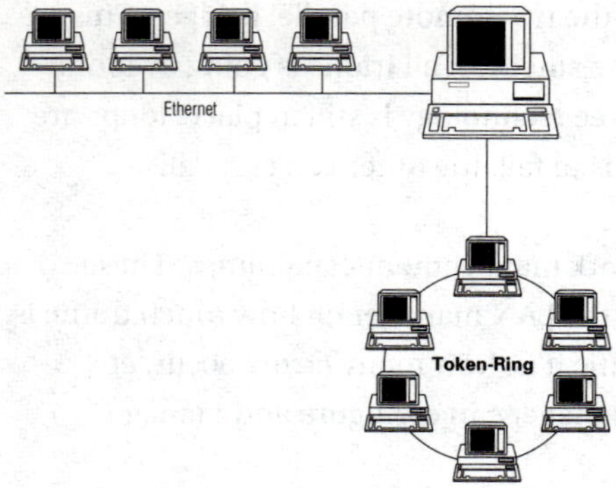

More Network Architecture:
Different topologies.

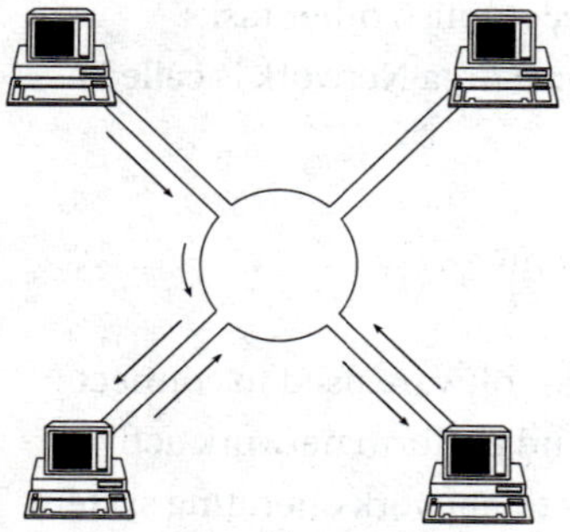

Token-Ring (logical topology):
How a Token-Ring is wired like a star.

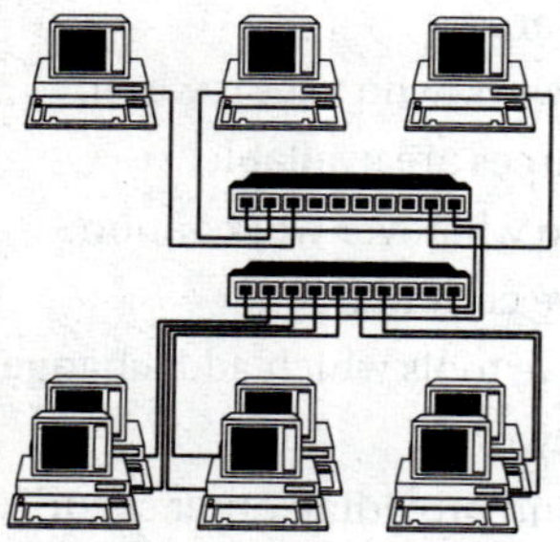

IBM Token-Ring Network:
With Token-Ring logical topology.

The leading systems software products include:

- *Novell's NetWare* The leading network operating system for medium to large networks or internetworks. A central file-server based operating system that includes mainframe-like security features. NetWare offers versions optimized for either 80286 or 80386 file servers. It can suport DOS, OS/2, or Macintosh workstations. Some versions have sophisticated transaction tracking.

- *3Com's 3+ system* 3Com's network program for dedicated DOS-based file servers. Because it works under MS/DOS, it offers capability with NETBIOS applications (those that rely on the network request-handling routines Microsoft built into its DOS). 3+ supports DOS and Macintosh workstations.

- *3Com's 3+ Open* 3Com's most sophisticated set of networking programs and utilities. Built to work on an OS/2 file server, 3+ Open can work with 3Com's LAN manager for sophisticated client-server applicaitons, or by itself for simpler network applications.

- *IBM's PC Network Program* IBM's peer-to-peer network program that works with IBM's broadband or Token-Ring network hardware.

- *IBM's OS/2 LAN Manager* Developed by Microsoft and IBM, this network program enables an OS/2 based machine to become a network file server. Although there's currently little software that takes advantage of LAN manager's features, future software will be able to fully implement the client server networking model with LAN Manager, using the file server to perform many of the calculations normally performed at the workstation, thus increasing overall speed.

- *Sun Microsystems' TOPS* TOPS makes this low-end networking program that can integrate Macs and DOS machines over low-cost LocalTalk hardware. Because it's a peer-to-peer network, users can share the contents of their local hard drives.

And for those of us who need to know more about network operating systems, here's some further expert information:

Network operating systems

The network operating system is a program for moving data around a network. It also controls the operation of the network—who uses it when, what they have access to, which network resources are available, etc. Think of the network operating system like you do DOS—loaded at bootup and working behind the scenes to provide services for users and application programs—only this time the services are on a network of machines, not just one PC.

At its most basic, the network operating system allows LAN users to share PC peripherals—hard disks and printers. Most network operating systems do much more, though. They provide data security by keeping people out of certain resources and files. They have administrative tools that add, change, remove users, computers, and peripherals from the network. They have troubleshooting tools that tell LAN managers what is happening on the network. They have internetworking support that ties several networks together. And so on. Let's see how these things are accomplished.

Redirection At the heart of the network operating system is a concept called redirection. Redirection is just what it sounds like: taking something headed in one direction and making it go in a different direction. You are probably familiar with DOS redirection. For example, the command DIR > FILENAME will redirect a directory listing to a file instead of to the screen. Try it. The > tells DOS to give the results of the command on the left to the entity on the right. Thus, the command DIR > LPT1: will send the contents of the directory to your printer instead of to the screen.

The important thing about redirection is that the program, in this case DIR, does not know or care where its output is going. It just sends it to DOS, which then takes care of it, depending on the redirection commands entered by the user. I'll say it again because this is important. With redirection the program does not know or care where its output is going. It sends it to the same place every time. Another program, in this case DOS, takes care of sending it where the user wants it to go. This is called DOS redirection.

Network operating systems depend heavily on redirection, only this time data is being redirected over the network instead of to files or printers. Nevertheless, the operation is almost identical. Here's how it works. Suppose you type the command COPY C:FILEA F: This copies

FILEA from drive C: to drive F:. For this to work, you must have a drive F:. You could have a drive F: if you had extra hard disks or RAM disks, but suppose you don't. Instead, you have a drive F: on another PC across the building attached via a LAN.

How does this work? Redirection. The network operating system makes it appear to the COPY program that drive F: is local. The COPY program doesn't know or care that drive F: is across the network. It sends the file to DOS just as it always does, only this time the network operating system steps in to reroute the file over the network to drive F: across the building.

The same redirection can be done with printers and other peripheral devices. Thus, LPT1: can actually be a printer on the network instead of a local printer. Same with COM1 (though this is a little harder). The network operating system takes care of redirecting all of these devices. Of course, the user doesn't need to know about redirection. He just types the drive designation or prints from his word processor as he always does. The network takes care of the rest.

The Server So far, we have talked about redirecting output from the user's PC. But where is the output going? The PC at the other end, the one with the drive we called F:, must be expecting data if our COPY command is going to work. It also must have offered its hard drive to users on the network. How else could we have used drive F:? It must have said,"Go ahead. My hard disk is available for use by PCs on the LAN." Again, it is the network operating system that takes care of this. It does so with a component called the server. The server does just what it sounds like. It serves up a computer's resources to the network, making them available for use by other PCs attached to the LAN.

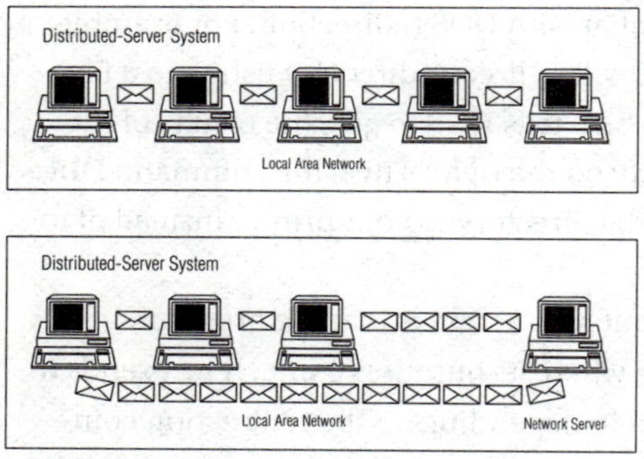

In a distributed-server system (top), node A can send a file directly to node C. In a dedicated-server system (bottom), node A must send it to the server first, and then node C must copy it.

Thus, we have a network operating system made up of two parts: a redirector and a server. Not all machines need run the server. But all machines must run some kind of redirector. Why? Because every machine has to be able to put data onto the network, and the redirector is the piece that does this. Not every machine needs to share its resources, so not every machine needs a server piece.

With some vendors' network operating systems, the machine with the server part of the network operating system cannot be used as a workstation. This is called a dedicated server machine. Novell uses this kind of setup almost exclusively. With other network operating systems, all machines on the network can be servers if desired. This is a nondedicated server setup.

There are advantages and disadvantages to these two types of server setups. Nondedicated servers allow for more flexibility. Users can make resources available on their machines as necessary. To share a file with another user a user might make his machine a server, which the other user could log in to and use the hard drive. On the other hand, since there are many servers on the network, it can be harder to administer all the resources that are available. Backing up all the shared data, setting up security to guard network resources, and just setting up who can use what resources on the network becomes more complicated. Another drawback is that nondedicated servers often suffer some performance drop as they are being used for two purposes at the same time: The user on the machine using the PC as a workstation and the other users on the network sharing the PC's resources.

"Your choice of dedicated or nondedicated operation will depend on the work your network is doing."

Dedicated servers have just the opposite advantages and disadvantages. They are easier to administer since all data is in one place. They are faster since they don't have a local user to serve. On the other hand, it is harder to make resources available on an ad hoc basis, since setting up a server is more difficult and time consuming. Your choice of dedicated or nondedicated operation will depend on the work your network is doing.

File Service The server we have been talking about is a file server. It is called this because its primary task is to make files available to users on the network, even though it also makes other resources available—printers, plotters, etc. File service allows users to share the files on a PC. The server PC says, "Here are the files I want to make available. Go ahead and use them." The server PC can make its whole disk available, certain directories available or only certain files available. Often, the network operating system can let the LAN manager determine which users are allowed to use which files, keeping the mail clerk out of the payroll file, for example. In any case, all that is happening with a file server is that its hard disk is becoming an extension of each user's PC. Here's how it works.

Suppose I want to use a file from the file server hard disk. I set up my local drive F: to be the file server hard disk. I do this with the network operating system. The process has many names. Some call it mapping the drive F: to the server disk. Others call it mounting. In either case I am setting up something called a virtual drive. My drive F: is not really local, even though it appears that way to my PC. It is actually the drive on the file server and the redirection part of the network operating system makes sure that everything destined for drive F: ends up at the file server.

Now, suppose the file I want from the hard disk is a word processor, say, WordPerfect. From the F: prompt I type the command for WordPerfect, WP. What happens next is that WordPerfect is loaded into the memory of my PC. The WordPerfect file is still sitting on the server while I am running it in my machine. The same is the case for a document file I open from drive F: using WordPerfect. It sits there while I edit it on my PC.

Meanwhile, other people can use WordPerfect from the file server (assuming we have a license that allows multiple users). As for the document I am using, WordPerfect must make it clear to other users that I am using it. It does so by locking the file. This prevents others from using it. With some programs, file locking might allow other users to read the document I am editing but they cannot make changes to it. They will have to wait until I am finished and open the file again. Some network operating systems will provide this kind of file locking for programs that don't. This keeps users from "bumping into" each other.

The important thing to remember about file service is that it is just an extension of the local PC. Programs work just as they would if they were on the local PC. There are some exceptions. Many database programs have been built to take advantage of a file server, allowing many users to work on the same database at the same time. Some, like Paradox, even allow one user to see changes made by another. Still, the file server itself is doing nothing more than doling out files. Of course, network operating systems provide much more than just file service—they also provide security, administration, printer sharing, tape backup, fault tolerance, etc.

"The file server port of the network operating system makes a PC into a multiuse machine."

Server Operation The file server part of the network operating system makes a PC into a multiuser machine. Instead of just one user on the server PC, there are many users. But we must qualify what we mean by many users. A network operating system allows many users to share the server PC's peripherals, its printers, its hard disks, its plotters, etc. It does not allow many users to share its processor. We will come back to this. For now let's see how the file server allows users to share its peripherals.

In most cases, the file server is running the PC's native operating system (like DOS or the Macintosh ***Finder***). It is also running the network operating system. When requests from users come in over the network, the network operating system receives them, interprets them and hands them, for example, to DOS for execution. So, if a file open request comes in, DOS will open a file and then give it back to the network operating system to take to the user. If many users are requesting things at the same time, the network operating system handles them by queuing them up and handing them to DOS one at a time, since that's how DOS works.

Some network operating systems are different. They do not run DOS in the file server. Novell and Banyan are two such vendors of this type of network operating system. They replace DOS with a multitasking operating system, thereby winning performance advantages. At the same time, they also lose something in compatibility and by requiring dedicated file servers.

Nevertheless, the operation of all file servers is similar and accomplishes the same thing: allowing multiple users to share the peripherals of the file server. Now let's see how the new network operating systems allow users to share a server's processor as well as its peripherals.

"Instead of just getting files from the server, the server can run programs that work with the programs users are running."

The New NOS While file service is a tremendous improvement over single-user operation, it pales in significance to the enhancements that come with the new network operating systems. Some new network operating systems are based on 0S/2, a multitasking operating system. That means users with 0S/2 can do several things at the same time and 0S/2 will make sure these things don't bump into each other.

The biggest advantage of this is that one of the services a server can offer is a task. That is, the server can offer its processor for use by other users, even while it is serving up files and printers. This means a fast server can be used to do onerous chores like program compiling, calculations, and database sorting. It also means new types of programs can be used to take advantage of the server processor.

Instead of just getting files from the server, the server can run programs that work with the programs users are running. The best example of this is a database server. The database server does things like sorting, searching, and indexing so the user program and PC don't have to. This cuts down on network traffic since not so many things are going back and forth between user and server. It also improves performance and security, since the server can handle the database centrally for many users.

The Platform There is not enough space right here to go into all the advantages of the new network operating systems. (For more see page 61.) Suffice it to say that all network operating systems are platforms upon which users build network applications that solve their problems. It is important to realize this. The network operating system is useless by itself. It exists only to make other programs work faster, more efficiently, and for more people.

When you go to buy a network operating system think about every feature only for how it can help you do what you have to do. There is no point in having sophisticated and expensive fault tolerance if you do not have extremely sensitive data on your network. On the other hand, if you do need the fault tolerance, don't skimp.

Connecting PC's to Macs

O.K. But what if you want to connect your Apple Macintosh to a PC-based Local Area Network system? Do you have to give up your Apple system?

Not anymore. It's possible to incorporate both Macintosh and PC equipment in the same LANs with a special network operating system. Here's how.

Connecting the Apple Macintosh to PC-based LANs has traditionally been a seat-of-the-pants affair. Mac users wanting to talk to a PC network either had to give up their familiar icon-based world for a forbidding DOS-style interface or, with more sophisticated systems like 3Com's 3+, commit to strictly PC-based servers and an unfamiliar network operating system.

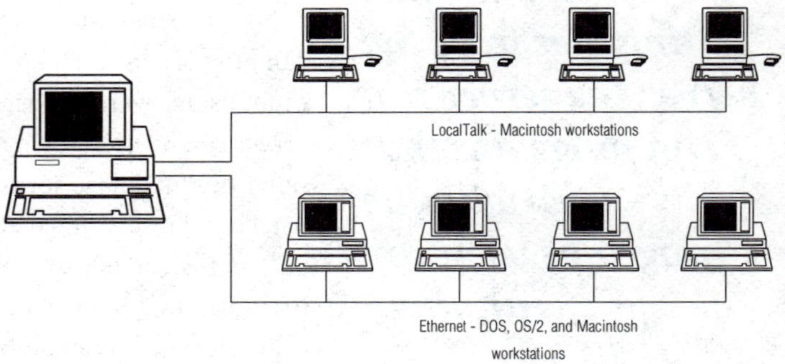

Netware for Macintosh: LocalTalk support.

Novell's ***NetWare for Macintosh*** dramatically changed that situation. The system allows Macintoshes to join a NetWare-based network with a transparency new to the PC LAN world. By implementing full compatibility with Apple's ***AppleTalk Filing Protocol*** (AFP)—the guts of the AppleShare network operating system—NetWare for Macintosh allows Mac users to join a PC-based LAN of DOS- and OS/2-based workstations without any changes to their familiar interface or their network client software.

This full AppleShare/AFP compatibility is the key to NetWare for Macintosh. It makes a PC-based NetWare file server look exactly like a Mac-based AppleShare file server. What that means is that a Mac user can use the same AppleShare client software to access the NetWare server that he uses to access an AppleShare server and that Apple packages with its new system software. The NetWare server looks and acts just like another AppleShare server. So Mac users have virtually nothing new to learn in the transition from using a Mac-based AppleShare file server to using a

NetWare server. The same software, the same interface, the same log-in procedure, and the same file security options remain. And since NetWare for Macintosh also implements Apple's ***Printer Access Protocol*** (PAP), even the printing procedure is unchanged. Finally, since the PC-based NetWare server functions as just another AFP-compatible server, it can be freely mixed with Mac-based AppleShare servers on a single network.

What Makes It Different These features are the differences between NetWare for Macintosh and a system like 3Com's 3+ for Macintosh. Though Macs can join a PC network and share files with a PC under the 3Com system, 3+ for Macintosh does not implement compatibility with AppleShare and AFP protocols. Instead, it offers only its own system of XNS protocols. This means several things.

"The NetWare server looks and acts like another AppleShare server."

First, the file server used by 3+ for Macintosh must be a PC—Mac-based AppleShare servers cannot be intermixed on a 3Com LAN. So integrating an existing AppleShare LAN into a 3Com system means junking any Mac file servers and committing entirely to PC servers running 3+. With NetWare for Macintosh, on the other hand, a current AppleShare LAN can be integrated with a NetWare LAN, Mac-based servers and all.

Since it doesn't support AFP, 3+ for Macintosh also requires 3Com's proprietary client software on the Mac. It cannot use the standard AppleShare client software that NetWare for Macintosh uses. While the 3Com software is easy enough to use, the interface to the network is not the same as AppleShare. Log-in and security procedures are quite different, and some retraining is required.

Of course full AppleShare/AFP compatibility is not anything radically new, nor is it somehow unique to Novell. AFP-compatible products for other operating systems are becoming more and more common, especially for the DEC ***VAX***. With products like ***AlisaShare*** from Alisa Systems (Pasadena, CA), the VAX looks and acts just like another AppleShare server, allowing a connected Mac to store and retrieve files on the minicomputer just as it would on a Mac server.

Full AppleShare/AFP compatibility is new to the PC LAN world, however. That won't last long—AFP compatibility is a feature few PC network operating system vendors can afford to ignore. 3Com has already announced plans to add full AFP compatibility to the Macintosh portion of its 0S/2-based 3+Open network operating system.

Physical Connections NetWare for Macintosh is built around a completely new version of NetWare—version 2.15. Older versions of NetWare—version 2. 1, for example—cannot run the new system. The

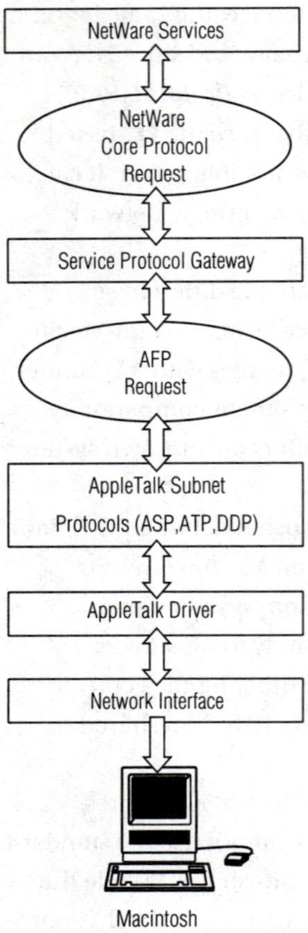

From AFP to NCP:
The process a Macintosh goes through to communicate with a NetWare file server under NetWare for Macintosh revolves around the Service Protocol Gateway, or SPG. The SPG does the actual conversion from AppleShare format to NetWare format. The SPG takes AppleTalk Filing Protocol (AFP) requests from the Mac and converts them to equivalent NetWare Core Protocol (NCP) requests, which the NetWare file server can understand and service. The data requested is then sent back through the SPG, which translates the NCP request back to an equivalent AFP request. Along the way back to the Mac, the data is processed through AppleTalk subnet protocol stack, which includes the AppleTalk Session Protocol (ASP) and the Datagram Delivery Protocol (DDP).

difference between version 2.15 and earlier versions is a variety of changes to the very basis of the NetWare filing system, to accommodate the Macintosh. Novell is currently only offering NetWare for Macintosh with ***Advanced*** and ***SFT*** NetWare version 2.15, but it has announced plans to offer it with its 2.15 version of ***Entry Level System (ELS) NetWare 11*** as well.

The mechanics of using NetWare for Macintosh are simple. Physically Macs can connect to the NetWare server either via their built-in LocalTalk hardware, or via additional EtherTalk Ethernet hardware. On the NetWare end, the PC-based server requires either a LocalTalk adapter to connect to LocalTalk-based Macs, or an Ethernet adapter to connect to EtherTalk-based Macs. LocalTalk adapters for PC servers are available from Novell, as well as from Apple and a few other third-party vendors. As for Ethernet connections to Macs, Novell currently only supports servers using 3Com's **EtherLink Plus** cards for AT-bus machines and **EtherLink/MC** cards for Micro Channel-based servers. It plans to support other Ethernet cards in the future, including its own **NE2000** and **NE/2** adapters. It also plans to keep up with hardware developments on the Mac side like Token-Ring. Of course, other network topologies are already supported by NetWare on the PC side, and PC workstations running Token-Ring, ARCnet and all other hardware schemes NetWare supports can all be part of a network with Macs attached via NetWare for Macintosh.

The physical connection to the NetWare network can be made either directly to the NetWare file server, or to a PC workstation functioning as a NetWare bridge. With the bridge approach, the NetWare for Macintosh software runs on a separate PC dedicated to that function, rather than on the main file server. This spares the file server any additional memory and processing overhead added by NetWare for Macintosh. Novell recommends bridges for larger networks, where the file server is heavily used; on the other hand, smaller networks, in situations where economics do not allow allocating an additional dedicated machine as a bridge, can run the NetWare for Macintosh software on the main file server.

Getting Down to Business With the physical connection made and AppleShare client software installed, a Mac on a NetWare for Macintosh network has all the usual AppleShare functions at its disposal. The main function, of course, is file service. Mac files and folders stored on the NetWare server look exactly like files and folders stored on an AppleShare server. The DOS- or OS/2-based PC files and directories stored on the server also look like standard Mac files and folders, and can be freely used by Macs, just as Mac files can be freely used by PCs. Plus,

Mac files and PC files can be mixed in a single PC directory, which maps transparently to a folder on the Mac side.

There are, however, some issues here. Though Macs and PCs on a NetWare for Macintosh network can have free access to each other's files, the files aren't always of any use. Depending on the format the file is written in, a Mac file might look like garbage to a PC user, and vice versa. ASCII files are usually readable by both machines, but a Lotus 1-2-3 file, for example, isn't automatically readable by a Mac, just as a ***MacPaint*** file would make no sense to a PC.

"One solution involves applications that run on both Mac and DOS- or OS/2-based machines."

The solution to this situation takes two forms. One form involves applications that run on both the Mac and DOS- or OS/2-based PCs, and that have compatible file formats so the two versions can freely use the same files. This is a big trend in the applications market. Already, packages like Microsoft's ***Excel*** and ***Write***, Symantec's ***ThinkTank/More*** and Aldus' ***PageMaker*** have versions for both Mac and PC, versions which allow Mac users and PC users to use the same files. Ashton-Tate's ***dBASE Mac*** for the Macintosh and dBASE III Plus or IV for DOS-based PCs can also freely share the same files.

The second solution to file compatibility between Mac and PC involves using a third-party conversion utility. With a conversion utility like Data Viz's ***MacLink Plus***, most popular Mac application file formats can be converted so that they are readable by a PC, and, vice versa. Obviously, this process isn't as transparent as using a package with compatible Mac and PC file formats.

Printing and Security NetWare for Macintosh also fully supports Apple's Printer Access Protocol (PAP), so printing from a Macintosh to a Mac-attached LaserWriter or **ImageWriter** is no different than printing under AppleShare. One difference is that printing output from a Mac can be routed to NetWare's print spooler, which offers a variety of queue settings to control the timing and order of print requests. Or a Mac user can choose to print directly to the printer, without the intervention of the spooler.

Meanwhile, NetWare for Macintosh allows both DOS-based and OS/2-based PCs to also make use of LaserWriters and ImageWriters. So a PC application that supports PostScript can print to a LaserWriter attached to the LAN via LocalTalk.

In keeping with its full AppleShare/AFP compatibility, NetWare for Macintosh also offers security features identical to AppleShare. The same access privileges available under AppleShare—"See Folder," "See Files," and "Make Changes"—are available to Macs under NetWare for Macintosh. These privileges are all mapped to equivalent security settings on the NetWare server.

Advantages So if NetWare for Macintosh is just like AppleShare, with all the same features, why bother using it? Why not stick with Apple's original network operating system and a Mac-based server? There are a variety of reasons. NetWare for Macintosh offers a host of advantages over AppleShare. To begin with, NetWare for Macintosh allows the integration of Macs and PCs; AppleShare offers no such integration. But that's obvious. What is less obvious is that Mac users under NetWare for Macintosh have not only the features of AppleShare at their disposal, but all the features of NetWare as well. A host of functions AppleShare users have never dreamed of—like fault tolerance and resource accounting—are available to Macs under NetWare for Macintosh. So while maintaining the familiarity and simplicity of AppleShare, NetWare for Macintosh adds a raft of new and sophisticated features.

"NetWare for Macintosh allows the integration of Macs and PCs."

Probably the most notable of these features is NetWare's native file security system. NetWare for Macintosh can provide Mac users with the same security system AppleShare does, by mapping AppleShare's three access privileges to equivalent NetWare access privileges. But it also offers them the option of using NetWare's security system, known as the most complete and effective in the microcomputer LAN market. Where AppleShare offers an anemic security setup with only three access rights, NetWare offers ten access rights, plus a much more robust group security system.

These additional security features are offered to the user via a ***Macintosh desk accessory*** (DA) supplied with NetWare for Macintosh. The DA gives the Mac user the full range of NetWare security, from access privileges to trustee rights. This is the one place in NetWare for Macintosh where end users used to AppleShare might have to learn something new. But if they feel uncomfortable with the NetWare DA, they can simply stick with the simpler AppleShare security system.

File security under NetWare for Macintosh is also more thorough than AppleShare in another way. Where AppleShare can only implement security at the folder (directory) level, NetWare can protect right down to the file level. Each file in a single directory can have its own access privileges; with AppleShare, all files in a single folder must have the same access. What this means is that files needing special access rights must be put in their own separate directories. That can throw a wrench into a clean and organized directory structure.

LAN security is more than file protection, however. Controlling access to the network itself is a crucial part of protecting it from hostile invaders. Again, NetWare for Macintosh provides more robust and complete security than AppleShare. Where AppleShare offers nothing more than simple password verification upon log-in, NetWare has a complex and flexible system of log in verifications. First of all log-ins can be restricted (on a per-user basis) to specific times, so that a user who shouldn't be playing around with the LAN at night, for example, can be denied access. At the same time, concurrent log-ins can be limited, so that users can't freely log in to as many machines as they like. NetWare also keeps an audit trail of log-in and log-out requests, so a system supervisor can keep track of users' activities and spot suspicious doings. And finally, a system supervisor can specify an expiration date for each user's account on the LAN, as well as how much disk space each user is allowed.

Passwords under NetWare for Macintosh are also more sophisticated than with AppleShare. Requirements can be set for the minimum length of passwords, as well as how often they must be changed. These precautions make sure users can't use overly simple and easily guessed passwords, nor can they keep the same passwords, when over time, a variety of unauthorized people have come to know them.

Since the release of version 2.1, NetWare has also included an impressive system of resource accounting. This feature allows a system supervisor on a NetWare network to closely monitor network usage, on a per-user basis. With resource accounting, an installation can keep close track of users' usage of specific network services—like time on the network or disk space used—and bill the users accordingly. Billing rates can be set to change according to the time of day or day of the week. This is a serious, mainframe-style feature that an AppleShare-based network would never have access to. But under NetWare for Macintosh, Mac users on a NetWare LAN can be monitored and billed just like PCs.

Running under NetWare for Macintosh also gives Mac users the protection of NetWare's robust fault tolerance. NetWare provides a variety of mechanisms to protect users from losing their data when network hardware fails. The system keeps redundant directories on each server, so if the primary directory is lost, the backup will keep the server going. NetWare also performs read-after-write verification on all disk writes, to insure that the data has been properly stored. With the SFT version of NetWare, the file server can also be configured to have mirrored drives and duplicate disk controllers, dramatically minimizing the possibility of data loss due to disk failure. Finally, NetWare has built-in ways to cope with power failures. Its Uninterruptible Power Supply (UPS) Monitoring facility signals the server when power is lost allowing it to safely close all open files and shut down before the UPS's battery runs out. These are features and protections Macs running under AppleShare simply do not have. If an AppleShare server crashes, users are out of luck.

Using Your LAN

Now that your LAN is operating, what can you do with it? How can you keep track of everything going on and keep it running smoothly? Tales of success and failure

Using Your LAN

Now that my LAN is working, what can I do with it?

We've now explained the basic ingredients of a Local Area Network system—the servers, workstations, connectors, and internal operating software. Now we need to approach the specific tasks you want to accomplish with this system.

Any software program that helps you accomplish such a task is called an "application." Application software should be distinguished from system software, the software used by the computer itself to accomplish tasks for application software, and also distinguished from network operating systems, which operate the various functions of the LANs itself. What we are talking about now, is the daily bread and butter of your business, what exactly your staff has to do to get the job done, including:

- Word Processing
- Communication and Electronic Mail
- Database
- Accounting
- Spreadsheets
- Desktop Publishing
- Printing

Please keep in mind that there *is* a difference between application software that is designed to be used in one computer and application software designed for a Local Area Network system.

If you are using your LAN just to share printers or hard disk space, there is no immediate need to change the applications software you have now. Any LAN operating system will allow single-user software to run, automatically intercepting users' local requests for disk or printer operations and carrying them out at the central "server."

However, technical constraints—and the license agreements you consented to by tearing the shrink wrap off your applications—mean that only one person at a time should run single-user software, whether it is stored on a central server or at a local workstation. Single-user programs often maintain default settings and other information in files meant to be opened by only one user at a time.

In any case, there is a big difference between software that's merely *usable* on a LAN, and software that actively uses the network. Switch to the special LAN version of your favorite programs, and you'll gain not just multiuser access to the applications, but also the ability to share databases, "boilerplate" text, and other information. Of course, you'll also be able to take best advantage of whatever peripherals are attached to the server.

Canny software companies almost always give you a price break on LAN versions. They know that installing software on a LAN will encourage new employees in a department to adopt the same product their colleagues are already using. It's cheaper to purchase a given program for your server, and then pay a license fee based on the number of users, than to buy a standalone version of the same application for each workstation.

Now here are some more specifics, for those who want to know more. And be sure to see our special Buyer's Guide on page 118 for more details along with some up-to-date prices.

LAN applications

The term "application" has several meanings. In its most generic sense, the term applies to a task. For example, a widget maker needs to take orders over the phone and transmit these orders to a warehouse where the widgets are shipped to customers. This whole procedure might be called an order entry and inventory control application. In this sense, other applications include list management, accounting, design, marketing, sales, etc.—the tasks of any enterprise.

More specifically, the term application refers to the computer software used to get a job done. Thus, database management software like dBase IV, Paradox and **Oracle** is called application software, as are other types of software like WordPerfect, **CrossTalk**, and Lotus 1-2-3. In this sense, application software is distinguished from system software, the software that makes the computer and LAN run. Think of the application software running on top and taking advantage of the system software (and hardware).

Finally, the word *application* refers to specific programs written to perform a task. For example, many users have written applications in the dBASE language. These are customized programs (a.k.a. applications) written by and for users, not by software vendors. This can get tricky, because some VARs and system integrators do write such programs to sell. The difference is they are not selling generic applications software like Microsoft, Ashton-Tate, etc. They, like the users themselves, are creating customized programs using the software of software developers like Ashton-Tate and Microsoft.

There is one more thing. Network operating system software, programs like NetWare, 10Net, and 3+, provide some applications. For example, the CHAT feature of 10Net is an application used for communicating over the network. Novell's **WHOAMI** program is a small application used to find out who a network user is. **3+Mail** is an electronic mail program used to send and receive messages and files. This presents some complications and indicates some changing directions for the PC LAN industry, which we'll discuss below.

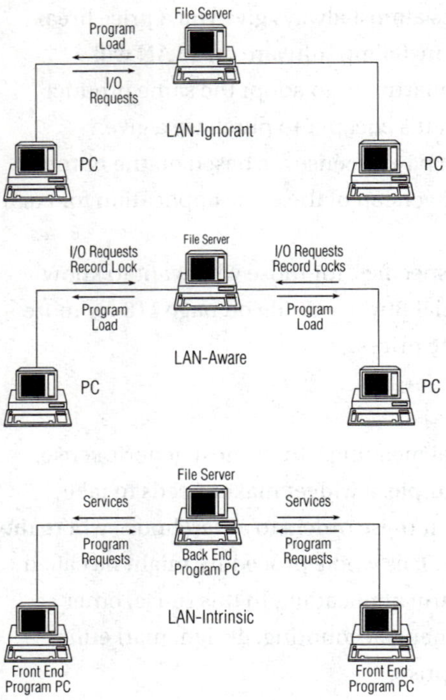

LAN Applications:
LAN-ignorant applications use the network in the most basic ways—trading I/O requests. LAN-aware applications take advantage of the LAN by establishing concurrency control and communications features like screen refresh or electronic mail. Finally, LAN-intrinsic applications begin to share processing power on the network, distributing data and compute power to open up a whole new range of LAN uses.

What does all of this have to do with LANs? Well, LANs exist for applications. That is, users install LANs to get a job done. They can have the computers, the cable, the interface cards, the file servers, the protocols—all the things we've talked about in the LAN Tutorial Series so far—but without applications software they aren't going to do much but copy things back and forth. LAN application software is what users really use. The LAN is just the base upon which they use it.

Application Types The following is going to sound somewhat philosophical, but hang in there. There are three types of applications—*LAN-ignorant, LAN-aware and LAN-intrinsic.*

LAN-ignorant LAN-ignorant applications are programs written for use on one computer by one user. However, these programs will often run on a network. That is, they may be stored on a file server and used by LAN users at their workstations. Most of the time there are severe limitations on what these applications can do. Moreover, if two people try to use the program at the same time, many horrible things can happen.

For example, if two people try to use Lotus 1-2-3 at the same time and work on the same spreadsheet, the person making the last change to the spreadsheet will overwrite all the changes made by the first user who saves. The program has no way of keeping the users from destroying each other's work. It lacks what is called *concurrency control.* On the other hand, Lotus 1-2-3 can be used by several people at the same time, if they are using different spreadsheets and if they have a license to do so. But Lotus 1-2-3 was not meant for this purpose and provides no functions that take advantage of the network.

LAN-aware LAN-aware applications are a step above LAN-ignorant applications. Usually, they are LAN-ignorant programs modified to run on a network. These programs recognize they will be used by several users at a time. They have concurrency control features like file and record locking to coordinate usage. For example, when a Paradox user begins to modify an address in a mailing list database, other users looking at the same mailing list at the same time, are prevented from changing that address record. This is called record locking.

When the change is complete, the change is displayed on the screen of every other user looking at the file. This is called *automatic screen refresh.*

Another LAN-aware feature is file locking. This is a less-sophisticated form of concurrency control. Instead of keeping users out of a particular record, they are kept out of the entire file altogether while another user has it open. Word processing programs are the primary users of this type of concurrency control.

LAN-aware programs like Paradox make up the vast majority of programs written for networks. They represent a big improvement over LAN-ignorant applications and have gone a long way to spur the growth of networking. In fact, they are becoming more and more sophisticated that the distinction between LAN-aware and LAN-intrinsic is being blurred.

LAN-Intrinsic Programs LAN-intrinsic applications actually share the processing power of several computers. Usually, though not always, this is done by dividing the application program into pieces. One piece is the server. The other piece is the client. The client piece is the part that talks to the user. The server piece does data processing. A database server is the best example of this type of application. Its principles can be generalized for other LAN-intrinsic applications.

"The client piece is the port that talks to the user. The server piece does the data processing."

In a database server, there are two pieces to the application—front end and back end. The front end is responsible for formulating requests and displaying formatted data to the user. The back end is responsible for managing and searching data, concurrency control, and security. At the front end program, users make queries, write reports, create databases—all the tasks they do with any other database management program. The difference is the way these tasks are handled.

For example, when a user asks for all the employees in the company database that make more than $50,000, this request is transmitted to the database server (back end). The database server then looks for all the employees making over $50,000. These records are then sent to the front end. This is different from the LAN-aware method.

In the LAN-aware method, there is only one program instead of two and it runs in the user's machine. When the request for high-paid employees is made, the user program gets the entire file over the network from the file server. It then has to go through the file to find the rich employees. This creates much more network traffic. The whole file is transferred from the file server instead of just a few records. Other network traffic needed includes the concurrency control commands to lock various files and records as needed. This creates even more network traffic.

With the database server the concurrency control traffic is eliminated. The database server (back end) takes care of it. Plus, only the requested records are sent over the network, not the whole database. The result is a more efficient, safer, better performing program and network.

The reason this can be done is that two programs are working together to create one application—a true LAN-intrinsic application.

There are very few LAN-intrinsic applications available now. New LAN environments created by operating systems like OS/2 and network operating systems like LAN Manager will help their development by providing multitasking, more memory, faster processors and programming interfaces that make writing LAN-intrinsic programs easier. But it will take time.

"Two programs are working together to create one application—a true LAN-intrinsic application."

The Future A category of applications we have not talked about is LAN utilities. Usually, these are programs written for LAN administration and management. Good examples are NetWare's ***SYSCON*** and ***FILER*** or 10Net's ***CHAT TALLYS***. Other LAN utilities include those for printer management, disk management, and network design. These applications are growing in sophistication and function.

Increasingly, LAN utilities are included in network operating systems. For example, NetWare comes with numerous programs to administer and manage the network. 3+Open, for OS/2 networking, has even more sophisticated network management capabilities. But, even more striking than this development, is the way in which application software and system software are coming together.

IBM's ***OS/2 Extended Edition*** is the most obvious example of this. Included are what most PC users consider applications—a database manager, a presentation manager, and a communications manager. Mainframe users expect this kind of integration, but to PC users it is a welcome development. By including these applications and integrating them closely with the operating system, IBM provides a more complete environment and a better set of tools for users and value added resellers to develop the applications (user programs) they use to solve problems.

Microsoft and its partners in developing ***SQL Server*** are doing the same thing in their efforts to integrate SQL Server with LAN Manager and OS/2. They are trying to create an environment, rather than just system software or application software. Hopefully, these developments will result in a whole greater than the sum of its parts—a whole that will change networking for the better and drive people to install more LANs.

Word processors

These days, every major word processing program is available in a special LAN version. These products make it easy for users to use a LAN server to store documents that need to be accessed by others, and they offer convenience in the form of a centralized dictionary, thesaurus, keyboard macros, and *style sheets* that can help a department standardize on formats for memos or correspondence.

Of course, LAN word processors also offer each user the full resources of any shared printer, even when it's a laser printer that requires careful management of downloadable fonts. Some *high-end* programs incorporate document management facilities, letting users track revisions of a document via a *redlining* option that shows additions or deletions on screen.

"A centralized dictionary, thesaurus, keyboard macros, and style sheets can help a department standardize."

WordPerfect 5.1 includes all the features mentioned above. It can combine separate files into one master document with a single table of contents or index, and imports a wide variety of graphics into WordPerfect documents. A particularly useful *intelligent printing* feature lets a user format text for a LAN printer, but preview it on a local dot-matrix device with the closest approximate fonts.

Microsoft Word 5.0, the latest version of the program that pioneered style sheets, adds on-screen preview of both graphics and multiple columns. It has new document management features that let multiple users attach comments to a single document. When all reviewers are finished adding comments, an included macro merges all of the annotations into a single file. Word 4.0 is the Macintosh version: this takes advantage of AppleShare and other AFP-compliant networks and is able to read and write files compatible with DOS Word, making it particularly useful on LANs with both Macs and PCs.

Although these feature-laden products were the first to support LANs, you can also purchase network versions of simpler, *executive-level* word processors. An excellent case in point is Software Publishing's ***Professional Write:*** it's an easy-to-use program that can trade files directly with ***Displaywrite***, Word, WordStar, and other formats.

Other LAN word processors include: IBM Displaywrite, Lotus ***Manuscript***, Multimate ***Advantage***, Samna ***Word 111 Sprint***, ***Volkswriter 4*** with ***Perfect Grammar***, ***Wordstar 5.5***, and ***Wordstar 2000+***.

Electronic mail

Electronic mail hasn't turned out to be the instant panacea to human communications problems that some visionaries claimed it would be, but it is making steady inroads, especially on LANs. A stable of excellent E-mail products is now available to LAN users, offering not only slick messaging features but powerful internetworking and gateway links to other mail systems.

Still, the LAN E-mail market is a confusing place, obscured by a haze of conflicting vendor claims. The following list of 11 pointed questions should help to clear the smoke and clarify the issues involved in buying a good mail package.

Does the E-mail package run on your workstation and operating system?

If you have an Apple Macintosh, you better not set your sights on a PC-only package. If you're running OS/2, you'd obviously do best to pick a product that supports that operating system. And if you have or plan to have a mixture of machines and operating systems, make sure the E-mail package you pick has versions for all of them. Several packages support both Macs and DOS-based PCs, while other products have both DOS and OS/2 versions. Finally, if your users are ***Windows*** fans, make sure you get a package like daVinci's ***eMAlL*** or Consumers' ***Network Courier***, which offer specfic Windows versions.

"If you have a mixture of machines and operating systems, make sure the E-mail package has versions for all of them."

What about LAN compatibility?

Obviously, you need an E-mail package that runs under your network operating system. But with DOS-based packages, there's more to it than simple compatibility. Most of the DOS-based E-mail packages on the market today are generic, meaning they'll run under any NOS that is DOS 3.1 or ***NetBIOS***-compatible—which includes basically all PC NOSs available. But there are also other E-mail packages available, packages that are tailored to specific NOSs and that take advantage of their specific features. Banyan's ***Vines Mail***, for example, is designed just for the Vines NOS, and is tightly integrated with Vines features like the ***StreetTalk*** global naming service. 3Com's 3+Mail and ***Tapestry Mail*** are similarly integrated with the 3+ and Tapestry NOSs. Da Vinci Systems still offers a generic DOS 3.1 version of its eMAlL package, but it also recently introduced a Novell NetWare-specific version as well. The new version is closely integrated with NetWare, meaning eMAlL takes its user and security information directly—and automatically—from the NetWare bindery. So LAN managers don't have to manually enter user and group names and security equivalences into both the bindery and the E-mail program.

There are advantages to both these approaches. Obviously, vendors of generic packages can sell to a wider base of LAN users than vendors of NOS-specific packages. And users don't have to worry about changing E-mail programs if they change NOSs. On the other hand, NOS-specific packages take fuller advantage of their specific environments than do generic packages. Where generics can only utilize the features shared by all DOS 3.1 NOSs, NOS-specific packages can use any feature their specific network operating system offers.

Whether these extra features make the NOS-specific package preferable to generic packages depends on the specific packages, the specific features—and the specific NOS. After all, if you have a NetWare-based LAN, you can't even consider buying Vines Mail.

With Mac-based E-mail packages, things are a little less complex. The Mac packages covered here all run on any network operating system compatible with the AppleTalk Filing Protocol (AFP)-which includes AppleShare and TOPS.

Is the package RAM-resident?

> *"A good, full featured E-mail program will eat up a minimum of 50k bytes of precious memory—and often more."*

If you can't pop up a form to write and send a message at a moment's notice—in the middle of an application—then you may end up never sending anything. Exiting an application to DOS, running the mail program, sending the message and, finally, returning to the application, is just enough wasted work and time to keep you from really using a non-RAM-resident E-mail program. But programs like da Vinci's eMAIL and Consumer Software's Network Courier, where a hot key pops up the whole program interface in the middle of an application, are so easy to use that our E- mail communications boom.

Of course, there are drawbacks to RAM-resident programs. For one thing, they're RAM hogs. A good, full-featured E-mail program will eat up a minimum of 50K bytes of precious memory—and often more. When running other hungry applications, like Borland's Paradox or Xerox's ***Ventura Publisher***, that extra RAM can be a serious problem. You might end up having to reboot or use a TSR utility like ***Referee*** in order to reclaim the E-mail program's RAM space, just so you can fit the big application into memory. If you use Paradox a lot, that little process could become a major headache.

Of course, all these problems are only an issue with DOS-based PCs, who have rigid 640K bytes RAM limits. Apple Macintoshes and OS/2-based PCs, with their much larger RAM limits, don't tend to have such memory problems. So E-mail packages for the Mac tend to be *desk accessories* which the user can pop up at a moment's notice. This is how Mac packages like CE Software's ***QuickMail*** and TOPS's InBox work. OS/2, meanwhile, can run multiple programs at once, so an E-mail program can easily be *RAM-resident*, coexisting with other resident programs. Of course, you do have to have enough RAM installed to handle all these coexisting programs.

There are other sides to the RAM-resident issue. For one thing, E-mail vendors who have squeezed their program into a 50K-byte TSR package may have had to squeeze on functionality as well. Features that more hefty non-TSR packages offer may have been eliminated from the TSR packages. Big packages like Conetic's ***Higgins*** couldn't possibly be RAM-resident, but they offer a wealth of E-mail and other features.

Probably the best solution is an E-mail package that can be both RAM-resident and non-RAM-resident. AT&T's ***PMX/StarMail***, for example, can be run as a regular program at the DOS prompt, with all features available, or it can be loaded into RAM as a TSR, with a reduced set of features so it will fit nicely into available memory. This way, a user has a choice, depending on his situation and preferences.

What about message notification?

Many users may find they don't need the convenience of a fully pop-up E-mail program. But they often find that they do need to know immediately when they receive a message, whether they're in the middle of an application or not. Most LAN E-mail packages on the market today offer this immediate and automatic message notification, whether the rest of the program is RAM-resident or not. Using a small TSR program (usually so small that it doesn't get in the way of other programs), these packages notify the user of an incoming message with an audible beep or some sort of pop-up visual prompt, like a status line or a pop-up window or, in the case of the Macintosh packages, a flashing icon. Usually, the user can set how he wants to be notified, or whether he doesn't want to be notified at all.

"Probably, the best solution is an E-mail package that can be both RAM-resident and non-RAM-resident."

Does the package offer message certification?

One important thing to watch for is some kind of certification feature. One type of certification, often called *return receipt*, works like real return receipt mail, where a user sending an important message can request an immediate and automatic confirmation message when his recipient receives the message. Retix's ***RetixMail*** actually lets the user know when the recipient has read the message. Another form of message certification involves the sending user checking a separate status list for information as to whether the recipient received his message. If used sparingly, a return receipt feature can be easier to use than a status list feature. But when used too freely, users may find themselves deluged with receipts and receipts to receipts. In these cases, where users only need return receipts on rare occasions, a status list feature may be more appropriate.

What about security?

Most E-mail packages offer at the least a system of passwords. The more secure systems have both passwords for each user and a master password for the LAN manager, so that only he can make changes to the overall system. RetixMail also allows only the LAN manager to change user passwords. Some packages, like Torus Systems' Tapestry Mail, offer encrypted passwords, so that even if an intruder with a Sniffer breaks into the system he won't be able to decode the password.

For the truly paranoid, many packages offer encrypted messages, either with a proprietary encryption method or via a standard like DES.

Again, this protects users from a hacker with a Sniffer, keeping him from being able to read sensitive missives as they travel down the wire. What about messages that have arrived, though, and are sitting on disk? Different packages handle security at the disk level in different ways. At least one package, da Vinci's eMAIL, keeps messages in a private directory on each user's local disk, where it is somewhat safe from the pryings of other users—and from some disaster at the central server. Most packages, though, keep the messages for the entire mail system on a central file server or *post office.* But if the messages are stored as regular unencrypted DOS files, this method can mean serious security problems—if intruders can get access to the file, they can read the message. Some products use encryption to protect these files. Others, like ***cc:Mail,*** use more extreme measures, encrypting and compacting all messages into a single database file. Even if an intruder could gain access to this file and decode part of it, he would be hard pressed to find the specific message he wanted.

"At least one package, da Vinci's eMAIL, keeps messages in a private directory on each user's local disk."

What other basic features does the package offer?

E-mail packages offer a wide variety of mail features beyond simple messaging. Watch for features like group distribution lists, where it is possible to send a single message to pre-determined groups of users. This can be a big time saver allowing a user to send a bulletin to all the users in, say, the Accounting department in a single send command, rather than laboriously sending separate messages to each individual.

Also watch for sorting and searching features. If you want to organize your messages a sorting feature can be invaluable, while a search feature can help you find a particular message.

A system of *enclosures* or *attachments* is also important. These allow other files to be included with—*attached* to—the basic message. So a message about this E-mail article to our publisher might have a copy of the article file attached to it. Most E-mail packages allow any type of file, from ASCII to binary, to be attached to a message, though a few limit themselves to ASCII-only attachments.

Some packages support graphic and bit-mapped attachments to messages. cc:Mail in particular is strong on graphics, allowing users to compose and send graphic messages, and automatically converting between different graphic formats, including everything from Hercules, EGA and VGA, to Macintosh PIC formats. So a Mac user could send a bit-map image and have a user running a VGA display see it pretty much the same way the Mac user did.

With attachments, most E-mail packages have almost no limits on the length of a single message. Though the basic message part of the transmission may be limited to some length—CE Software's QuickMail, for example, has a message limit of 20K bytes—with attachments, the entire message can be as big as the user likes.

"With attachments, most E-mail packages have almost no limits on the length of a single message."

What features beyond E-mail does the package offer?

While many packages covered here stick to strict electronic mail functions, others are more ambitious, adding other functions. Conetic's Higgins, for example, is a wide-ranging office automation and group productivity package. It includes features like group scheduling, calendaring, to-do lists and expense reports—all in addition to and integrated with E-mail. ***WordPerfect Office*** offers a similar set of office automation functions in addition to its basic E-mail functions. Action Technologies' ***The Coordinator*** package integrates individual scheduling and activities tracking with electronic mail for something called "Conversation Management." These packages often don't think of themselves as E-mail, but as something larger that just makes use of E-mail.

A few E-mail packages are experimenting with integrating themselves with other vendors' products. Da Vinci Systems, for example, is working to interface its eMAIL package with Information Research's (Charlottesville, VA) ***Syzygy*** scheduling product, via Novell's Message Handling Service (MHS).

How about internetworking and remote communications?

Most E-mail packages can run on several servers on a single LAN, allowing users running from different servers to pass messages as if they were passing them to users on their own server. Some packages, though, go beyond this, allowing users on different LANs—connected physically, via phone lines or via another transmission medium—to exchange messages with each other.

Different packages accomplish this in differing ways, and with differing success. The best packages make the process of inter-LAN communications totally transparent, where a user doesn't even realize the user he is sending a message to is attached to a different LAN, a LAN that may be 10 meters or 10,000 kilometers away. The E-mail package transparently does the routing of all messages between the internetworked system's different servers or *post offices,* freeing users from having to know anything about the physical details of the system or how his messages are delivered, including things like phone numbers for dial-up links. AT&T's PMX/StarMail's internetworking feature takes things a step further, allowing users on DOS-based Starlan networks to transparently exchange messages with the AT&T mail systems running on both local and remote *UNIX*-based **3B2 minicomputers.**

Some vendors provide these internetworking features as integral parts of their basic packages. Da Vinci Systems, for example, bundles an internetworking feature called ***Internet*** with every copy of its eMAIL package. Other vendors, like Consumers Software with its Network Courier package, require the purchase of a separate internetworking *module.*

"The best packages make the process of inter-LAN communications totally transparent."

Another related feature, often included in E-mail vendors' internetworking packages, is remote communications for standalones. With this feature, a standalone PC, one not attached to a LAN, can dial up via modem and become a full-fledged user on a remote LAN's mail system. From there, the standalone user can exchange messages with LAN users just as if he himself were locally attached to the LAN. With its Modem Mail module for its Network Courier package, Consumers Software offers a particularly sophisticated remote standalone feature, where standalone users can transparently receive mail in the background, even as they work on a different application. Other less sophisticated packages require more work on the part of the user. Still others don't offer a specific remote standalone feature at all, and require the use of a less-than transparent third-party remote product like ***pcAnywhere, Close-Up,*** or ***Carbon Copy*** to access the mail system.

What about gateways to other E -mail systems?

The internetworking features described above are all for linking LANs running the same type of E-mail systems, for example, linking one LAN running 3+Mail in New York to another LAN running 3+Mail in Boston. But when it comes down to running different LAN E-mail systems, for example linking 3+Mail to Vines Mail, or for linking a LAN E-mail system to a public E-mail system like MCI Mail or to a mainframe E-mail system like ***PROFS***, things become more complex. These simple internetworking modules just can't handle these more demanding requirements. Gateways, however,can.

E-mail gateways are a complex and confusing subject. One important thing to remember about true E-mail gateway is that they are transparent to their users, that they fully integrate the two different mail systems that they set out to connect. While it's easy for a 3+Mail user to use a standard SDLC mainframe gateway to dial up an IBM mainframe and run PROFS, or for a Network Courier user to dial up an asynchronous DEC VAX host and run the ***All-in-One*** E-mail system, these are not true E-mail gateway connections. A true E-mail gateway offers a much slicker, vastly more seamless link. It fully integrates the two mail systems so that their users don't even realize they are sending messages to and receiving messages from a totally different type of system. A good 3+Mail-to-PROFS gateway, for example, would allow both 3+Mail and PROFS users to exchange messages with each other, just as if they were exchanging them with users on their own local systems. PROFS users look like local users to users of 3+Mail, and vice versa. The gateway handles not only the physical connection between the machines, but the logical connection between users.

"E-mail gateways exist to link a dizzying range of LAN-based and non-LAN-based E-mail systems."

E-Mail gateways exist to link a dizzying range of LAN-based and non-LAN-based E-mail systems. For most popular LAN E-mail packages, there are gateways to other LAN E-mail systems, to public E-mail systems like MCI Mail and EasyLink, and to a wide variety of mainframe and minicomputer-based E-mail systems, like IBM's PROFS, DEC's ***All-in-One,*** Hewlett-Packard's ***HP-Desk,*** and Wang's ***Wang Office.***

How these gateways are implemented and sold varies widely. Some LAN E-mail vendors offer their own proprietary gateways for links to specific E-mail systems. Consumers Software, for example, sells its own gateway between Network Courier and PROFS, while cc:Mail sells its own gateways to both MCI Mail and PROFS. Many E-mail vendors, though, rely on third party gateways and gateway services. Users of Conetic's Higgins, for example, must rely on third-party gateway links from gateway vendor SoftSwitch (Wayne, PA) to make connections between Higgins and other systems. The SoftSwitch **SNADS Gateway/Higgins** links the Conetic system to a wide variety of other LAN, public, mainframe, and mini E-mail systems. Banyan Vines Mail uses a similar SoftSwitch product called **SNADS Gateway/Banyan Mail.** SoftSwitch and a variety of other third parties offer gateways for 3+Mail to bolster 3Com's own proprietary **MCI Mail gateway**.

But these SoftSwitch gateways—and many other third-party gateways—are complex and expensive affairs. SoftSwitch ***Central,*** the company's big E-mail gateway product and the one that the SNADS gateways mentioned above require, runs on an IBM mainframe, provides links to dozens of different mail systems and carries a very hefty pricetag. But LAN E-mail vendors' own gateways, like those from Consumers Software and cc:Mail, as well as some third-party gateways like SoftSwitch's ***MailBridge*** products, are much simpler. Besides linking just two mail systems—rather than dozens—these gateways run on PCs and are priced accordingly. So don't go setting up a sprawling SoftSwitch Central system when your vendor's or a third party's little one-gateway, one-link product will do the trick for your needs. On the other hand, if you need connections to everything from Wang Office to DEC's ***VMSmail,*** big third-party gateways like SoftSwitch's may be the only way to go.

There are also E-mail gateway *services,* which offer dial-up gateways via phone lines. CE Software's QuickMail, for example, can utilize the DASnet/I-Net service to offer gateway links between the Mac-based package and a variety of public and mainframe E-mail systems. These services can be expensive, however.

> ❧ *"There are also E-mail gateway services, which offer dial-up gateways via phone lines."*

What about X.400 and MHS?

You may also find vendors offering a different species of E-mail gateways, gateways not to specific E-mail systems but to E-mail protocols. X.400 is the CCITT's international standard for messaging. In theory, any E-mail system that fully supports the X.400 protocol can transparently exchange messages with any other X.400-based system. Similarly, products supporting Novell's Message Handling System (MHS) protocol can transparently send and receive mail among themselves. Protocols like these are the future of electronic mail. They spell the eventual death of the scores of specific E-mail gateways on the market. In a world where all E-mail packages are X.400-compatible, you only need one gateway—an X.400 gateway.

But X.400 is still something of an unrealized potential, with only a few vendors beginning to support the protocol in the PC LAN world. Retix is beta testing its RetixMail package, which is built directly on X.400. That means it can communicate with any existing X.400-compliant mail system—which includes systems like PROFS, All-in-1 and many others—all without an additional gateway. But it is the only such native-mode PC LAN E-mail package available. Consumers Software, meanwhile, should be shipping its X.400 gateway by press time. Several other vendors have X.400 gateways in the works (see box). So when shopping for a an E-mail package, keep future X.400 compatibility in mind.

As for MHS, it will never be as broad and encompassing a standard as X.400. Still, a variety of vendors of both E-mail and other applications are embracing the MHS protocol. LAN E-mail vendors Action Technologies (the developer of MHS) and da Vinci Systems offer MHS interfaces for their programs, as do many non-E-mail applications like Ashton-Tate's *Framework.* These packages can theoretically all pass messages among each other as if they were passing them to their own local users. MHS also provides a standardized protocol to write gateways to. SoftSwitch, for example, offers an MHS gateway called **MailBridge Server/MHS** that links MHS-based applications like The Coordinator and da Vinci eMAIL to both SoftSwich Central systems (and thus dozens of E-mail systems) and to other SoftSwitch MailBridges for specific systems like PROFS and MCI. Alcom also offers MHS gateways. Whether MHS has enough momentum

> ***Communications Software***
>
> A LAN is a convenient way for many users to share modems connected to a server. However, to access the modem pool, you need communications software that works via the NetBIOS protocol instead of insisting on a local serial port. Such programs include DCA's Crosstalk Mk4, Hayes' Smartcom III, and Relay Communications' Relay Gold.

and gains enough adherents to make supporting it important is still up in the air, but MHS support is definitely something to consider in an intelligent E-mail purchase.

Database

Let's take it as given that your company, like most companies installed or is thinking of installing a LAN for three reasons: to share hardware and software resources, to communicate and, most importantly, to disseminate every single piece of relevant information to every single relevant person. Let's also assume you've taken care of the first two by buying network hardware and a network operating system with electronic mail. Finally, let's assume your company is like most: constantly straining to expand and improve access to information.

These are reasonable assumptions, because you can never get enough information. Take Federal Express, the package shipping company. Using a sophisticated bar-code system and worldwide distributed database, the company can locate your package in a matter of minutes, no matter where in the world it actually is. That's why it's the fastest growing company in the package shipping business.

But the company could do more. First, it could lower the response time to seconds. Next, it could offer customers direct, online access for package searches. Finally, it could provide other forms of communication using its network, e.g., E-mail nodes and facsimile machines in every Federal Express street office. Each of these improvements could expand and improve access to information, for both Federal Express and its customers.

The airlines are another example. Their networks provide fast access to information about reservations, flights, weather, meals, crew, traffic patterns and much more. At United's Terminal of Tomorrow in Chicago's O'Hare International, an employee can get information about the clocks at each gate or the flashing signs announcing arrivals and depatures from any computer in the terminal, as well as information about reservations, flights, etc. Add United's nationwide links and a reservations operator in Los Angeles can find out what the sign at Gate 23 in Chicago says.

Of course, not every business needs nationwide networks and distributed databases across mainframes. Ultimately, however, every business, including yours, wants its very own airline reservations system or its own package tracking system. Your business might be reserving tables at a restaurant or tracking the parts at a lamp factory. But either way, your company rises or falls on its ability to get the information you need, when you need it, where you need it, and in the form you need it.

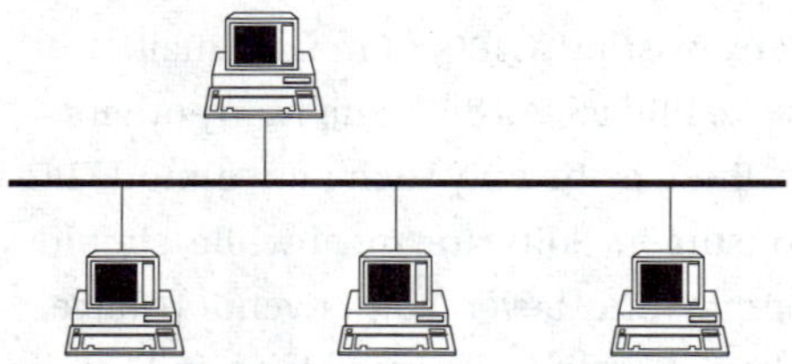

Client-Server Databases:
In general, an OS/2 database server will provide higher performance than a DOS-based server. The best OS/2 database server is one that can support both OC/2 and DOS clients. Under the client-server model, the front end resides on the clients and is responsible for displaying data and redirecting the users request. The server is most likely a more powerful machine, since its duties include processing all user requests and maintaining data integrity and reliability.

The obvious question is, how?

With LANs and databases, of course.

LANs are the physical connections used to connect sources of information: people, bar code readers, keyboards, computers, video cameras, etc. They come with software to help get the job done, but their primary task is the connection. It's what you do with the connection—the database software part—that makes life fun. That's what the rest of this article is about.

What is a Database? Simply put, a database is a collection of information organized for easy access and manipulation.

An address book is a database. So is a recipe book, a catalog, a dictionary, or a calendar. Ususally a database holds representative information, information that refers to something else, like food, people, clothing, words, or days of the year in the example above—information we need to get our jobs done and live our lives.

> *"It's what you do with the connection—the database, software port—that makes life fun."*

Information kept in a database is only half the story, though. The other half is the *road map* explaining what individual pieces of information mean and how they relate to each other. By itself a phone number is meaningless. For it to stand for useful information we need to know that it's our customer or our friend's. Creating a road map is an important component in building a database, and keeping that map up to date is how we keep it relevant to the real things it is describing.

So here's our working definition of a database: A database is an organized collection of pieces of information, together with a road map that helps us understand what individual pieces of data mean and how they relate to one another.

Database Management Systems The task of building the road map and then the necessary database into a computer can be formidable. Some databases are staggering in size. Fortunately, this is an important enough task that a branch of computer science has grown up around the subject, and any number of commercial database management systems (DBMSs) may be purchased to provide database-related services. These services include database definition (building the road map), database conversion (importing data from a variety of sources into a database, or exporting it from the database into one of a variety of forms) and database management (keeping the data current, correct, and safe from loss or harm).

The rise of the information sciences has also had an interesting side effect—namely that businesses and corporations now view their databases as resources with definite, mission-critical value, much like the people, money, and fixed assets that they always recognized as vital to their operations. They have learned the lessons of Federal Express and United Airlines.

"Business and corporations now view their databases as resources with definite, mission-critical value."

Among the many things DBMSs do, controlling access to data, protecting data from accident or malicious intent, manipulating data and providing tools for the interpretation of data are the most important. A DBMS must provide fast, easy access to data, but it must also keep that data consistent and useful. The following list of features summarizes important capabilities found in most DBMSs:

- *Database design and maintenance tools* These usually consist of a programming language-like environment, called a data definition language (DDL). It is used to build the database, defining the things it will hold, their relationships and the way they will be maintained. Associated with the DDL are tools, including a utility appropriately named a data dictionary. It is actually a database that describes another database and is used to store existing definitions of the database elements and relationships.
- *Data administration and control mechanisms* These tools confer varying levels of privilege to users and restrict access accordingly. Three principal levels of access exist: read access (look, but don't touch), write access (change the contents of the database), and administrative (change the composition and distribution, as well as the contents, of the database). This last type of access allows a supervisor to change the structure and relationships of a database, something most users should not be able to do since it can have grave affects on the integrity of data.
- *Data entry management utilities* These are for entering data into the database. They range from simple prompt/response routines to elaborate screen forms that include all kinds of data-checking and relationship management information. For instance, checking to make sure the phone number has the correct number of digits or the salary of an employee is more than a few dollars and less than a few million.
- *Report design and generation utilities* These allow database programmers to design and name particular reports to be extracted from the contents of a database. For instance, a customer list, including names, addresses, and telephone numbers. Once defined, a report can be generated at the push of a button, each time with the latest data available.
- *"Ad hoc" query facilities* These let database users question a database on the fly. For instance, you can ask how many people in your database are named Fred or how many live in Wisconsin. In a sense, query facilities permit users to obtain reports without having to design them.

> "Query facilities permit users to obtain reports without having to design them."

- *Backup and recovery utilities* These permit a database to be restored to a pristine state when hardware, electrical or human failure causes its data to become suspect or corrupted. For instance, suppose a lightning strike powers down the computer and disk drive just as some new information is being added to the database. It is not clear if the changes were complete and recorded in the database. By rolling back the database to a state when everything was certain and reentering the changes, users can be sure their changes were made. This process is called *transaction rollback* and *recovery.*

Together, this collection of capabilities comprises a complete cradle-to-grave environment for setting up and managing databases.

New Developments The biggest development in the LAN database arena is the PC database server. Suddenly, every major database vendor has announced a PC database server or support for a PC database server. The first PC database server came from Gupta Technologies (Menlo Park, CA) more than two years ago. Minicomputer databases implemented the client-server architecture long before that. Only recently, however, has the architecture caught anyone's attention now that large software companies with even larger marketing budgets have entered the fray.

More exciting than database servers are distributed databases. Database servers form the basis for distributed databases, but they are not the same. Database servers have one server and many users. Distributed databases have many servers and many users. The differences are profound. For now, it is enough to say that one company, VIA Information Systems, is shipping a true, LAN-based distributed database system and several other companies will ship similar products soon. The adoption of NetWise's Remote Procedure Call Tool by several LAN database vendors should speed the development of distributed databases.

The advantages of a database server over a file-server-based DBMS are well known. Database servers perform better, use less network bandwidth, save on workstation resources, and are more reliable and secure in mission-critical applications. They allow for the use of database information by programs other than database management applications, for example, Excel, Lotus, and PageMaker.

Distributed Databases As mentioned, database servers and distributed databases are not the same. Distributed databases require the ability to work transparently with data, regardless of where the data resides.

A distributed database has two key features. The first is the ability to do a relational join with two tables from two database servers. The second is the ability to write updates to two or more sites as part of one transaction.

"Distributed databases require the ability to work transparently with data, regardless of where the data resides."

VIA DRE, for example, uses a dual data dictionary. Each database server operates independently (there is no "master") and includes a dictionary describing the data it holds. Each user has a dictionary handling application requests by connecting the user to the appropriate database server. The user dictionary knows where the data is so the application and the user need not. Data can be moved to the most convenient location without rewriting applications.

Tricky Stuff LAN database servers are here. Distributed databases are here. Applications may be built, though programming expertise is required. Front-end programs will reduce the knowledge barrier. However, even with such programs as Paradox, dBASE, ***Advanced Revelation,*** and ***Focus,*** programming will still be a necessity. Large, sophisticated, mission-critical, transaction processing applications will always require programming.

The fundamental flaw in the whole concept is that users want complicated, tricky stuff, but they want it to be done easily. Application generators, form generators, and report writers make simple things simple. Users have to add the tricky stuff.

Luckily, the pieces needed to conquer the tricky stuff, in the form of database server programmatic interfaces, high-level languages, libraries, and development tools, are available or will be soon. Better learn to program. It will make life much easier.

Accounting

For many companies, accounting software may be the reason for installing a LAN. Accounting information—Accounts Payable, Accounts Receivable, Payroll, Inventory, etc.—comprises a company's most important information. A network allows your books to be kept up-to-date by several data entry operators simultaneously, and means that completely up-to-date reports may be produced at any time.

Of the hundreds of accounting programs on the market, not all run on LANs. With its ***AccPac*** line, however, Computer Associates has a full range of network accounting software. AccPac BPI modules include Accounts Receivable and Payable, Payroll, and Inventory Control. To run them on a LAN, you install the AccPac BPI Lan Pack, which confers file and record locking plus password protection.

Data Pro's line of accounting programs is LAN-ready, and significantly more complete than most. It includes General Ledger,

Accounts Payable with Checkwriting, Purchase Order Entry with On-Order Processing, Payroll (again with Checkwriting), and Job Costing with Time Billing. Point of Sale and Inventory Management modules support hardware add-ons including cash drawers, bar code readers, and even speech synthesizers. The Data Pro modules, which have a consistent user interface, can either stand alone or operate as part of an integrated system.

Great Plains accounting software is another flexible, powerful series. You need Network Manager software to enable LAN use. ***Open Systems,*** as its name implies, offers purchasers source code in Basic for its accounting modules. To run them on a LAN, the ***Network Resource Manager*** is a required option. UNIX versions are also available.

If you're particularly interested in tailoring accounting software to your own business, take a look at the ***SBT Database Accounting Library.*** SBT offers a particularly wide range of modules—including Professional Time and Billing, Project Accounting, Purchasing, and many others-written in dBASE source code. Users can modify the programs and run them using any dBASE interpreter.

Spreadsheets

Spreadsheets are fundamentally *personal* productivity tools, so their LAN versions aren't dramatically different from the single-user ones. But network versions of spreadsheet programs offer a savings in cost and workstation disk space, and they are more convenient to load. Most important, they always prevent multiple users from changing the same worksheet concurrently by mistake.

"They always prevent multiple users from changing the same worksheet concurrently by mistake."

Computer Associates' *SuperCalc5* is a good example of the advantages a LAN spreadsheet can confer. With the ability to hot-link up to 255 worksheets, and manipulate as many as three at once on screen, SuperCalc5 supports network file locking. It also provides each user with his or her own personal default settings, and can automatically search multiple server directories to root out SuperCalc or 1-2-3 files.

Underlining the growing importance of LANs, both of the new versions of Lotus 1-2-3 include network support as a standard feature. 1 2-3 Release 3, which allows loading multiple spreadsheets into as many as 16M bytes of memory (on 80286 or '386 PCs). features file locking and support for either DOS or OS/2-compatible LANs. It comes in a single-user edition, but a server edition will lower the price of adding workstations. 1-2-3 Release 2.2, which now comes with the ***Allways*** print formatting program built in and has been tailored to the existing base of DOS networks and 8088 PCs, comes in a server edition; the workstation edition (consisting of a software license and documentation only) is relatively inexpensive.

Microsoft's ***Excel*** also runs across LANs, printing to network devices via its Windows user interface. Thanks to the size of the Excel program files, it's particularly useful to be able to offload them to a LAN server; because of differing workstation configurations, though, it's best to keep Windows itself on local disk drives. Only a single person may have read/write access to a worksheet at any one time, but Excel optionally lets others look at it without making changes. The very-similar Macintosh version can trade worksheets with PC Excel using the SYLK format. It now stores spreadsheets up to an incredible 8M bytes in size, provided your Mac has the RAM.

Desktop publishing

Though most desktop publishing programs may be installed on LAN servers, and run from one workstation at a time, it's still rare to find one that is multiuser. With its ***Network Edition,*** however, Ventura Publisher can make that claim.

The file server software allows all workstations to share a printer, "chapters," and source text files. A special alert notifies a user when a file within a chapter has been modified by another user, and multiple workstations can share the same read-only style sheets. Ventura does have rather stringent hardware requirements: Each workstation must have a full 640K bytes of RAM, plus at least 256K bytes of expanded memory.

Printing

Theoretically, a LAN user should have quick, transparent access to every aspect of the network. That includes peripherals, such as modems and printers. Especially printers. It's a safe bet that employees use the printer more than any other device in any office, barring the phone and coffee machine. Yet NetWare, the most popular of all the LANs out there, is notoriously obstructive when it comes to printing.

First of all, NetWare will only print to a printer attached to a file server. Secondly, the user has to explicitly tell NetWare to intercept the print data before DOS gets it and tries to send it to a possibly nonexistent local printer. Finally, and most annoyingly, NetWare will not allow you to control network printers from within an application.

NetWare's Printing Jungle To print using NetWare alone, you have to type CAPTURE at the DOS prompt to redirect printer output to the network file server. You either have to execute another CAPTURE, or specify ENDCAPTURE to release the print job to the file server's printer. Without an ENDCAPTURE command, NetWare will automatically time out after a specified amount of time. Before version 2.1, NetWare required that you type SPOOL and ENDSPOOL before the document could be printed.

Enter printer utilities, those third-party solutions to network printing headaches. The earliest were designed to allow users to print from within their applications, either with a pop-up menu selection or a hot-key combination. Later, utilities were designed to allow users to print to *any* printer on the network, not just one attached to a file server. Nowadays printer utilities handle everything from downloading fonts to using the right paper, as well as managing queues and controlling printer configurations. And usually, this can all be done with simple, intuitive menus that eliminate endless typing.

"Printer utilities handle everything from downloading fonts to using the right paper."

Do You Really Need One? Later versions of NetWare, however solved some problems. Although users still can't control network printers from within an application, in NetWare 2.1, Novell has added advanced queue management functions that, among other things, let users create queues, manipulate jobs within them, and assign priorities. With all this new functionality, there's some question as to whether users really need a printer utility that can cost anywhere from $100 to $600.

Through its CONSOLE commands, NetWare handles network printing by setting up queues, or waiting areas for jobs that have been sent to the printer. NetWare automatically assigns one queue to each printer. Print jobs are sent from the queue to the printer on a first-in-first-out basis. NetWare allows one printer to service more than one queue, and conversely, one queue can be serviced by more than one printer. NetWare allows extensive queue management as well. Users with a supervisor's clearance can delete jobs from queues, assign queues to printers, or printers to queues, and create new print queues. Supervisors can also assign priorities to whole queues.

Although NetWare's queue management features may be more than adequate, there's still the problem of accessing them. To delete the second job from the PERSONNEL queue, for example, you'd have to type QUEUE PERSONNEL DELETE JOB 2. Parts of this command line are optional, but even in the best of all possible cases you'd still have to type Q PERSONNEL D 2. To add a queue to a printer, you have to specify the printer number, the queue name and, optionally, the priority level you want to assign the queue, so you end up typing PRINTER 1 ADD PERSONNEL AT PRIORITY 3, or, at least P 1 ADD PERSONNEL.

Also, there are plenty of problems that NetWare 2.1 doesn't solve. The first is that the network printer still has to be attached to the file server. (Netware 2.15, Rev.C, includes a utility for setting up remote print servers.) File servers, especially in large companies, may not be located on the same office or even floor as a user who wants to print. More importantly, file servers are often kept under lock and key for security reasons. To retrieve a printed document, users either have to travel to some remote part of the office, or find a network manager to retrieve it for them. This is a waste of everybody's time, not least of all the network manager's.

Furthermore, different users are going to need different kinds of paper in the printer, from company letterheads to labels. (The current version of NetWare can handle multiple form types on network printers). Add the running back and forth to the printer to make sure that the right paper is loaded, to retrieving the document from the file server, to managing the queues with NetWare's laborious CONSOLE commands, and network printing with NetWare is still a nuisance rather than a convenience.

Still, whether or not you need a printer utility, depends (like everything else) on your needs. If very little printing goes on over your network, it's well worth it to suffer occasionally with NetWare than spend lots of money on a utility. However, if you do a lot of printing or have a large network or do a graphic-intensive printing, the money spent on a utility will be worth the time and annoyance saved.

"If you do a lot of printing, the money spent on a utility will be worth the time and annoyance saved."

Things To Consider While even the most basic printer utility makes life considerably easier, not all are created equal. There's a range of options to choose from depending on your needs. Some utilities do little more than pop up in the middle of a program and send your job to the appropriate printer. Others will allow you to manipulate jobs within queues, feed the appropriate paper to the printer and notify you when a certain job has been printed. Here's a rundown on some things to consider.

[1] *VAP or not VAP?* Since the great majority of the printer utilities are for NetWare, ask if the utility is a ***Value Added Process*** (VAP). A VAP is software that is loaded when the server is booted up. Processing takes place on the file server, thus lessening the burden on the workstation's CPU. There's some debate, however, as to whether it is necessary, or even beneficial for a printer utility to run as a VAP.

Currently, ***LANSpool*** from LAN Systems (New York, NY) is the only printer utility that runs as a VAP. According to Jim Rosen, vice president of Network Products at LAN Systems, with LANSpool running as a VAP, the user doesn't need to be logged into the server to share its printer: "The memory overhead is much lower, since the bulk of the processing is done at the file server and not at the workstation. You can add functionality without increasing overhead."

Danny Schulmann, a technical representative at Cybertek (Culver City, CA) agrees that running as a VAP takes less time on the workstation, but also warns, "You have another vendor's product living inside your file server. If you have a problem, you won't be able to determine what's causing the problem that easily." Greg Gianforte, president of Brightwork Development (Red Bank, NJ) said that his company found that they could provide the functionality they needed without loading any memory resident software on the file server.

"Just because a program uses a lot of RAM doesn't necessarily mean that it provides more advanced print features."

[2] ***Memory requirements*** The major selling point of most utilities is the fact that they're RAM-resident, so find out just how much RAM they need, both on the workstation and the print server. It can be anywhere from 10 to 100K bytes. Examine the products carefully, though. Just because a program uses a lot of RAM doesn't necessarily mean that it provides more advanced print features. Sometimes they're just greedy.

You may want to consider whether or not you need a RAM-resident utility. Several packages do have an optional pop-up module. Some users are comfortable with NetWare's commands: a pop-up program will just use up precious RAM. Utilities that don't run from within an application will still allow you to print to any printer on the network, as well as control the printer set-up and font control codes. In that case, find a package, like LAN Systems' LANSpool, that takes full advantage of NetWare's CONSOLE commands.

Even if you're not a NetWare whiz, it might be worth it to give up pop-up features to save yourself the memory overhead. Network Enhancement Tools' (Houston, TX) ***PrintTamer*** requires 58K bytes, but the user has a choice of loading it as RAM-resident or not. Other products that focus more on the printer setup than on managing print jobs, like Brightwork Development's ***PS-Publish*** and LaserAge Software's (Los Angeles, CA) ***PrintWare***, also offer optional pop-up modules.

[3] ***The mighty printer*** These are *printer* utilities after all, so in your excitement over VAPs and RAM residency don't forget about the printer. A functional utility will let you send to the printer of your choice from within an application. A truly useful utility will also let you download font control codes and even specify what kind of paper you want to print on. Also consider what kinds of printers it supports, like laser printers, Postscript-compatible printers or plotters.

PS-Publish from Brightwork Development allows users who already have a Hewlett-Packard Laserjet to upgrade it to a Postscript printer. Postscript printers use a different printer language designed to support what-you-see-is-what-you-get graphics. PS-Publish attaches to any workstation on the LAN so that all network users can access a Postscript printer.

The only drawback to PS-Publish is that it is not software alone. There is an interface card with a video interface, supplied by OMS Imaging (Mobile, AL), that has to be dropped into the printer server (that is, whichever machine the Laserjet is attached to). It makes PS-Publish a little expensive, although you can purchase the OMS card separately for less, and it also means that you have to buy a copy of PS-Publish for each printer that you want to upgrade.

However, PS-Publish is totally integrated with PS-Print, Brightwork's printer utility, so you don't lose your Laserjet capability. When you submit a job, just specify if it's a graphic or text job and Brightwork's utilities will send it to the appropriate queue. There is also a new installation procedure for both PS-Print and PS-Publish that creates a default queue and printer configuration, so that with a few keystrokes the whole thing is set up ready to use. PS-Print is also notable for its forms-handling capability, which lets users specify what kind of paper the job is to be printed on.

"You should be able to change the priority of jobs within a queue."

While PS-Publish is exclusively for NetWare LANs, ***PrintWare*** from LaserAge Software (Los Angeles, CA) controls printer configurations over any DOS-based network. PrintWare has a data dictionary of printer control codes and allows the user to establish a configuration for any printer on the network. PrintWare consists of ***PrintWare Manager*** and ***PrintWare Utility.*** PrintWare Manager is used by the network manager or supervisor to create a library of printer configurations.

When there are several people using a network printer, there's no guarantee that the printer has been left in the configuration you need. PrintWare lets you reestablish the appropriate configuration. It also supports the printer command sets of over a hundred different printers. You can also configure printer drivers for other applications. Printer configuration is all that PrintWare does, however.

[4] ***Miscellaneous*** There are several other differences between the utilities. Although almost all say they allow queue management, all that means in many cases is that users are allowed to delete print jobs from the queue. Ideally, you should, depending on your clearance level, be able to change the priority of jobs within a queue, and assign priority levels to whole queues. You should also be able to decide which queues are serviced by which printers.

Find out if the utility notifies you when a job is finished. It's not the most crucial feature in the world, but it does save you the trouble of checking the print queue to see if the job is still in it or worse still, is travelling to the printer to search for your document.

A good utility will let you decide whether or not you want a banner page printed before your job. A banner page is just a sheet of paper that comes out before your job is printed that specifies which user's job follows. They can be invaluable in separating different documents, especially in larger companies, when many jobs are sent to any given printer.

Check which version of NetWare the utility runs on. This may seem like an obvious suggestion but most users will trust that their utility has been upgraded to the proper version. Some like Riverbend's ***HotSpool***, don't support version 2.1 of NetWare, but only support up to version 2.0a.

Actually, although we've focussed primarily on printer utilities for NetWare, there are utilities for AppleShare as well since AppleShare does not include print spooling in its services. Print spooling is especially important for Macintosh users, since they do a great deal of desktop publishing. The AppleShare printer utilities are primarily spoolers that free up your Macintosh so that you can keep working instead of waiting for the printer to be free. Utilities like ***NetPrint*** from TOPS (Alameda, CA) let users on a DOS-based network print to an Imagewriter.

"You have to make sure you send the whole set up string each time you print."

Printer Problems

Shared printing, although at times clunky, is not exactly riddled with unsolvable technical problems. Once installed , printer utilities are fairly intuitive. Even those that use hokey combinations to control printing, as opposed to pop-up menus, are relatively trouble free once you learn how to use them.

That's not to say that users don't have problems with their utilities. Cybertek has even put together a tip sheet that leads users of their ***Network Assistant Plus*** step by step through the printing procedure. That way, not only can users isolate where their technical troubles lie, but also tech support has an easier time diagnosing users' problems.

Jim Rosen, vice president of LAN Systems, recommends testing your PC's serial and parallel ports on a standalone printer before you attach it to the network. People are quick to blame the network for what actually could be a local problem. Also, Rosen warns,"Don't assume that the printer has been left in a certain way. You have to make sure you send the whole set up string each time you print."

Creating a print server can also be on the complicated side. Danny Schulman, a tech representative for Cybertek, had one user on the network who found out that everybody could print to the printer attached to his machine except him. It turns out he had defined a private printer on his machine, as well as the network printer. When he tried to send print data to the printer, the system was trying to send it to a nonexistant second printer.

Greg Gianfore, president of Brightwork Development, says the biggest problems that he encounters relate to the quality and locating printers on the network. According to Gianfore, "The industry's evolving and the users are demanding more and more. On a network where you have plotters and desktop publishing, quality is becoming a real issue. Users are complaining about the time it takes and the quality of the output. Also, LANs are starting to have the same problems that you find with minis and mainframes, where there are services on the system that users simply aren't aware of. There may be a postscript printer on the network, but who knows where it is?"

Integrated software

Integrated software packages combine word processing, database management, and spreadsheet applications in one product. The advantages of integrated software include its consistent commands and menus, and the easy transfer of information from one module to another. They can, however, benefit from networking in the same way as their stand-alone counterparts.

Ashton-Tate's Framework III LAN offers the functions listed, plus telecommunications and even electronic mail. Lotus' Symphony includes a locking utility that supports worksheet sharing over the LAN, and has graphics built-in. Open Access II Plus includes a multifile database, spreadsheet, word processor, and desktop utilities.

Informix Software takes a modular approach with its ***Smart Software System.*** This LAN integrated software, including a word processor and spellchecker, spreadsheet, and database manager, may be purchased as separate modules or all at once. Adding workstations is easy; just purchase access software for each machine you want to attach.

Among the very cheapest LAN applications on the market is Microsoft's ***Works,*** a simple integrated package whose spreadsheet reads and writes 1-2-3 files. The Macintosh version of Works runs over AFP-compatible networks, letting several users access data files in "read-only" mode. Software Publishing's ***PFS:First Choice*** is similar; its graphics module is actually a subset of the respected Harvard Graphics.

Groupware

The term "groupware" covers a wide range of new software products, not easily classified. What all have in common is taking isolated PC users and bringing them into a group. Thanks to these programs, which are usually priced on a per-server basis, members of a group need not be in the same place—or time—in order to work together.

Conetic Systems' Higgins handles office administration, allowing users to coordinate their schedules. It includes to-do list and expense report modules, and desktop accessories such as note pads, calculators, expense reports, to-do lists, tickler files, and phone directories. Higgins Exchange can link LAN E-mail to external E-mail services such as CompuServe.

Office Works, a program from Data Access, offers similar functions and adds built-in database software that allows users to share name-and-address files and other lists. Chronos Software's ***Who-What-When Enterprise*** integrates people, project and time management. When you start the program, it displays a calendar, but users can switch to linked views of the projects they are working on or people they work with. Finally, The Coordinator, an elaborate electronic mail system, includes a system of management tools that track work commitments. It forces workgroup members to be explicit about what they promise to do and nags them to meet deadlines.

Word Perfect Office, as its name implies, is ideal for those already using Word Perfect for word processing. This product features a shell that can simplify LAN operation, allowing a user to switch applications and move text between them with a *clipboard.* Word Perfect Office also has macros, electronic mail, and a scheduler that automatically finds *open times* when department meetings can be scheduled. Its simple flat-file database module, ***Notebook***, saves mail or telephone lists as Word Perfect merge files.

More often than not, users in a group are collaborating on perfecting a document. Broderbund's ***For Comment*** takes word-processed documents and distributes them over a LAN, inviting reviewers to make comments in the "margins." The program makes it easy for the author to collate the comments and choose which suggestions to incorporate.

Other groupware products: ***ActionTracker Plus, Shoebox, Telephone Note Taker Plus, TimeTalk,*** and ***Word Perfect Office for PC Networks.***

How can I keep track of everything going on my LAN and keep it running smoothly every day?

By now you're beginning to appreciate the tremendous potential of a Local Area Network system—and how complex it can be.

Servers, workstations, cabling, bridges, gateways; sophisticated systems software that moves the data around and controls the operation; specific application software that makes it possible for you to do whatever task that needs to be done: using a database, communications, word processing, printing—there are many, many potential elements in a Local Area Network system, proportional to how large a staff you have and how many jobs are running concurrently.

With so many pieces to this puzzle, how can you keep track of the whole picture? As a manager or department head, how can you audit all or any specific part of your network, both geographically and statistically monitoring the configuration, cost, and performance of your LANS in operation? How can you keep constant tabs on the efficiency of your hard and software inventory, your usage, traffic, file management, menuing, archiving, and security?

There *is* a way. There's something called LAN Management Software. This is single-task or integrated network management software systems which can both monitor and diagnose every aspect of your daily work.

This LAN Management Software offers a graphic roadmap of your LAN's components, providing a wide range of information you can use to find out exactly what's going on around the network, including utilities which specialize in:

[1] **File and Directory Management** Helping you find what you need in the maze of directories and files of the file server's disk; getting an overview of the server's directory structure and allowing you to utilize, change, and manipulate everything stored on the hard disks of your LANS; providing also special menuing and archiving capability.

"The more complex your LAN, the more sophisticated the LAN management you need."

[2] **Usage Monitoring** Telling a manager which applications are being used, who is using them, for how long, and from which workstations.

[3] **Traffic Monitoring** Allowing you to measure data such as how long spent at a specific task and how much work is flowing past a certain point; recording and reporting traffic to and from workstations, displaying specific problems throughout the system.

[4] **Accounting** Reporting and allocating the cost of your network to specific users in the system.

[5] **Troubleshooting** Reporting and correcting equipment on the blink; setting off alarms when there are network errors.

[6] **Security** Restricting access, recording user activities and auditing data; also providing file locking to protect unattended workstations and file encryption, which creates passwords to keep out unauthorized users.

The more complex your own LAN, the more sophisticated a LAN Management Software system you need.

LAN management software

Network products vendors finally are responding to user demands for solutions to the network management problem. Many of them offer what can rightfully be called *integrated* network management systems, stations, centers, or managers. They're integrated because they combine many management capabilities—from performance monitoring to audit-trail accounting to changing configuration parameters—into one package. Whatever a vendor calls its integrated network management product, it's designed to provide network managers with the up-to-date, real-time information they need to understand, and thus manage better the network's operation.

Network Management Traditionally, network management products have been divided into five categories:

- Security management (or variations of password-protection schemes).

- Performance management (monitoring network capacity and loading).
- Accounting (audit trail) management (capturing and allocating costs of the network to network users).
- Fault management (troubleshooting, finding and correcting failing equipment).
- Configuration management (network installation, booting, tracking hardware/software configurations).

"These systems offer a graphic look at all or parts of a network."

Providing as many of these capabilities as possible in one software package is the goal of vendors offering integrated network management systems. These systems, usually made up of hardware and software components, offer a graphic look at all or parts of a network, both from a physical and statistical point of view. They generally overlay the LAN's components on a geographical or logical map displayed on a color graphics monitor, and provide a wide range of statistical information the LAN manager can use to find out what's going on around the network, and then reconfigure the components on the LAN to avoid potential future disaster. An integrated network management product, unlike the myriad standalone applications available, could automatically tell a LAN manager that a server or remote bridge is overworked, then allow taking that component out of operation, changing its operating parameters, then putting it back in service. It could also let the manager see how many bad packets are crossing an Ethernet—thus slowing it down—or set danger thresholds that automatically beep or display an on-screen message when a network component is experiencing trouble or about to fail.

An ever-increasing number of these integrated systems are now or soon will be on the market. Not all of them are appropriate for every network, and in fact none may be appropriate for a particular installation. Most likely, however, one of these products can help you manage your network more efficiently, in less time, and from a central location.

DECnet NCP Although not a standalone system, Digital Equipment's ***DECnet Network Control Program*** (NCP), when used in conjunction with a number of optional DEC-provided software tools, offers many capabilities.

NCP, which operates in tandem with two agents, the network management listener (NML) and a *mirror*, offers commands that allow examining and controlling all the layers of the DECnet architecture, and helps manage X.25 features when available.

The NML accepts connections from NCP or user-written applications that *speak* the NICE network management protocol, an application layer protocol similar to the OSI CMIP.

Optional network management products available for use with DECnet, including an ***NMCC/DECnet Monitor***, an ***NMCC/VAX Ethernim*** (Ethernet network integrity monitor), a LAN traffic monitor that presents traffic stats in graphical form, a remote system manager, and remote bridge management software for use with DEC's LANbridge 100.

LAN Manager/NetView IBM, in a use of terminology certain to confuse a lot of people, offers a local network management product called the LAN Manager that, with one exception, operates only in tandem with IBM's mainframe-based NetView application.

"Service points make network components visible to the network manager sitting at the focal point."

The ***LAN Manager***—it is offered in two versions, a LAN Manager Version 2.0 and a LAN Manager Entry Version 1.0—is what IBM calls a *service point* within IBM's overall network management structure. A service point is one of four entities defined within IBM's network management structure; the others are the focal point, entry point, and target.

A focal point, which sits atop a hierarchical model of a system, manages all of the remotely and locally attached network components in its domain from a central location. This centralization provides a global view of the network, and helps the network administrator better understand the relationships between network elements.

Service points make network components visible to the network manager sitting at the focal point. They handle the transportation of management data between the network component—what IBM calls *targets*—and focal point. An entry point moves both network management information and data around the network. Within this structure, LAN Manager provides network management functions as a service point.

Unlike earlier versions, LAN Manager Entry Version 1.0 does not provide a user interface at the local network level—management functions are available only at the central mainframe console running NetView Release 3. The LAN Manager Entry Version 1.0 application can manage a single IBM Token-Ring or IBM PC Network (broadband or baseband) network segment; it supports both 4- and 16M bit/sec Token-Rings. By porting the Entry version from DOS to OS/2, IBM has eliminated DOS's 640k byte memory restraints and the need for a dedicated LAN management server.

The entry LAN Manager uses the OS/2 Communications Manager to communicate with NetView operating in a host, acting as a NetView agent; communication must be through a gateway—for example, a 3174—or SDLC.

In operation, the LAN Manager Entry Version 1.0 monitors the LAN for the detection of hard errors; displays ring status information; and monitors functions such as the detection of soft errors and the display of REM tables. It also provides six commands that generate network and adapter profiles and status, permit removing an adapter from the network, and restarting the LAN Manager. It can verify the connection between two stations, list the active adapters, and display or print an event logo.

The LAN Manager Version 2.0 is designed for use in a mixed-LAN environment. It also operates under OS/2 Extended Edition 1.1, and can be executed in three modes: as a standalone application, a LAN management agent for NetView running in a host, or as an independent application to NetView/PC Version 1.2 while providing service point functions for multiple applications or subsystems.

"This lets the LAN administrator closely monitor resources that are essential to the operation of the network."

The LAN Manager Version 2.0 allows a network administrator to specify a network node he or she wants monitored; when the node loses contact with the network, LAN Manager puts out an alert. This lets the LAN administrator closely monitor resources—printer servers, key file servers, or gateway servers—that are essential to the operation of the network.

LAN Manager Version 2.0 also allows applications to generate and send alerts to a focal point such as NetView. In addition, LAN Manager Version 2.0 allows users to change a host of bridge configuration parameters, including hopcount limits, link passwords, bridge number, and LAN segment number per adapter.

Both versions of the LAN Manager require a PC or PS/2 running OS/2 Extended Edition 1.1. The Entry version also requires the computer to be equipped with an IBM Token-Ring adapter, an SLDC or IBM PS/2 multiprotocol adapter, 500K byte of memory, and a monitor.

LattisNet NMS ***The LattisNet Network Management System*** (NMS) from SynOptics Communications (Mountain View, CA) gives LAN managers tools to manage network traffic, isolate network faults, and plan for network growth. The system manages the physical and data-link layers of SynOptics' ***Ethernet LANs*** from a central console, presenting realtime management data via a Windows-based interface.

The LattisNet NMS provides a programmable report generator, a realtime graphics-based display of SynOptics ***System 3000 Concentrators*** that offers an expanded view down to the board and port levels, and media-access-control (MAC) level statistics-gathering capabilities.

The LattisNet NMS allows identifying every network connection by its station address and characterizing the station by its data activity and MAC-level statistics and errors. Network managers can program the system to automatically disconnect stations that exceed predefined performance or MAC-level error thresholds.

LattisNet NMS modules are connected to a dedicated network management bus on each SynOptics System 3000 Concentrator backplane; these modules gather and transmit specific data to a central control console adapter, installed in an IBM PC/AT or compatible computer. SynOptics' LattisNet management software then presents the data as a graphical map of the network.

The management functions built into the System 3000 Concentrators and host modules give the LAN manager a detailed picture of network activity at the concentrator, module and port levels. The LattisNet NMS software report generator creates a visual or printed log of network events, alerts, performance, and diagnostic data that the network manager wants.

"Network managers can program the system to automatcally disconnect stations that exceed predefined performance."

The network manager can use these statistics in a wide range of ways—pinpointing overworked sections of the LAN, deciding where new concentrators are needed, maintaining network integrity, and providing for cost-effective network growth.

LattisNet NMS components generally run about 10 percent of the network per-port cost, say SynOptics officials; a LattisNet port typically ranges in cost from $350 to $500, depending on transceiver options, so the incremental cost of a LattisNet Network Management System would be from $35 to $50 per port.

NCS AT/2 3Com's ***Network Control Servers*** monitor and manage the Santa Clara, CA, vendor's internetwork bridges and gateway and communications servers. 3Com offers two versions of the NCS: the 286-based **NCS/AT**, which can support 512 servers, and the 68020 Sun-3-based **NCS/2**, which can handle up to 4,096 servers. With few exceptions, they operate identically, and can be purchased in a "kit" form that allows adding them to an existing system. They currently operate under a proprietary protocol, but will support SNMP "in the near future," says 3Com.

The NCS products offer realtime monitoring of major network events, audit trail records with time/date stamps, and a variety of reports that display and analyze the activity of 3Com bridges and communications and gateway servers.

The NCS systems provide command-file facilities that let the LAN manager automate sequences of network management tasks; they provide an access-control database that permits the manager to set up and manage network access rules—that is, user rights to access particular components. They also allow the manager to boot up a remote communication from a central NCS.

They also generate a variety of statistical data: peak traffic periods, session statistics (connection source, destination, and duration), network utilization, and serial line traffic rates. The NCS/AT sells for $12,000, and the NCS/2 for $35,000.

DCA's ONMS ***DCA's Open Network Management System*** (ONMS) gives network managers a graphical view of their entire, multivendor DCA network. ONMS can operate in standalone fashion or as a *middle manager* in tandem with large networks with end-to-end network management systems.

"They provide an access-control database that permits the manager to set up network access rules."

Based on OSI CMIP/CMIS standards (it also supports AT&T's Unified Network Management Architecture), ONMS is made up of *plug compatible* software modules that run on a Sun workstation. ONMS is controlled by a system manager that provides graphical, textual, and relational database facilities. The ONMS manager works in cooperation with three agent-management modules to control DCA's ***System 9000*** backbone and ***Series 300*** products as well CMIP-based products. These modules transmit management information between the manager and other network components.

In operation, ONMS allows the network manager to view all or parts of the network; point-and-click capabilities allow *zooming* in on specific elements of the network. ONMS' ***Unify*** database controls storage and access to network components.

ONMS allows ten users to access it simultaneously, and it can be accessed from a VT100 modem-equipped terminal for remote troubleshooting.

OpenView Hewlett-Packard's ***OpenView*** is a modular set of OSI-compliant network management tools that presents the user with a graphical map of a network. The core product, HP ***OpenView Windows***, runs on an **HP Vectra PC** that serves as a central management point for both local and wide area networks. OpenView lets LAN managers monitor and troubleshoot local and remote networks through a comprehensive line of OpenView WAN and LAN modular products. Among those available are a bridge manager, a network command interpreter, a data line monitor, an NS diagnostic monitor, a digital data test set, and a Windows developer's kit that allows creating custom-designed OpenView tools that are consistent with the OpenView interface.

Among the capabilities OpenView products provide are monitoring the status of and collecting network performance data on remote HP 3000 computer systems and managing bridges to optimize communications bandwidth use.

HP plans to port its DOS-based OpenView products to UNIX, thus bringing multitasking capabilities to its network management line.

"OpenView lets LAN managers monitor and troubleshoot local and remote networks."

OverVIEW Proteon calls its ***OverVIEW*** a "turnkey network management system designed for monitoring and controlling multivendor ... multiprotocol internetwork systems." OverVIEW runs on a 286-based AT-compatible computer and supports SNMP and its predecessor, SGMP.

It offers a multilevel, graphic view of a network, with zoom capabilities for isolation of problem areas. Its capabilities allow a network manager to define an internetwork topology in hierarchical levels, simplifying what are generally complex internetworks.

By polling SNMP-compatible devices at regular intervals and collecting pertinent data, OverVIEW creates a realtime picture of the internetwork's operation. OverVIEW's graphic representation of network elements lets a manager move rapidly from component to component.

OverVIEW provides WAN data definition for point-to-point serial, **DDN, PDN X.25** and **ARPANET DDN 1822** connections, and local data definitions for **IEEE 802** networks and Proteon's own Token-Ring products.

OverVIEW's network database allows the network manager to add, modify, or delete information about network segments and standard network items—for example, node names, physical node addresses, and interface types. OverVIEW also maintains a history of network alerts and important operational events. An alert log, containing types of errors and traps generated by network nodes, is accessible from OverVIEW's color-coded network map.

One key OverVIEW feature, called the performance monitor, presents a "histogram" of network traffic and errors. OverVIEW network management stations are priced at $9,995.

NYSERNet's NMS NYSERNet's ***Network Management Station*** (NMS) is an SNMP-compatible application that consists of 18 tools, many of them graphical. These tools range from topology maps that help oversee network operation to tools that indentify activity of various network objects of interest to the network manager. NYSERNet licenses its NMS source code to commercial and end-users.

AT&T's STARLan AT&T's ***STARLan Network Manager*** (SNM) offers versions for managing both STARLan and STARLan 10 networks. SNM release 1.0, for STARLan-only networks, runs on AT&T's 3B2 or 6386 WGS computer; SNM release 2.0, for STARLan and STARLan 10 networks, runs on the 6386 WGS. A LAN manager can also operate the program at an **RS-232** terminal or an **AT&T PC6300** or compatible PC with terminal emulation.

The STARLan NMS allows LAN managers to administer and reconfigure network nodes, monitor equipment status and performance, collect and study report data, and troubleshoot and isolate network problems.

The STARLan SNM is based on an ***Informix*** on-line database, called the network configuration database (NCD), that contains user-defined information about the network. The database allows the LAN manager to display all or part of the network graphically, and show reports on a variety of events, such as node error counts.

"SNM's fault-detection-and-monitoring facilities give the administrator a number of specific test procedures."

SNM's fault-detection-and-monitoring facilities give the administrator a number of specific test procedures—for example, a communication test routine that exchanges packets between the SNM and faulty node provides error statistics—for troubleshooting the network.

The product also produces daily reports and is easily customizable. For instance, the user can determine the node-status polling frequency, severity levels for alarm generation, and the daily maintenance times.

WIN/MGT Wollongong's SNMP-compatible ***Integrated Networking/Management*** (WIN/MGT) products give users the ability to analyze, monitor, alter, and manage large interconnected, multi-vendor networks. They also provide end-to-end management services for gateways and hosts. Wollongong offers WIN/MGT agents for DOS, NCR Tower, and Macintosh computers. Wollongong sells a WIN/MGT station for the **SunOS** and agents for **VMS** and **386 STREAMs**.

WIN/MGT allows network managers to determine the status of network components; review error situations in network links and interfaces; remotely verify the location and status of network nodes and services; and detect and identify the sources of incorrect routing information.

These capabilities let the WIN/MGT user diagnose and correct common faults and bottlenecks, assure the availability of basic services, and automatically generate network activity reports. A WIN/MGT station for the SunOS is priced at $10,000, a WIN/MGT agent for VMS sells for $1,500 to $8,200, depending on the CPU platform; the WIN/MGT agent for 386 STREAMS is $300.

Protocol analyzers

The essence of networking is communication. On the average network where many users share resources, exchange files, and cooperate with each other, millions of pieces of data are flying across the network. Even with the most primordial printer-sharing network, information has to pass from one node on the network to another.

Computer communications can be likened to a phone call at work. You pick up the phone and dial a number, thus gaining the phone company's permission to use its trunk line. When you dial the number, you include an exchange that routes the call to the proper geographic area and office. If the call is long distance, you include an area code as well. A receptionist answers and checks to see if your call will be accepted by the person on the other end. Finally, you are transferred to the person and communication begins.

"Networks need a formal, organized, detailed method of communicating information."

Just as a phone call cannot be made without dialing the number or a letter mailed without an envelope, address, and stamp, data can't be sent willy-nilly over the network. Networks need a formal, organized, detailed method of communicating information. Network protocols provide the *language* for communication between computers.

The Lexicon of the LAN Protocols make up strict rules governing communications between computers. It's important that steps for communication be taken in a certain order. A node first must gain access to the physical medium. This usually is controlled by the hardware you've chosen. Ethernet networks, for example, rely on a contention method of network access, where requests for use of the network are generated as needed. In case of a simultaneous request, also called a collision, each device waits a random amount of time and tries again. In the phone analogy, it would be similar to a party line, where you pick up the phone to see if the line is free. If it is, you can make your call; if not, you try later.

After the machine has access to the network, it must surround the data it's sending with information about where the information is going (like the exchange in a phone number). If the packet is going over a wide area network, further routing information (like the area code) has to be added. Also, a specified format adds information, such as start and stop bits or synchronization and error checking bits, onto the data. Protocols specify everything from the transmission rate to how data will be used by an application or end user. If any part of the packet is not in a format recognizable by another device, the two cannot communicate.

Protocols often are likened to human language. But in a language spoken by humans, a rich variety of dialects pervades. Accents and idioms used by someone from Happy, TX, might vary drastically from those used by someone in Trenton Bridge, ME. Nevertheless, the two can probably understand each other. Although *dialects* can exist in the same protocol, two machines running different dialects of the same protocol cannot communicate, depending on which vendor's version is used. Computers, being less bright than tree stumps, don't make the same attempt at reasoning or logic that a human would. Their protocols need to be designed strictly and consistently adhered to.

The Tangled Web As a network grows more and more heterogeneous, matching protocols exactly is more difficult. Vendors may develop protocols that vary slightly from the published standard and from one another. Other vendors may develop proprietary protocols, independent of all standards. Still others combine protocols from various standards to take advantage of the best features.

Even in a completely homogeneous environment, things are bound to go wrong, independent of the protocol but affecting communications nonetheless. A faulty network interface card can suddenly generate bad packets, for example, or not generate packets at all. The only way to determine what is causing network failure is to examine the packet on the most basic bit level.

"Computers, being less bright than tree stumps, don't make the same attempt at reasoning or logic that a human would."

Three network troubleshooting tools are available. The most basic are testers that check for faulty physical media. These can vary from primitive boxes with diagnostic LEDs to sophisticated monitors that isolate a cable break to within ten feet. On the high end of the tools are the network monitors that keep an eye on the network independent of what protocols are running on the LAN. How many frames are generated per second may be important to a network manager, but it may not care which protocols run on the network.

Seeking Therapy Protocol analyzers fall between testers and network monitors. While it allows for sophisticated system analysis like the network monitor, it is primarily a diagnostic tool, as is the cable tester. It provides detailed information about the information traveling over a network, but it can't warn of impending failure on its own. Protocol analyzers locate the source of a network problem. The human using the analyzer can then take action.

Protocol analyzers were used originally by software and hardware developers who needed to make sure that their product conformed to a specification. The only way to do this was to analyze the packets bit by bit to see where the problems were. A protocol analyzer takes the convoluted bit pattern in each frame and converts it into English (or at least hex) so that a user can easily see what's going on with the network. It displays the information in a usable format.

Protocol analyzers are not proactive tools, like network monitors. They sit on a shelf until the network has a problem. A creative system manager can take a proactive approach to network management with a protocol analyzer, however. Most protocol analyzers include features that allow LAN managers to predict when something might go wrong or be aware of a problem earlier.

"Protocol analyzers locate the source of a network problem. The human using the analyzer can then take action."

Those Wonderful Triggers Protocol analyzers don't have to be restricted to intermittent use. Says Paul Vitello, senior product manager at Racal-InterLan, "Protocol analyzers can be proactive in that you can use one to monitor network performance on a regular basis. You can then become familiar enough with the performance characteristics of a network to anticipate when there's going to be a failure. "

A protocol analyzer can be programmed to detect a multitude of conditions. Most protocol analyzers have filters and triggers that capture data on the basis of its characteristics. By using filters and triggers to detect and record network conditions, the network manager collects information on network performance. From this history, he can gain an understanding of the traffic patterns and better recognize deviations.

A trigger tells the protocol analyzer when to start or stop collecting data. For example, you can set a trigger to stop collecting data as soon as an error condition is registered. You can then go back and examine every bit of data before the error condition occurred, collecting information about which patterns you can expect before a failure. Consequently, you could set a trigger to warn you the next time the pattern is encountered.

Triggers are not limited to looking for error conditions. They start or stop collecting data at a certain time. A government agency might want to monitor all sensitive data and could set a trigger to start collecting data whenever it registers packets marked "secret."

A filter is similar to a trigger in that it collects specific data. However, a filter continuously screens for data you're interested in. Also, whereas a trigger used alone captures the full network bandwidth, a filter can capture parts of a packet or only packets coming to or from a certain destination. Or if you're interested only in one set of protocols, a filter can ignore all others and only capture those. A filter is like a traffic cop sitting behind a billboard, watching the cars on a freeway and only chasing those exceeding the speed limit.

Filtering can be done in hardware or software; each has advantages and proponents. Hardware filtering is faster, but less flexible than software filtering. When packets are filtered in software, the board collects all the packets and the software must screen through them anyway, which affects the performance of the protocol analyzer.

Filtering in hardware saves some buffer space, which is crucial when considering protocol analyzers. Analyzers can collect data at a much higher rate than it can be written to a hard disk. With a heavily utilized 10M bits-per-second network, a 250K bytes buffer isn't going to go very far if you use a pure software filter. The protocol analyzer will drop packets after a while. With a hardware filter, you lose some flexibility because you can't readily program the protocol analyzer to screen for the same variety of packets as with a software filter.

The best method of filtering is a combination of hardware and software. A hardware filter can reduce the number of packets captured so that it can be handled by the software. Then, without the risk of dropping packets, the software can fine tune the filtering process and report only relevant information to the user.

"The best method of filtering is a combination of software and hardware."

If you don't need realtime filtering (that is, if you don't need immediate information about how many TCP/IP packets are traveling from a node to the file server at this very moment), another alternative is to capture all packets and stream the data to a hard disk. You can then filter through that data at your leisure and remove extraneous information.

Disk storage is crucial for serious users of protocol analyzers. With information on network use stored on disk, you can have a continuous record of network performance, through any changes and upgrades.

Invest in a protocol analyzer that can export information to other programs such as Lotus 1-2-3 or Paradox, so that you can manipulate data. Most analyzers produce rudimentary reports, charts, and bar graphs showing network utilization, but advanced number crunching is always useful.

A filter is useful in proactive network management by collecting statistics on network use. You can filter for everything from error bits to specific protocols and glean and analyze information to determine where recurrent trouble spots are.

You're not limited to creative use of filters and triggers to determine when your network might fail. You can spend endless hours analyzing the information you gather when collecting packets. Although the information is useful, there's no way of definitely knowing from the statistics alone when your network or parts of your network will fail. Many protocol analyzers can generate and monitor traffic. To be truly prepared, a network manager must know which component in a network will fail, when it will fail, and what will cause it to fail. He or she also has to be aware of the network's capacity; that is, at what level of utilization does network performance degrade seriously. Network performance usually falters somewhere between 20 to 30 percent of capacity, but that can vary enormously. Depending on configurations and applications, networks can fail at 5 percent or 50 percent. There's no way to actually be sure without stressing the network and measuring results.

Some protocol analyzers also have emulation capabilities. This means that it can generate traffic that looks as though it's coming from a particular workstation. Emulation capabilities become important as your network increases in complexity. You have to begin to test for problems that you can't anticipate. You also have to keep an eye out for problems that may not be catastrophic.

"To be truly prepared, a network manager must know which component in a network will fail, when it will fail, and what will cause it to fail."

For example, you could have two Token-Ring networks bridged to one another, with the first connected to a mainframe through a LAN gateway and cluster controller. To communicate with the mainframe, a PC running terminal emulation on the second network must route its conversation over a bridge, through a mainframe gateway, to a cluster controller, and finally to the host. It might not be a problem but a lot of other communication is going on, the gateway becomes a bottleneck and you will see timeouts because the PC didn't respond in time. It's not a mammoth disaster but it can affect performance in the long run. A protocol analyzer can emulate such traffic before you run the applications. You would then know if you need multiple gateways.

Capacity planning is a large part of a network manager's job, not just when the LAN is installed but as upgrades and changes are made. With a protocol analyzer that includes traffic generation and emulation, you can benchmark each equipment and know at what point that device is going to fail. Says Zett, "If you know when each component is going to break, then you have a target level of utilization at which performance is no longer acceptable, when your network is going to break it makes you just a little bit smarter."

When the Time is Right A protocol analyzer is not an insignificant investment. They range in price from $10,000 to $25,000. Some of them are turnkey systems in the body of a portable computer and others come in the form of a board and software that plugs into a portable computer. Software-only analyzers are able to be loaded onto any workstation on the LAN but these are far less efficient than their hardware-based counterparts. They are cheaper and easier to manipulate so if you don't need intensive or continuous monitoring of data packets then consider one. However, if you're serious about LAN troubleshooting, buy a hardware-based analyzer.

Since protocol analyzers are expensive and are used infrequently, you may wonder whether you need one. You might investigate renting one. It depends on how critical your network is to your business and how critical your data integrity is. "Figure out the dollar value of your downtime," says Zett. "You may not care what the cost of the analyzer is if your data's important enough. It'll pay for itself relatively quickly."

Another factor that could determine whether you need a protocol analyzer is the complexity of your network. Again, the more devices you have and the more applications you run, the greater the chances that something will go wrong. Unfortunately, most people don't realize that the intricacy of their network requires a diagnostic tool until there's a catastrophic failure.

Backup

Making copies of the program and data files on the network is called backup. Backup is the most important thing you can do for the LAN. You can buy the best file server, the slickest workstations, the newest operating system, and the fanciest application software, but without backup, the network could very easily become nothing.

Catastrophic failures aside, people make mistakes. Users regularly delete files by accident. Even network administrators are not immune from slips of the fingers. Sometimes they inadvertently delete entire directories. It's one thing if that file held a short memo. It's another thing if those were the figures for the shareholders meeting tomorrow. Sure, people can print files so they always have a hard copy, but then someone has to rekey all that data. And hard copy does nothing when a program's executable files are deleted. Humans make mistakes. So does hardware. Even though hard disks have a meantime between failure around 100,000 hours, the server disk could experience a head crash, rendering your company's vital information nonsense. The power does surge, blowing disks left and right. There are plenty of shocks strong enough to crash the heads, even though disks are made to withstand several Gs of force.

Network operating systems have glitches. Mysterious system errors do cause files to disappear. Viruses don't just make good copy for journalists. They do exist, albeit in small numbers, but when they strike, they wreak havoc.

MIS departments wouldn't dream of running minicomputers or mainframes without backup systems and procedures. The PC LAN is no different.

Backup Options Before we discuss the options, let's get the terminology straight. When used as a verb, the correct words are "to back up." When used as an adjective or noun, it is "backup."

> *"Most people back up to tape. Tape is inexpensive and convenient."*

There are basically two options: back up to disk or to tape. The simplest method, to back up to floppy disk, is really only suitable for standalone PCs with small hard disks. If a server has a 40M byte drive, and 20M byte are used, it would take 14 floppies to back up that information, and that's only if you use 1.44M byte diskettes, the highest capacity available. Imagine the time you spend swapping 14 floppy diskettes everyday. And most servers have storage ranging into the hundreds of megabytes. Even gigabytes of storage aren't an anomaly anymore.

Backing up to floppies is marginal even for users. It's okay, because they have less disk storage, but it's hard for the network manager to ensure that the users really will back up. Most users will only back up their disks after they've lost important data. And then only until they feel invincible again. There are programs which will automatically save the user's changes to disk, usually when they detect the user is not using the computer. Many people won't like auto-savers, because it takes the control out of their hands. It can save changes the user did not intend to make.

In practice, it is ridiculous to back up the server to floppies. You can back up the server to another hard disk, either removable or in another machine. Removable disks are handy because if the server disk fails, you can just pop out the ruined disk and pop in the new. However, removable disks such as **Bernoulli Boxes** don't go above 40M bytes.

Another option is to back up to disk in another machine. You can set up a batch file to copy all the files or all new files to a hard drive in another machine on the network.

Most people back up to tape. Tape is inexpensive and convenient. Network managers may complain bitterly about tape and its ills but basically the vast majority use tape for backup.

A new option in the backup bag of tricks is optical disks. The write-once, read-many drives are more useful for archiving than backup since you cannot change the data once it is on the disk. The newer rewriteable optical disks are handier for backup since they boast of a huge amount of storage and are reusable. Optical disks don't wear out as fast as tapes but they cost lots more money.

Tape Formats The most common tape format is standardized by the Quarter Inch Committee. The tape is a quarter-inch wide with nine parallel tracks enclosed in a metal and plastic housing a little smaller than a VCR tape. 3M's **DC600** is the most popular of the formats. A DC600 fits into a standard 5¼-inch form factor so it can be mounted internally in a PC although the vast majority of drives are attached externally. The *standard* tape length is 600 feet; the *extended* length cartridge has 1,000 feet of tape. The **DC2000** format uses the same ¼-inch nine-track medium but the cartridge fits into a 3½-inch form factor which is perfect for a PS/2.

"DAT can store gigabytes of information on a cassette the size of a pack of cigarettes."

Digital Audio Tape is the newest backup medium. DAT for data is the same DAT tape that provides the superior sound that audiophlies are oohing and ahhing about. DAT can store gigabytes of information on a cassette the size of a pack of cigarettes. DAT will offer terabytes in the future. The difference is DAT uses digital recording.

The traditional method uses analog recording. The data from the disk already in digital form has to be converted into analog and then laid down on the tape. Analog isn't nearly as exact. When restoring a file the tape unit may come across some questionable areas where it isn't sure of the value. DAT is an absolute measure; it's either a 1 or a 0.

Under the traditional method the quarter-inch tape is moved across the stationary read-write head. The data is laid down in a serial track until it reaches the end of the tape. When the end of the tape is reached it reverses itself and lays down another track parallel to the first.

A newer method is helical scan. In this method both the tape and the read-write head move. The tape is wrapped around a cylindrical drum on which there are several read-write heads. The data is laid down in diagonal strips on the tape. Helical scan not only increases the capacity of the tape but it increases the throughput rate. Both the newer 8mm tapes and the 4mm DAT can use helical scan.

Tape Methods There is very little difference among the various tape drives. Basically they are made by a small number of manufacturers and resold by companies that make backup software. This is in the process of changing since a few tape drive manufacturers are beginning to go direct to the user.

There are two methods of operation: *image* and *file-by-file.* Image is the more primative and less desirable form. A drive doing an image backup takes a complete image or a snapshot of the server disk not concerning itself with the disk's file structure. It just copies all the bits on the disk onto the tape. Due to this lack of overhead, image backup is the fastest method. It is not the most efficient. Say a user has lost only one file and you want to restore it from tape. You'll have to restore the entire disk which takes a considerable amount of time and effort. There can be problems restoring an image backup to a disk other than the one it was backed up from.

"A good rule of thumb is back up the files that change every day, and back up the program executables once a week."

File-by-file backup is much better than image backup. With file-by-file data from each file is copied to tape before moving onto the next file. It takes a bit longer to reconstruct the fragmented files into whole units because the disk head has to jump around from place to place reading the different fragments of the file but you can restore individual files more easily. With the file-by-file method you can back up only selected files since only a percentage of the files on the disk change in a given day.

What And When Backup is not effective if you do it occasionally. It's like exercise. It doesn't matter what you do as long as you do it regularly. You aren't going to have the body of Mel Gibson if you have the workout routine of PeeWee Herman.

A good rule of thumb is back up the files that change every day, and back up the program executables once a week. Then, the worst that could happen would be that the users would lose one day's work. But even if you don't take the time to back up every day, at least do a complete backup once a week.

Don't use the same tape every day. A generational backup system is the best. The ideal is to have tapes marked Monday, Tuesday, etc., and use them accordingly. Then save those tapes for three weeks before reusing them. That way, if a user needs the file he deleted from last Tuesday, you'll have it. If you don't want such an elaborate system, at least alternate the tapes every other day. That way if you discover that the drive can't read yesterday's backup, at least there is the tape from the day before yesterday. MIS doesn't have the right attitude on a lot of things, but when it comes to backup, they're right on target. Tape is cheap. Rotate it.

Night is the best time to do backup. Sending all the files that were changed that day will bog down the network. The more important reason is that open files can't be backed up. Some software packages will simply skip the open files, inviting a catastrophe. Others will wait until those files close, which could leave the tape system waiting forever. Either make sure all users are logged off the system by a certain time, or buy a package that lists the open files, so that you can back them up later. In addition to allowing you to run backup unattended, the software you buy should let you back up the server from any workstation. This way, the network administrator can perform backups from his workstation, and the server can sit safely in the closet. Backup directly from the server takes a lot of RAM and CPU overhead. The backup software should allow the local workstations to be backed up. Users can't be trusted to back up their own hard disks.

Security is a major issue. You don't want someone with a tape drive to walk off with the contents of the server disk. Therefore, the software should require a password. Some products require that the backup software log in as the supervisor. This is bad, because the person performing the backup should not necessarily be able to access every bit on information on the network.

Beyond Backup If you do it right, backup will ensure that you will lose only a day's work. But that can be too much. In that case, you move into the fault tolerance world, and use disk mirroring or disk duplexing. Disk mirroring uses two disks and one controller. Any writing is made to both disks. Disk duplexing takes fault tolerance one step further, and duplicates both disk and controller. It affords twice the protection (at twice the cost). In either case, a copy of the server disk is ready to go on line at any time. Depending on the software package and hardware configuration, the switchover time could be a few minutes to instantaneously.

However, backup is sufficient for most LAN installations. And tape is the cost-effective method for the vast majority of them. Use It.

LAN security

Just as there are many ways to skin a cat, there are many ways to invade a LAN. Therefore, the subject of LAN security is very broad, encompassing everything from physically locking each and every workstation to scanning the retinas of all employees. Obviously, prevention is the key word when it comes to LAN security. Stopping intrusion, in all its forms, is what security is all about.

There are three basic threats to LAN equipment and data: physical theft, electronic tampering, and unauthorized access. Physical theft includes people stealing computers, taking floppies with data and tapping into the cable. Electronic tampering covers computer viruses and other sorts of malicious reprogramming. Unauthorized access, the most common threat to security, occurs when people see information they shouldn't.

There are literally hundreds of approaches to dealing with each of these threats. Just as there are many forms of home security, from a lock on the front door to a 24-hour guard, there are many forms of LAN security. And just as the type of home security you use depends upon the neighborhood you live in, the valuables you own, the insurance you carry, and the money you have, the type and amount of prevention your LAN needs depends upon the importance of the data you're projecting, the network equipment you use, and the money you wish to spend.

"Doesn't a travel itinerary tell intruders when you'll be out of town?"

There is no formula for calculating your security needs. In some cases, the threats are obvious—banks, Department of Defense, insurance company files—and the security measures clear. In other cases, the threats might be more obscure. For example, you might think your personal schedule doesn't hold valuable information, but doesn't a travel itinerary tell intruders when you'll be out of town?

Clearly you don't need retinal scanners to keep people out of your electronic date book, but making the file read-only gives you some measure of added security. Again, the amount of security will depend upon the threat you perceive.

Physical Security The most basic form of physical security is keeping equipment behind locked doors or bolting it to the floor. All sorts of products exist to prevent intruders from taking equipment. Most of these involve physically locking equipment with metal bars, in steel cabinets or with large chains. These products only keep equipment from being physically stolen.

The next step is preventing physical access to the data stored in your equipment. The most obvious form of security along these lines is the keyboard lock that comes on most PC ATs. Other measures include locking file servers in closets, thus preventing direct access and forcing intruders to circumvent network security to get at data. Closets might also be a good place for printers and other output devices since printed data may be as sensitive as electronic data.

Biometric devices are yet another way to prevent physical access to computer equipment. Some of these devices use fingerprints for identification. Others use voice recognition. Still others will scan a user's retina, which is in the back of the eye, for a blood vessel pattern as identification. What almost all of these devices have in common is a large price tag. Only Her Majesty's Secret Service has the need and the pocket book for such toys.

Another physical security step is removing PC floppy disks, which prevents users from walking off with data. Many manufacturers have gone farther to sell diskless PCs, void of floppy disks and hard disks. These get their boot information and data from network file servers. Thus, there is no way of physically removing data. Some of the diskless PCs have serial and parallel ports. These can represent a physical threat as intruders may connect printers or modems to remove data from the network.

The last physical security measure is to secure the cable. Copper cable gives off electromagnetic emissions. These can be tapped by listening devices, with or without cutting into the cable. If they don't cut into the cable they are virtually impossible to detect. One solution is to switch to fiber optic cable, which is much more difficult to tap without detection. Another possibility is to keep cable out of reach. A final measure is data encryption, which we'll get to below. With encryption, even if intruders are successful at tapping the transmission, they will not understand what they're getting.

"The most common type of intrusion is unauthorized access to data, which can take myriad forms."

Electronic Protection Protecting your LAN against a computer virus is much the same as protecting it from unauthorized access. The theory is that if an intruder can't get access, he or she can't unleash a virus. However, this is not always enough. Authorized users can unwittingly introduce viruses to the network. Therefore, there are programs designed to keep a lookout for viruses and limit the havoc they wreak. At this point, no program can prevent a virus. It can only deal with the symptoms.

The efficacy of virus-limiting programs varies. Jay Nickson, president of On Disk Software in New York, NY, and inventor of **Quarantine**, one such program, says, "Only very high security or high-risk networks need protection against viruses. Usually, a good backup program will limit any major damage."

While viruses are potentially the most dangerous and costly type of intrusion, they are rare. The most common type of intrusion is unauthorized access to data, which can take myriad forms.

> “With access privileges the LAN manager creates a network profile for each user.”

The first line of LAN defense should be set up at each workstation. User log-in passwords is the simplest measure. Virtually all network operating systems will not give workstation users access to network resources without the correct password. To make passwords more effective, assign them and change them at random intervals. Don’t let users write their passwords on Post-It notes stuck on their monitors. Use mnemonic devices to help them remember.

Another method to stop unauthorized access uses an add-in card inside each workstation. This card forces the workstation to boot up from a particular drive every time. It can also enforce some kind of user validation, like a password. If the card is removed, the workstation is automatically disabled.

Once a user has workstation and network access, there are other security barriers that can be put in place. Most network operating systems have many levels of security. These limit what resources are available, which data can be accessed and what operations can be performed with those resources and data. For example, it is possible to allow users only to read a data file without changing it. Or, users may not be allowed to create or copy files.

Such access privileges may be assigned by file or by user. Usually, there is some combination of user and file security. For example, a file may be completely open to all users with a certain security level. Those with lower security levels might be restricted to reading the file. Many of the same types of privileges can be assigned to non-storage devices, too, like printers, modems and plotters.

With access privileges, the LAN manager creates a network profile for each user. This profile, which is implemented when the user logs on, limits the activity of that user, restricting him or her to authorized data and devices. Profiles may also be set up for data and devices, limiting their access to only authorized users. Profiles make managing security easier since they provide a consistent method of assigning and maintaining network privileges.

Back at the workstation, still another barrier can be erected to hinder intruders. A screen-blanking program that requires a password can prevent someone from walking up to an idle PC and using it. This program blanks the screen after a user-defined period of time and requires the entry of a password to renew activity. Many of these programs are available and some LAN operating system vendors include them.

Workstation file systems may present another threat to network security. DOS is notoriously easy to circumvent. Intruders can use many available programs to get at a hard disk and remove data, even if security programs are at work. For this reason, high security installations may want to use a different operating system, one with a different file system.

UNIX is the most obvious alternative. It has sophisticated file security and additional programs are available for even more protection.

Encryption Sometimes, steel plates, anti-virus programs and network access privileges are not enough to deter intruders. Data encryption might just be the answer in such situations. With encryption, data is encoded before it is sent, making it unreadable, even if it is intercepted. An electronic key is used transforming the data before it is sent. In short, the bits that make up the data are changed around in some pattern. The data is then sent in this transformed and unintelligible form. At the other end, another electronic key is used to decrypt the data, so it may be read by the receiving device.

"To further enhance encryption's effectiveness, keys should be changed at randomly spaced intervals."

In almost all cases, encryption requires extra hardware because of the processing power required. It also helps that the encryption procedure is more difficult to access when it is on add-in card ROM rather than a network hard disk.

The most common data encryption standard is that used by the U.S. government called DES, for Data Encryption Standard. Another standard used by the government, called CCEP, is more recently developed than DES, and will someday supplant the older standard. This will take sometime, however.

DES defines how the data should be encrypted and the specifications for an electronic key. It uses one 64-bit key for encryption and decryption. This can cause problems because the key must be in the hands of both sender and receiver. The only way to get it from place to place is to send it. Transmitting the key, however, might present a security threat.

The Public Key System is a solution to this. Under this setup, each user has two keys, one public and one private. The public key is made available to all senders. It is used only for encryption. The private key is used only for decryption and remains exclusive to the receiver. Thus, there is no need to transmit private keys. Encryption may be done in two places on the network: at storage devices and during transmission. Some networks only encrypt data when it is sent. This makes wire-tapping more difficult. It does not keep intruders from taking data from a hard disk, however. Other networks also encrypt data on the hard disk. Data is encrypted as it is written and decrypted as it is read from the disk. Having encryption working in both places keeps network data much more secure.

To further enhance encryption's effectiveness, keys should be changed at randomly spaced intervals. This prevents intruders from discovering either the key or the time the key is changed. Alternative key should be available, too, in case the original set of keys is compromised.

The best network encryption schemes hide much of the encryption hassle from end users by taking care of key management and encryption automatically.

Be Reasonable No matter what type of security you implement, diligent watchfulness is important to its success. To help in this regard, several LAN operating systems include audit trails. These keep track of all activity on the network, including which station has tried to log in to a file server three times unsuccessfully, or which files are being changed when they shouldn't be.

Some audit trails can be set to produce alarms when certain network events take place. For example, the system manager may want to know when certain files are open, or when unusual traffic takes place. Audit trails will also keep a running log of all that takes place, so the LAN manager may be able to detect a pattern of intrusion.

An aspect of network security that is often overlooked among all the technical talk is its effect on people. Security imposes restrictions which can cause friction. Users may feel frustrated by security procedures that hinder their ability to do their job. This might make them more willing to circumvent those procedures and violate security.

"Security imposes restrictions which can cause friction."

The only solution to this problem is to motivate people to cooperate. Here are four suggestions from *Securing NetWare LANs*, by Mike Hurwicz, president of the MTI Group:

- Explain the reasons for security procedures. When people understand why controls are necessary, they are more likely to cooperate.
- Make it clear to prospective and current employees that everyone is expected to cooperate. Establish clear consequences for failure to cooperate.
- Be specific about policies and procedures. Write them down and give everyone a copy. Make sure each individual knows what to do.
- Don't overdo it. Insofar as possible, make it easy to cooperate. Says Hurwicz, "Enlisting the support of employees is probably the single most cost-effective security precaution a company can take."

Biometric devices Biometrics are futuristic. Biometrics offer unparalleled security and safety. If security is a priority, you want biometrics, even at their cost. What are biometrics? Simply put, biometric devices identify people through unique body characteristics. Fingerprints, retinal patters, voice patterns, hand prints and signatures are particular to an individual. These can be recorded, analyzed and compared. With biometrics, the key to the lock on the LAN is literally at the users' fingertips.

Besides being convenient, biometric devices offer unparalleled security. Passwords are mastered. Card keys are lost. But hackers have yet to find a way past biometrics. It's a new hurdle which hasn't been crossed. Everyone has a unique fingerprint, voiceprint, retinal pattern, and so on. Changing your biometric (what's being scanned) is more expensive, dangerous and difficult then simply copying a key or typing in a password. Moreover, it's usually impossible. And while biometrics alone may not be sufficient, they are a vast improvement over virtually any other security product on the market. That's why government installations, labs, banks and anyone serious about security goes with biometrics devices.

"Signature recognition has the highest acceptance rate of the biometric devices."

Biometrics do have their drawbacks. Most notably is cost. Most if not all biometric devices exceed $1,000. Thumbscan's (Lombard, IL) fingerprint reader costs over $1,000. So does Ecco's (Danvers, MA) voice recognizer. That's a lot for securing each node on a LAN. But it's far cheaper than the cost of the company's data. A second drawback is that users may be intimidated. Retina scans are the most daunting. Signature recognition has the highest acceptance rate of the biometric devices.

The biggest concern is the reader's accuracy. In the past, biometrics have had a reputation for ineffectiveness. People who should have been accepted have been rejected. Those who should have been rejected have been accepted. However, recently, notes Bill Zalud, editor of *Security Magazine*, "Biometrics continue to improve their accuracy. After two decades, an important goal has been reached. Biometric devices—overall—admit the wrong person less than one percent of the time and reject the right person a little more often." Moreover, some products like Ecco's **VoiceKey** can even improve with use.

There are two stages to the biometric process: *enrollment* and *logon.* During enrollment a computer generated template is created. The process takes at most a few minutes. Afterwards the device is ready to go. Whenever a person wants to gain access to the room or use the computer, he scans his biometric. The data gathered is compared against the information on disk. If there's a match, the user is admitted, otherwise he's rejected. The entire process requires a few seconds.

All biometric devices can be used for securing a room. Some manufacturers have products for securing PCs. All the manufacturers mentioned here make products for both room and computer security. Ecco is the only exception. However, even Ecco is developing a version of their voice recognizer for computers.

Biometric devices include an identification pad. After matching his biometric, the user enters his secret identification number. If both the number and the biometric are verified he's admitted. Otherwise he's rejected. EyeDentify's (Portland, OR) **EyeDentification** system and Autosig's (Irving, TX) are the only exceptions. They rely solely on the reading process.

Securing each node on the network is expensive. An alternative is securing a particular group. Recognition Systems (San Jose, CA), for example, enables users to have one hand geometry reader per room or department. After scanning the users are assigned a password. The password is only effective for a few minutes at a particular workstation. Every password is randomly generated. This way you get the security of biometrics for a fraction of the cost.

The Readers A bevy of biometric readers are available. *Fingerprint readers* are actually among the more mundane. They identify a user by the shape and number of minutiae points on a finger. The minutiae points are the points where ridges fork or end. This is the same process used by the Federal Bureau of Investigation (FBI). However, while FBI's system is designed to search for fingerprints, fingerprint readers are designed to identify fingerprints. Thumbscan and Fingermatrix manufacture fingerprint readers for PCs. The Thumbscan **AMS-PC (Access Management System PC)** with **Fingerprint Reader** costs $1,520 per PC. The **Ridge Reader Mint** is Fingermatrix's new reader for PCs. It ranges in cost from $1,300 to $3,300 per entry point dependent upon configuration.

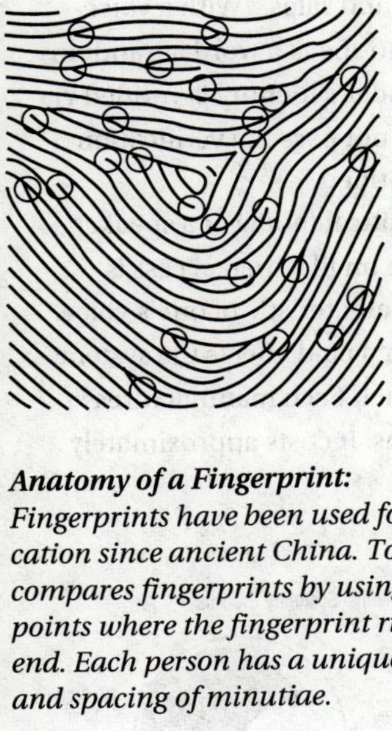

Anatomy of a Fingerprint:
Fingerprints have been used for identification since ancient China. Today, the FBI compares fingerprints by using minutiae, points where the fingerprint ridges fork or end. Each person has a unique number and spacing of minutiae.

Fingerprints are unique to each person; that's common knowledge. But retinal patterns? *Retinal Scanners* scan the pattern of user's retinas. Barry Becker, EyeDentify's vice president of international marketing, explains, "Every person, even an identical twin, has a unique blood vessel pattern in the retina." The EyeDentification System measures this unique pattern. A low-intensity infrared light is bounced off 320 data points within a 45-degree scan (see illustration, p.112). The amount of light reflected is converted into a template number. The quantity of light is not even affected by a person's contact lenses, because contact lenses are clear. Even tinted contacts don't present a problem. Eyeglasses, however, are a different story. The user must remove them during enrollment and log-on.

How safe is scanning people's retinas? Very. The light's intensity is about equal to one Christmas tree bulb.

A number of organizations have used readers without a problem. EyeDentify has been approved by major safety organizations, including Underwriters Laboratory, Sweden's National Institute of Radiation Protection, the Health and Safety Section of the Australian Radiation

Hand Geometry:
Recognition Systems manufactures a hand geometry reader. The ID3D constructs three dimensional images of a user's hand. If there's a match between the template and the user's hand, then he's admitted.

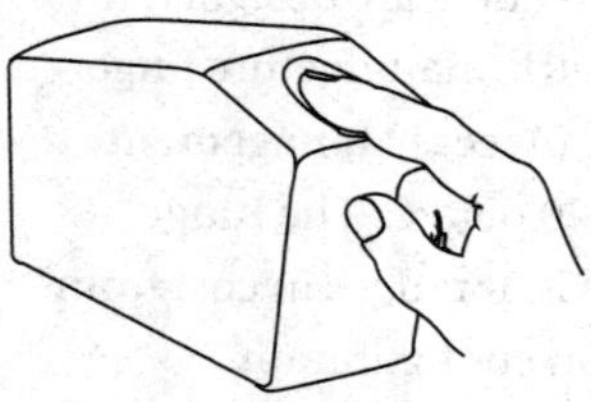

Fingerprint Reading:
The Ridge Reader Mint from Fingermatrix scans fingerprints, thereby controlling physical access to computers. It uses an individual's minutiae points for positive identification.

Laboratory, Oregon Health and Sciences University, and Workers Compensation of the State of Oregon. EyeDentify also has the stamp of approval from American Airlines, Argonne Labs, Brookhaven Labs and the FBI.

Eyedentify manufactures two retina readers. EyeDentification systems is a standalone unit retailing for about $6,000. It's generally used in securing room access. **EyeNet** is EyeDentify's PC unit. It varies in cost dependent on the particular installation.

Another area where biometrics have become popular is voice verification. Voice verification is the ability to identify the speakers by their vocal tract. Voice recognition, on the other hand, is the computer's ability to understand what is being said. Voice recognition is a bit of a ways off.

Voice verification is here and flourishing today. In fact voice verification has some interesting applications. One is electronic monitoring of criminals incarcerated at home instead of in prison. Says Michael Backler, Ecco's vice president for marketing and sales, "With a voice-equipped system, the offender is prompted to speak a word at random time during the day or at a curfew. The offender's identity is verified via voice pattern matching. If the offender does not pass the verification process, local correctional authorities are notified."

A voice verifier constructs a mathematical model of a speaker's vocal tract. If the vocal tract matches the one on file, then access is granted. It works by analyzing the unique characteristic of one's voice. According to Backler, neither a recording nor a cold affects the system. The voice itself isn't the key, but the vocal tract. Ecco manufactures VoiceKey for securing rooms and installations. It costs approximately $1,000 to $1,500 per reader.

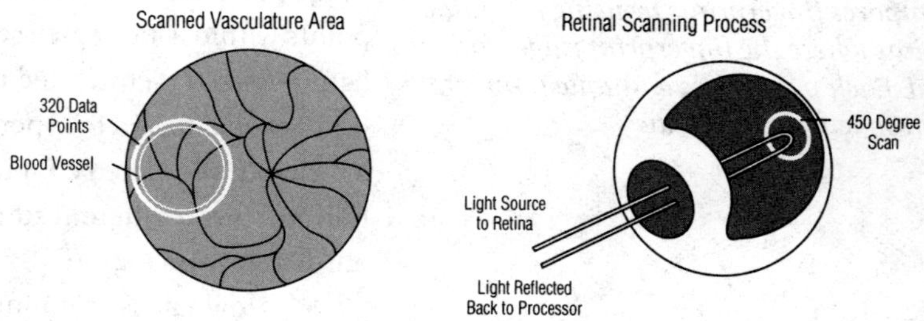

Retina Patterns: *Every person has a unique shape and spacing of his or her blood vessels. Retina readers use this pattern for identifying people. The reader bounces light off of the retina. The 320 data points are measured within the 450-degree scanning range as shown in the illustration. The amount of light reflected indicates the pattern. Since contact lenses are clear, they don't affect the retina scan, but glass eyes do.*

Signing Off While biometric devices substantially improve a LAN's security, they are not a solution in themselves. Other security problems exist beyond proper user identification. Users accessing secret data is a prime example. More important is user integrity. People can log on and then share their account with others. Proper data security, user education, transaction tracking are equally important. But biometric manufacturers will tell you that. They are not purporting to be the answer to every security threat, only to a specific type of threat. And you know what? They might just have the solution.

What makes a network work: Two tales of success and failure

What makes a network work? Is it planning, implementation, type of equipment, number of users, software, hardware, or people? There are many horror stories of LAN or attempted LAN installations, but there are also the success stories. What is the fine line that separates the two? Let's consider two fictional cases.

Lucifer & Piranha (a devil worship emporium and sushi bar) decided to link together their five PCs and ATs. They had waited a long time, after hearing the tales of woe from colleagues and other associates regarding their attempts at networking (or NOTworking, as it turned out). A meeting with the computer consultant who had helped them in the past provided guidance. After detailing how many computers were to be linked, how many new computers were needed, and which software was to be used, they developed a plan of attack (or attach, in the case of a network).

The consultant carefully planned the layout of the network, designed a cost-effective LAN installation, and ordered the necessary equipment. A cabling company ran the coaxial cables to the various locations of existing and future workstations. The cable installers marked all cables for easy identification in the cable closet, and left a few extra feet at each station in case someone wanted to rearrange the furniture.

Finally, the big day arrived. The consultant formatted the server and loaded the software. He configured the network adapters, made a log of all switch settings and serial numbers, and installed the adapters in the computers. After he connected the cables, he flipped on the power switches.

Did it work? Well, yes and no. One workstation displayed the message that the server could not be found. The other six logged right on without a hitch (or glitch). As it turned out, the lost workstation was a pseudo-luggable that had a slot, but wasn't a true compatible, and no upgrade ROMs were available, since the manufacturer had discontinued the model. Oh well, it wasn't that necessary anyway. Except for minor "gotchas," things ran very smoothly (they did find that single-user software doesn't run very well on a network). They're happy with how they can share files easily and share their printers.

Approximately a year later, the company added three diskless workstations. Because they had planned ahead, they didn't have to worry about network address conflicts; they just referred to the configuration log from the initial installation. The next upgrade includes plans for a larger, faster tape backup to run off the server.

"The latter company was partially a victim to being on the 'bleeding edge' of technology."

Steelhead, Bass, and Dolphin (a floundering firm with little porpoise in life) also installed a network system, but two years earlier. The company realized there were potential benefits from sharing resources such as expensive daisy wheel printers (times change rapidly in the computer industry) and hard disks. Not having existing microcomputers, the company contacted several retailers in the area. After finding one they liked, the salesperson/consultant recommended and installed the three computers and related peripherals. In-house experts ran the cabling. After making the connections, the consultant turned on the computers.

It worked! Except that SuperCalc3 wouldn't work—so they went back to SuperCalc2. And the workstation would randomly lose the server. After months of troubleshooting, the company hired a new consultant. After running diagnostics on the network adaptors and the self-tests passing, the consultant suspected the cabling. Since the original consultant had only specified coaxial cable, the in-house experts made a quick run to Radio Shack for—yes, you guessed it, TV antenna coax cabling! It does look the same, you know. After running network grade cabling, things seemed slightly more reliable. But the vendor announced new network boards, labeled the old ones "mature technology," and dropped support for them!

Well, the problems never did get ironed out and Steelhead, Bass, and Dolphin opted to dump the network idea and buy two hard disks for the workstations. They are still running this way today, although they did buy an automatic switch box to share a printer with three computers. Several vendors have approached the company to install a different networking system, but the company is still very gun-shy of networks in general. Although they can print from some of their computers, they can't share files (except through their "sneaker-net"—running floppy disks from station to station). And they still can't have more than one person updating accounting records at a time.

The first company did many things correctly—good planning and consulting with someone with network experience. The latter company was partially a victim to being on the "bleeding edge" of technology, further impeded by having a poorly planned installation set up by someone not knowledgeable or experienced in setting up networks. So the moral of the story is: Plan carefully, use people with knowledge and experience, detail the configuration of the system, and expect some problems or incompatibilities even with the most careful planning.

Oh, and don't go fishin' when the going gets tough.

Buyer's Guide

An expert Buyer's Guide to LAN software and hardware

Buyer's Guide

HERE´S AN UP-TO-DATE consumer's guide to the latest LAN hardware and software. Some of the material in the software section of this buyer's guide has appeared earlier (in our discussion of LAN applications) but we decided to include it again here, this time complete with current prices, to provide this comprehensive and useful tool for shopping.

A local area network (LAN) is the ideal way to tie a company together. It will allow employees to share printers, disk space, programs and data files. As a business grows, your LAN can keep pace, keeping people in touch via E-mail, making sure they all have up-to-date information, and coordinating their efforts with workgroup software.

All this has, of course, been explained in ample detail elsewhere in this book. If you've already taken the plunge into networking, you know the advantages already. But if you're still at the planning stage, you might have worries such as these:

"A LAN can't help being expensive."

"Once I choose one manufacturer's solution, I'll be stuck with it."

"The software applications most people use don't really take advantage of a LAN."

Legitimate concerns. However, the industry has long since laid them to rest. First of all, the low-end LANs are now very affordable. If all you want to do is share a PostScript printer or move files between PCs and Macs, you'll find a wide selection of "twisted-pair" LANs for just several hundred dollars per PC.

Second, though there are different LAN systems, they don't so much compete as exist in parallel. There is merely a variety of different solutions, from which you can choose according to your need and your budget (we don't know of any LAN today that can't be connected to any other in some way).

Third—and most significant—all of today's major software packages now come in special LAN versions. Multiple users can now routinely share databases in real time; data protection (file, record and field locking) is handled automatically. LANs also facilitate workgroup computing, which means being able to coordinate projects via LAN-specific scheduling, conferencing and electronic mail software. In short, today's hottest, state-of-the-art programs don't just benefit from a LAN: They require one in order to run.

In this Buyer's Guide, we examine LAN applications software and LAN hardware—in that order (if you're impatient to read about hardware, flip ahead to page 133). This isn't putting the cart before the horse; quite the contrary. After all, it's the applications software— word processors, spreadsheets, databases, and so on—that will determine what your LAN can do. It's the applications software that handles your data, which is, after all, your most important investment. And it's the applications software that you can purchase and become familiar with, before the first screw is turned to install a LAN interface card.

There are two general classes of LAN applications software. The first class, which is the most common, consists of popular programs such as 1- 2-3 and Word, which have developed from stand-alone versions into products that are LAN-aware. These LAN versions of major applications, as well as giving users extra power, usually offer a buyer significant cost savings. The second class consists of programs that—because they depend on E-mail service or "client-server" distributed computing—run only on LANs.

LAN Software

LAN VERSIONS OF MAJOR APPLICATIONS

If you are planning to use your LAN just to share printers or hard disk space, there will be no pressing need to change the applications software you have now. Any LAN operating system will allow single-user software to run, automatically intercepting users' local requests for disk or printer operations and carrying them out at the central server.

However, technical constraints—and the license agreements you consent to by tearing the shrink wrap off your applications —mean that only one person at a time should run single-user software, whether it is stored on a central server or at a local workstation. Single-user programs often maintain default settings and other information in files meant to be opened by only one user at a time.

In any case, there is a big difference between software that's merely usable on a LAN, and software that actively uses the network. Switch to the special LAN version of your favorite programs, and you'll gain not just multiuser access to the applications, but also the ability to share databases, "boilerplate" text, and other information. Of course, you'll also be able to take best advantage of whatever peripherals are attached to the server.

LAN applications software for DOS machines uses the NetBIOS protocol, an IBM/Microsoft addition to DOS ever since version 3.1. NetBIOS, which enables a standard method for file and record locking, is supported by almost all LAN system software, so you'll be able to run applications no matter what system you choose. For example, Novell's popular NetWare, though it has many extra functions, is compatible with any NetBIOS application—including everything we list in this Buyers' Guide (Novell also offers special message handling and packet exchange services, themselves supported by many LAN applications). Similarly, Macintosh multiuser software Macintosh users should look for software that supports the AppleTalk Filing Protocol (AFP), a standard used by Macintosh networks.

Canny software companies almost always give you a price break on LAN versions. They know that installing software on a LAN will encourage new employees in a department to adopt the same product their colleagues are already using. It's cheaper to purchase a given program for your server, and then pay a license fee based on the number of users, than to buy a stand- alone version of the same application for each workstation. When it comes time to upgrade software versions—not an infrequent occurrence these days—you just load new software on your server. This beats having to ship disks and manuals to twenty or thirty different people, and then leading each through the process of reinstalling the software.

WORD PROCESSORS

Almost everyone needs to use a word processor at some time, making word processing the most universal application. Naturally, every major word processing program is available in a special LAN version. These products make it easy for users to use a LAN server to store documents that need to be accessed by others, and they offer convenience in the form of a centralized dictionary, thesaurus, keyboard macros and "style sheets" that can help a department standardize on formats for memos or correspondence.

Of course, LAN word processors also offer each user the full resources of any shared printer, even when it's a laser printer that requires careful management of downloadable fonts. Some "high-end" programs also incorporate document management facilities, letting users track revisions of a document via a "redlining" option that shows additions or deletions on screen. No longer does some poor soul need to print out a dozen copies of a document, circulate them, and then labor to collate all the suggestions.

***WordPerfect* 5.1**, which costs $695 for a server program, and then $150 per workstation, includes all the features mentioned above. It can combine separate files into one master document with a single table of contents or index, and imports a wide variety of graphics into WordPerfect documents. A particularly useful "intelligent printing" feature lets a user format text for a LAN printer, but preview it on a local dot-matrix device with the closest approximate fonts. WordPerfect for the Macintosh ($395) allows files to be exchanged, formatting intact, with the PC version.

Microsoft's *Word* 5.0 features on-screen preview of both graphics and multiple columns. Priced at $450 (and $250 for each subsequent additional workstation), it has new document management features that let multiple users attach comments to a single document. When all reviewers are finished adding comments, an included macro merges all of the annotations into a single file. Right out of the box, Word 5.0 will also run as an OS/2 application, on any workstation that uses that operating system. Under OS/2, it can multitask and gains extra RAM, for even faster operation.

***Word* 4.0** for the Macintosh (a flat $395 per workstation) takes advantage of AppleShare and other AFP-compliant networks and is able to read and write files compatible with DOS Word, making it particularly useful on LANs with both Macs and PCs. It also has a edge in that links to Microsoft's E-mail program, Mail, are built right in. Choose "Send Mail" from the File menu, and Word opens up Mail, with your document title already in the subject area, and the document already included as a message.

Word for Windows, Microsoft's newest word processing program, is destined to be of particular interest to LAN users. For one thing, it is ready to run under Windows 3.0, the company's graphical interface that is network-ready and can make a LAN much easier for a novice to use. For another, **Word for Windows** can locate and convert word processing documents—in a variety of file formats—wherever they reside on a LAN. Users can cut and paste numbers and graphics from spreadsheets such as Excel, while Word for Windows is also able to compare document versions and collate comments appended to a file by multiple users. With its extensive macro language, Word for Windows allows a system administrator to create menus that load and save documents from a server without a user having to learn any new procedures.

IBM's *DisplayWrite* 5 for DOS also emphasizes connectivity. It has built in LAN support for IBM, Novell, and 3Com systems, and employs the Revised Form Text Document Content Architecture (RFT/DCA) file format, allowing documents to be exchanged with most other PC word processing programs, along with larger IBM systems. DisplayWrite 5 for DOS' new "WSYIWYG" page preview feature provides nine levels of zoom. Other versions of the program—all file-compatible—include ***DisplayWrite 5/2*** for OS/2, and ***DisplayWrite* 5.2 *Composer***, with sophisticated page layout capabilities.

Although these feature-laden products were the first to support LANs, you can also purchase network versions of simpler, "executive-level" word processors. An excellent case in point is Software Publishing's Professional Write. It's an easy-to-use program that can trade files directly with DisplayWrite, Word, WordStar and other formats. Professional Write costs $729 in a five-user LAN pack.

Other LAN word processors include: Lotus Manuscript, Multimate Advantage, Samna Word III and Ami Professional, Sprint, Volkswriter 4 with Perfect Grammar, Wordstar 5.5 and Wordstar 2000+.

SPREADSHEETS

Spreadsheets are fundamentally personal productivity tools, so their LAN versions aren't dramatically different from the single-user ones. But network versions of spreadsheet programs offer a savings in cost and workstation disk space, and they are more convenient to load. Most important, they always prevent multiple users from changing the same worksheet concurrently by mistake.

Computer Associates' SuperCalc5 is a textbook example of the advantages a LAN spreadsheet can confer. With the ability to hot-link up to 255 worksheets, and manipulate as many as three at once on screen, SuperCalc5 supports network file locking. It also provides each user to maintain his or her own personal default settings, and can automatically search multiple server directories to root out SuperCalc or 1-2-3 files.

SuperCalc5 can open up and work with worksheets created by earlier versions without conversion. It can now hold up to 255 files in RAM at a time, and its linking capabilities are prodigious. Create links between the files in RAM, those on your local hard disk, or those anywhere on your LAN—SuperCalc5 won't even care whether they were originated by SuperCalc or by 1-2-3.

SuperCalc5 also offers 3-D, adding depth to your models with multiple pages. It's also one of the few spreadsheets to produce 3-D graphs— just one choice out of a huge range that even includes a "radar" graph using polar coordinates.

Via an optional 1-2-3 command mode, Lotus addicts can use the menus and macros they're familiar with. SuperCalc can also pick selected fields and records out of dBASE files. For database files larger than will fit in RAM, you'll need ***Silverado***, Computer Associates' $149 add-in that adds relational capabilities and multiple ways to view information.

SuperCalc5 costs $495, and a ***LanPak*** adding three extra users costs only $495 extra. Unlike many other programs today, it will run well even on workstations with only 512K bytes and an 8088 microprocessor—you need not junk these older machines. At the other end of the spectrum, Computer Associates also offers a mainframe version, CA-SuperCalc5.0, for those whose LAN is connected to a mainframe.

With more than 5 million users, Lotus Development has faced a real challenge in upgrading 1-2-3. Some people now want to upgrade to—and get the most out of—new state-of-the-art LAN workstations, while others want to connect those old dual-floppy PCs they have hanging around. All need 1-2-3 compatibility.

The Lotus solution? Several different 1-2-3s. Release 2.2 is for users with basic 8088 PCs, floppy disk drives, and as little as 320K of RAM. Release 3 is for 80286 or 386 PCs with hard disks and 1M byte of RAM. And ***1-2- 3/G*** is for 80286 or 386 machines running OS/2 and ***Presentation Manager***. All these 1-2-3s are compatible with existing keystrokes. macros, and worksheets.

Even the most "modest" upgrade, Release 2.2, has many new features. Though it holds only one worksheet in RAM at a time, Release 2.2 lets you write formulas that link to values in worksheets on disk. Incorporating add-ins that were previously optional—the Learn macro recorder and Speedup—Release 2.2 also features minimal recalculation.

Also new are an Undo function and the ability to search and replace globally. The Macro Manager function lets you keep a quiver full of macros in memory, ready to run and no longer confined to a single worksheet. The new command makes graphing a block of data quicker, and the program now automatically spaces legends and X-axis labels.

1-2-3, Release 3 is not just an upgrade, it's a whole new program. It can store spreadsheets in up to 16M bytes of extended memory. It can access 32M bytes of EMS 4.0-compatible expanded memory. And it can run as a OS/2 protected-mode application, taking advantage of the operating system's multitasking capabilities.

Release 3's linking facilities are top-notch. You can reference cells or ranges in stored worksheets by name, or—using Release 3's ability to display three different worksheets on screen—just "point and shoot" to establish your hot links. Release 3 also is one of the few 3-D, multipage spreadsheets. You can add new pages just as easily as you'd insert rows and columns. Among the many improvements to 1-2-3's database functions are the ability to perform relational operations on different database tables. You can access, query and update data in dBASE III files using the included DataLens driver.

Both Release 2.2 and Release 3 include network support as a standard feature. 1-2-3 Release 3 features file locking and support for either DOS or OS/2-compatible LANs. It comes in a $495 single-user edition, but a $695 server edition will lower the price of adding workstations to $395 each. 1-2-3 Release 2.2 comes in a $595 server edition; the workstation edition (consisting of a software license and documentation only) is just $295.

Finally, 1-2-3/G ($695 for a single user—server and node edition pricing was not available at press time) employs the graphical user interface of OS/2 Presentation Manager. It features all the capabilities of 1-2-3 Release 3 plus the Solver, an advanced goal seeking technology for answering sophisticated "what-if" questions. There is built in support for

LAN security and file access; OS/2 LAN Manager users can run the product across OS/2- based networks and query database servers. Incidentally, Lotus has also developed versions of 1-2-3 that run on Digital Equipment VAX/VMS computers—relevant if your LAN includes these systems.

Microsoft's Excel is an ideal spreadsheet for those who have DOS, OS/2 and Macintosh machines connected to the same LAN. It comes in versions for all three operating systems, boasting the same interface, file structure and macro language. Training is easier, and it's a cinch to transfer worksheets and graphics between PCs and Macs. Mac Excel, priced at a flat $395 per workstation, now stores spreadsheets up to an incredible 8M bytes in size, provided your Mac has the RAM. *Mac Excel* allows transferring charts and worksheets into Word: When you update data in Excel, the linked document in Word gets updated too.

The PC Excel runs across LANs and accesses network devices via the Windows user interface. Thanks to the size of the Excel program files, it's particularly useful to be able to offload them to a LAN server; because of differing workstation configurations, though, it's best to keep Windows itself on local disk drives. Only a single person may have read/write access to a worksheet at any one time, but Excel optionally lets others look at it without making changes. The PC version of Excel costs $495, while a workstation pack is $250.

Excel creates and maintains links between multiple worksheets easily. You can load multiple worksheets into RAM or—though it's slower— retrieve your linked values from worksheets on disk or from a network server. It's easy to create a graph: Just use your mouse to select the worksheet data you wish to chart, and then open a chart window. Change data in the worksheet, and your chart will automatically redraw to reflect the changes.

All Excel versions can read and write other file formats, including Lotus' ***.WKS, .WK1***, and dBASE III (enough RAM to hold the data is required). By selecting a range within a worksheet, you can define a database; Excel then lets you enter data into new records just by filling in a form.

DOS and OS/2 versions of Excel (both $495) take advantage of ***Dynamic Data Exchange*** (DDE), which may be used to "hot link" selected spreadsheet cells to other applications running at the same time. With a DDE-aware word processor such as Word for Windows or Ami Professional, you can import Excel data into a document. DDE then makes sure the data is updated every time the source worksheet gets changed. OS/2 Excel can consolidate worksheets from up to 256 sources, wherever they reside on the LAN.

Borland's ***Quattro Pro***, which sells for $495, plus $295 for each extra user on a LAN, offers a distinctive mix of features. Even with its extensive functions, though, Quattro Pro will run on machines with as little as 512K bytes of RAM. The program offers linking, and can open as many as 32 worksheets at once. Of course, you'll start out with a single worksheet. When this gets unwieldy, break the worksheet into parts, and Quattro Pro will keep track of all references and formulas. A special "workspace" function lets you open and close linked worksheets in unison.

The spreadsheet may be operated with a mouse, or via 1-2-3-, Quattro-, or Quattro Pro-style menuing systems. File compatibility is a strong point: Quattro Pro reads 1-2-3 files and macros, and may be used to query dBASE IV, Reflex, and Paradox databases. Since Quattro Pro conforms to Paradox's multiuser protocols, it can work with a Paradox database that's "live" on a LAN.

Informix' ***Wingz*** is a high-end Macintosh spreadsheet, perfect for LAN system administrators who want to create customized applications. Users on a LAN will be able to manipulate spreadsheet data, via customized formats that need not look like traditional spreadsheets. All the Macintosh menuing tools—dialog boxes, "radio buttons," sliders, and pop-ups—may be used to prompt users for input. You can use these to customize a screen so the spreadsheet rows and columns are hidden entirely. For example, the display might show just a pie chart and several sliders: You'd change values by using the mouse pointer to select and move sliders, causing the chart to be redrawn. To protect a worksheet from the klutzy, you can hide or password protect any of its elements. You can also compile programs written in Wingz' programming language

Users will find graphics easy to create. After selecting a range of cells, you just click on the charting tool icon, then drag a box to where you want your chart to go—the chart goes onto the same worksheet as its data. Chart types include 3-D graphs one can rearrange using elevation, rotation, and vanishing point sliders. To fine-tune your worksheet further, add free- floating text and graphics imported from other Mac applications, or use Wingz' freehand drawing tools.

Wingz ($395) may be run under Apple's UNIX (A/UX) now. More significantly for LAN users, versions are under development for Sun and DEC workstations, and a Wingz for Windows version will be released during 1990. In other words, this spreadsheet is yet another good choice if you plan to link a variety of different machines.

DATABASES

Today's sophisticated LAN databases allow multiple users to consult the same database files. Data integrity is ensured by record locking: Multiple users may open the same file, but only one at a time can change any given record. Some products lock right down to the field level, and can password-protect selected items.

LAN databases now also can update the screens on all workstations at any preset interval. After all, if a clerk in your mail-order business changed a customer's request from a pink tie to a blue one at the last minute, you wouldn't want the shipping department to be still looking at an outdated screen after the order had changed.

It's not necessary to adopt a fancy multi-file database product for your LAN if all users will be sharing one file. Symantec's ***Q&A*** bundles a "natural language front-end" with a word processor and flat-file database management. It offers record locking and five levels of password protection; combining the basic $349 Q&A and $299 ***Network Pack*** gives four users simultaneous access.

Multifile database products allow relating multiple files, usually a good idea when relationships between data items are complex. dBASE, the best-known of multifile databases, used to require sophisticated programming to work well on a LAN. The latest version, dBASE IV, features a host of improvements, many related to making network operation more functional. You can enable an Autosave facility, which continuously saves changes to a database, and a "rollback" function allows you to backtrack to save records in the event of a system crash. dBASE IV users can also switch into a Structured Query Language mode, creating and querying databases using SQL. The program costs $795, and a $995 LAN pack permits you to add five users.

FoxBASE+ ($595 in a multiuser version) is a dBASE-compatible database program that claims to run dBASE programs faster than any other interpreter on the market. A $700 run-time version lets you add an unlimited number of workstations without paying additional fees. The Macintosh version, FoxBASE+/Mac, allows users to share databases on AppleShare compat ible networks. Priced at $395 per workstation or $300 for an unlimited runtime version, ***FoxBASE+/Mac*** is compatible with dBASE III+ program and data files, but also has the ability to store graphics in its database files. Finally, Fox Software's ***Foxpro/LAN*** database manager ($1,095) features a character-based windowing interface, and programming language extended to include many new functions—including manual/automatic file and record locking. Users can share data with, and run programs written for, FoxBASE+ and FoxBASE+/Mac.

Borland's Paradox 3.0 also runs programs originally written for a single-user system on a LAN with few changes, because file and record locking are automatic. If you encounter a locked record within a file, you can get the name of the person who is using it. You can also find out the names of all Paradox users on the LAN. Paradox can even set up a graph that automatically changes on screen as users add data. This capability allows real-time monitoring of a process such as order-taking. Paradox costs $725, while a $995 ***Lan Pack*** provides manuals and licenses for five additional users.

R:Base for DOS or ***OS/2*** features ***Query By Example***, a "pseudo-compiler" that speeds up program operations, a reliable SQL interface, and automatic multiuser support. It costs $725, including a license for three workstations. R:Base takes care of record locking automatically. If two users attempt to change a field at once, the changes are put in a queue and the first user effects the change. The other is notified of the change and is given the opportunity to make, or abandon, his own changes. R:Base for DOS also features on-line help specially written for network users.

An exciting development in LAN databases is client-server architecture. Instead of running fundamentally identical copies of database software on every workstation, this scheme puts a specialized database engine only on the server. The other workstations get client software, which translates user requests for information into a form the database engine can understand.

When a user asks the database engine for information, all that goes over the LAN is the initial request, and then the server's reply. Because network traffic is significantly reduced, performance increases can be spectacular. Some server products will run on a DOS machine, such as Gupta Technologies' $1,995 ***SQLBase Server***, but others require an OS/2 server, such as IBM's $830 0S/2 Extended Edition. Many other companies are preparing future client/server products.

Other LAN database products include: ***Advanced Revelation, Clarion Professional, Dataease, Dataflex, DBXL/LAN, dBASE/Mac, Fourth Dimension, Omnis Quartz,*** and ***Professional Oracle.***

ACCOUNTING

For many companies, accounting software may be the reason for installing a LAN. Accounting information—Accounts Payable, Accounts Receivable, Payroll, Inventory, etc.—comprises a company's most important information. A network allows your books to be kept up to date by several data entry operators simultaneously, and means that completely up-to-date reports may be produced at any time.

Of the hundreds of accounting programs on the market, not all run on LANs. With its AccPac line, however, Computer Associates has a full range of network accounting software. AccPac ***BPI modules*** ($395 each) include Accounts Receivable and Payable, Payroll, and Inventory control. To run them on a LAN, you install the $395 AccPac BPI Lan Pack (also $395), which confers file and record locking plus password protection.

Data Pro's line of accounting programs (mostly $750 apiece) is LAN-ready, and significantly more complete than most. It includes General Ledger, Accounts Payable with Checkwriting, Purchase Order Entry with On-Order Processing, Payroll (again with Checkwriting), and Job Costing with Time Billing. Point of Sale and Inventory Management modules support hardware add-ons including cash drawers, bar code readers, and even speech synthesizers. The Data Pro modules, which have a consistent user interface, can either stand alone or operate as part of an integrated system.

Great Plains accounting software is another flexible, powerful series, priced at $695 per module. You need $395 Network Manager software to enable LAN use. Open Systems, as its name implies, offers purchasers source code in Basic for its $795 accounting modules. To run them on a LAN, the $795 Network Resource Manager is a required option. UNIX versions are also available.

If you're particularly interested in tailoring accounting software to your own business, take a look at the ***SBT Database Accounting Library.*** SBT offers a particularly wide range of $395 modules—including Professional Time and Billing, Project Accounting, Purchasing, and many others—written in dBASE source code. Users can modify the programs and run them using any dBASE interpreter. Via FoxBASE/MAC or Nantucket Software's $295 ***McMax***, the SBT programs will even run on a Macintosh.

Though DOS machines do enjoy the largest base of accounting software—particularly if multiuser operation on a LAN is what you're interested in—the Macintosh is now definitely a viable option too. Great Plains has versions of its accounting series that are TOPS and AppleShare compatible; they're priced at $795 for the required Network Manager and then $795 per module. Chang Labs' popular ***Rags to Riches*** series also runs on Macintosh LANs; it's priced at $895 for Accounts Receivable and Accounts Payable. Additional modules are $795 each.

INTEGRATED SOFTWARE

Integrated software combines word processing, database management, and spreadsheet modules into a single product. Some companies are installing network versions because they provide "one-stop shopping", economy, and ease of use.

Ashton-Tate's ***Framework III LAN*** offers word processing, database, and spreadsheet, plus telecommunications and LAN-ready electronic mail. Complete with file locking, it costs $995 for five users.

Lotus' ***Symphony*** ($695) includes a locking utility that supports worksheet sharing over the LAN, and has graphics built-in. ***Open Access II*** Plus ($895, for five users) includes a multifile database, spreadsheet, word processor, and desktop utilities.

Informix Software takes a modular approach with its Smart Software System. This LAN integrated software, including a word processor and spell-checker, spreadsheet, and database manager, may be purchased as separate modules or all at once. Adding workstations is easy; just purchase $179 access software for each machine you want to attach.

Among the very cheapest LAN applications on the market is Microsoft's Works ($149, and then $97.50 per additional workstation), a simple integrated package whose spreadsheet reads and writes 1-2-3 files. The Macintosh version of Works ($295) runs over LANs too, letting several users access data files in "read-only" mode. Software Publishing's PFS:First Choice is similar: Its graphics module is actually a subset of the respected Harvard Graphics. It costs $159, but a LAN pack adding five more users is just $475.

FutureSoft's ***Right Hand Man*** is a LAN personal productivity tool that runs in terminate-and-stay-resident mode, occupying as little as 4K bytes when it isn't popped up. Users can receive E-mail, take notes, and access dBASE-compatible database files. Right Hand Man also can read messages as they are received via computerized voice. It costs $189 per user, or $899 in a 10-user pack.

COMMUNICATIONS SOFTWARE

A LAN is a convenient way for many users to share a pool of modems connected to a communications server. Not only does this give every user access to a modem—for dialing up online databases, checking mail on MCI Mail and CompuServe, and so on—even in sites where outside phone lines are difficult to obtain, but it also means that the cost of high-speed 9600 or 19,200 bps modems becomes much easier to justify.

However, off-the-shelf copies of PC communications software will not work, because they expect to find a modem attached to a serial port on the local workstation. To get around this problem, you might choose to buy a specialized network redirector card that captures the software's request for a serial port and sends it over the LAN. However, a better solution is to select communications software that works via NetBIOS or another LAN-specific protocol instead of demanding a serial port. Data will automatically flows through the LAN to the communications server where the modem is physically attached.

Available communications programs designed to work with an ACS (Asynchronous Communications Server) include DCA's $249

Crosstalk Mk* 4** and Hayes' ***Smartcom III (also $249), and Relay Communications' ***Relay Gold*** ($525 for five workstations).

Procomm Plus for Networks (from Datastorm Technologies) is a easy-to-use program built around a simple phone dialing directory, it requires little initial attention to parameter settings such as "Xon-Xoff" or "full duplex-half duplex," yet makes settings easy to change when you need to. ASPECT, Procomm Plus's script language, might not be as powerful as the one in Crosstalk Mk 4, but it certainly can automate all common communications sessions.

A nice feature for people who have no interest in writing scripts is Procomm's learn mode, which records keystrokes during a session and then turns them into scripts automatically. Although some script writing is necessary for complicated tasks, record mode is perfect for teaching Procomm to call a service, sign on to it, check for mail, and so on.

Softklone's ***Mirror III LAN*** is compatible with script files already written for Crosstalk XVI (long the standard in many companies), but has an extended language called PRISM that even allows construction of custom data-entry forms and menus. It also provides a wide range of terminal emulations and file transfer protocols. The $595 price includes a license for up to eight workstations.

DESKTOP PUBLISHING

Though most desktop publishing programs may be installed on LAN servers, and run from one workstation at a time, it's still rare to find one that is multiuser. With its Network Edition, however, Ventura Publisher can make that claim.

The $1,295 file server software allows all workstations (each of which must be running its own $595 Ventura program) to share a printer, "chapters," and source text files. A special alert notifies a user when a file within a chapter has been modified by another user, and multiple workstations can share the same read-only style sheets. Ventura does have rather stringent hardware requirements: Each workstation must have a full 640K bytesof RAM, plus at least 256K bytes of expanded memory.

Although details were not available at press time, Ventura Publisher will also be released this year in a Windows-specific version. Thanks to Windows 3.0's built-in compatibility with Novell, 3Com, and other LANs, Ventura users will be able to access memory above 640K bytes, making the program faster and facilitating assembly of publications from documents LAN-wide. Of course, the new Windows release is likely to benefit Ventura's arch-rival, Aldus PageMaker, as well.

LAN-Specific software

LAN-SPECIFIC SOFTWARE

With the exception of the new client-server database products, all the applications we mentioned above are ones that were already familiar on standalone PCs. But LANs may also be used to run exciting new software: that which brings users together into a workgroup.

Workgroup software includes simple electronic mail—so users can exchange messages—and "groupware," a host of other applications that are really only effective on a LAN, including scheduling, document processing, time management, and conferencing.

ELECTRONIC MAIL

Electronic mail software can send messages from one user to another instantaneously. E-mail programs set up an in-box you can check at your leisure, and let you send messages without leaving the application you may be using. Some also feature a "bulletin board," where all users can read and leave comments. "Rude" messaging capabilities mean that messages can flash on screen no matter what application the recipient may be in the middle of using.

Because the Macintosh's LocalTalk connector has made simple Mac LANs so common, Mac users enjoy a wide choice of E-mail software. The popular ***Inbox*** costs $350 in a three-user starter kit, while software for additional users is $125. Microsoft's Mail, which installs as a desk accessory available at any time, costs $395 for the server component, with a license for 1 to 4 users. Extra workstation packs are $125 each.

CE Software's QuickMail actually allows Macintosh users to send and receive multimedia messages—up to 90 seconds of sound, along with a text message and clipboard color graphics. Sound recording is via Farallon's ***MacRecorder,*** though users do not need a copy of this software in order to play back messages. QuickMail costs $399 in a five-user package; additional workstations cost $89.95 each (the product is also available in 50- and 10-user bundles).

PC users may choose their own version of QuickMail ($299 in a five user package). Another option is ***Inbox/PC*** ($99 for a three-workstation LAN), which links to the Macintosh version, producing a display mimicking a "while-you-were-out" notepad. The Network Courier ($295 for six users) lets you select a 60K byte RAM-resident configuration, a full-fledged standalone version with a 1-2-3-style command line, or an edition with the Windows user interface. It can attach any kind of file to a message, so you can send someone a "here's the spreadsheet you asked for" note along with a worksheet.

Da Vinci eMAIL is a leading E-mail program for PC compatibles, with versions for both DOS and OS/2. Da Vinci eMAIL was the first electronic package to have been released in a Windows version, worth noting in view of the current popularity of Windows 3.0 as a LAN user interface. The program is available in slick Windows or OS/2 Presentation Manager versions, although it also comes in a version that employs text-based pull-down menus for compatibility with old 8088 workstations. Thanks to its hardware-independent design, Da Vinci eMAIL runs with any networking software, on any server, and via any LAN cabling hardware. For anyone who isn't already using Novell NetWare, Da Vinci Systems offers an optional interface to the MHS Message Handling System, enabling users to send mail to remote networks (Novell users get MHS when they buy NewWare). Character-based Da Vinci eMAIL costs $295 in an eight-user pack; the Windows version is $445.

cc:Mail is another very popular E-mail program, one which runs on DOS, OS/2, and Macintosh platforms. It has a built-in text editor, a main menu and two status windows at the top of the screen that list received messages and the number of messages stored in folders. cc:Mail can support compound messages made up of text, files, screen images, graphics, and even fax messages. The sender need only know the recipient's name in order to send a message; proper addressing gets handled by the cc:Mail "post office." With available options, cc:Mail can link to external E-mail systems such as MCI, and also to IBM's PROFS and DISOSS plus DEC's VAX/VMS mail systems. Typical prices are $495 for Mac and OS/2 server applications, and $695 for a DOS sever.

GROUPWARE

The term "groupware" covers a wide range of new software products, not easily classified. What all have in common is taking isolated PC users and bringing them into a group. Thanks to these programs, which are usually priced on a per-server basis, members of a group need not be in the same place—or time—in order to work together.

Conetic Systems' $995 Higgins handles office administration, allowing users to coordinate their schedules. It includes to-do list and expense report modules, and desktop accessories such as note pads, calculators, expense reports, to-do lists, tickler files, and phone directories. Like some of the products previously mentioned, Higgins Exchange can link LAN E-mail to external E-mail services such as CompuServe. Users can send information to those on other Higgins systems without having to specify the location of the recipient.

Office Works, a $1,395 program from Data Access, offers similar functions and adds built-in database software that allows users to share name-and-address files and other lists. Chronos Software's Who-What-When Enterprise ($695) integrates people, project and time management. When you start the program, it displays a calendar, but users can switch to linked views of the projects they are working on or people they work with. Finally, The Coordinator ($995), an elaborate electronic mail system, includes a system of management tools that track work commitments. It forces workgroup members to be explicit about what they promise to do and nags them to meet deadlines.

WordPerfect Office 3.0, as its name implies, is ideal for those already using WordPerfect for word processing. This product ($695 for a five-pack) features a shell that can simplify LAN operation, allowing a user to switch applications and move text between them with a "clipboard." WordPerfect Office also has macros, electronic mail, and a scheduler that automatically finds "open times" when department meetings can be scheduled. Its simple flat-file database module, Notebook, saves mail or telephone lists as WordPerfect merge files. Via the optional Office Connection Server, WordPerfect Office can communicate with other servers and external E-mail systems worldwide; users will also be able to dial in to collect messages from a home PC using the $149 Word Perfect Office PC.

More often than not, users in a group are collaborating on perfecting a document. Broderbund's For Comment ($995) takes word-processed documents and distributes them over a LAN, inviting reviewers to make comments in the "margins." The program makes it easy for the author to collate the comments and choose which suggestions to incorporate.

Just a few of the many other groupware products: ***ActionTracker Plus***, ***Shoebox***, and ***Telephone Note Taker Plus***.

LAN hardware

LAN HARDWARE

If we had listed each software application that runs on a LAN, this book would already have reached *War and Peace* dimensions. But your appetite should've been whetted sufficiently by the intriguing programs listed above. If you haven't already got a LAN, and are eager to run all that good stuff, then tighten your seat belt for an "If It's Tuesday, This Must Be Belgium" tour of LAN hardware and system software—from the simplest to the most elaborate.

Each workstation, and, of course, server machine, will requires a local area network adapter board, and LAN system software to support file and record locking and confer password protection. But the days when a LAN had to be complicated or expensive are long gone. The LAN marketplace now offers an embarrassment of riches, ranging from easy-to-install systems for two or three users to those that can form the spine of an entire corporation. We've divided today's offerings into four levels:

- Cluster, meant for a group of three or four people who just need to share a printer or disk drive;

- Workgroup, for four or five people who need to work together with multiuser software;
- Departmental, for five to fifty people running multiuser software and, electronic mail;
- and Corporate, where gateways link multiple departmental systems.

You need to understand that these categories are meant only as a rough guide—there's no clear dividing line between the classes. In fact, a hallmark of today's LANs—with their emphasis on expandability and interconnectivity—is that they won't lock you in: You can start with a basic system, and later make it faster or larger by upgrading either the LAN hardware or the system software. Also, thanks to common standards, it's generally possible to mix LAN hardware from different companies just as you'd mix different manufacturer's stereo components.

CLUSTER LANS

Non-dedicated servers for sharing disks and printers

The widest-used cluster LAN is Apple's LocalTalk, built into every Macintosh. Right out of the box, it allows users to share any laser printer with an AppleTalk port (such as Apple's LaserWriter II NT and NTX, or IBM's Personal PagePrinter II). LocalTalk runs at 240K bits/sec. (100 times the speed of a 2400 bps modem) and can relay a signal only 1,000 feet. However, you can extend its reach by installing Farallon's PhoneNet, whose $60 adapter supports ordinary RJ-11 telephone cable over distances of up to 4,500 feet.

If you want to share disk space as well as printers, you will have to upgrade the Mac system software. The most popular way to do this is by using TOPS ($249 per Mac). With TOPS installed, users can copy files freely from machine to machine, sharing disk storage. TOPS gives any Macintosh on an AppleTalk network the ability to share files with any other. It also is now compatible with the AppleTalk Filing Protocol (AFP), the standard for Macintosh multiuser applications. When your needs develop, and you wish many workstations to share the same data file concurrently, TOPS will be ready.

If you want to add DOS machines to the cluster, you can attach PC compatibles to a LocalTalk network using Tops for the PC software ($189). There are several ways to add the required LocalTalk port to a PC workstation, including Apple's **Local Talk PC Card** ($150) and TOPS' **Flashcard for the PC** ($239). "Translators" included with TOPS can convert files between PC and Mac formats. If you want the PCs to print on a networked ***PostScript*** printer, you will need to add the TOPS ***NetPrint*** software ($189).

Entry-level LANs made solely for DOS machines are, like TOPS, simple "peer-to-peer" systems. This means they allow any workstation to give disk space, a printer, or other resources to the LAN. A good example is Waterloo Systems' PORT Lite, which costs $495 for software supporting up to five users ($795 bundled with two ARCnet adapter cards). PORT Lite is easy to install and gives the choice of either an icon-driven user interface or DOS command line operation.

WORKGROUP LANS

True multiuser software with non-dedicated or dedicated servers

Upgrading a LAN for multiuser software is not so much a matter of changing the hardware as it is of changing to LAN system software that supports file- and record-locking. This LAN operating system will also endow other security features such as different passwords and privilege levels for each user.

Grapevine LAN Products' ***Grapevine***, a 3.6 M bits/sec, peer-to-peer network, is compatible with the NetBIOS standard for DOS multiuser software. The $595-per-node price covers both a LAN adapter card and operating software, including an excellent electronic mail facility. An interesting aspect of Grapevine is its compatibility with ***PrinterLAN***, a $295 software-only product that uses an identical user interface to link laptop computers—or any other PC with only a serial port—to the network at 115,200 baud. PrinterLAN confers remote access via modem, too, so telecommuters may use it to check their Grapevine E-mail from afar.

Novell's ***ELS NetWare*** ($695 for four users), in contrast, requires a central machine as a dedicated server. ELS NetWare is fully NetBIOS-compatible, but it uses a special file system tuned for maximum performance and security. If you need to use your server as a workstation simultaneously, this is still permissible, provided the machine has a spare megabyte of memory set aside to hold NetWare.

3Com's 3+Share ($595 for five users) also uses a central file server that you can operate as a workstation concurrently. Unlike Novell, 3Com gives you the option to farm out certain server functions—printing, filing, and dialing in remotely—to workstations. However, the company warns that performance can suffer if you do this too much.

ELS NetWare and 3+Share both run on a wide variety of Ethernet adapters, including the $395 **Novell NE1000**, the AST **Ethernode** ($395), the 3Com **Etherlink II** ($445), and the Western Digital **Ethercard Plus** ($395). In addition to its line of adapters for standard PCs, Pure Data offers a $595 **Ethernet** card for Toshiba laptops. The company also sells many adapters for the popular ARCnet networking system, ranging from a $295 8-bit model to a $695 Micro Channel version. All feature switchless installation.

ARCnet is a token-passing system running at 2.5M bits/sec. that performs surprisingly well under load, and has proven itself for more than ten years. The system runs over either simple twisted pair wiring or via coaxial cable. Thomas-Conrad offers what must be the industry's widest range of ARCnet adapters. It includes simple 8-bit adapters at $249, and ranges on up to a $395 card for Micro Channel machines and a $495 card for the Macintosh II.

For multiple users to access a file stored on a central Mac concurrently, Apple's AppleShare File Server and Print Server software ($799 and $299, respectively, with no per-workstation charges) is required. DOS machines can use an AppleShare server too, with Apple's $149 AppleShare PC. This allows LocalTalk-equipped PCs to store files on the server and to share an attached laser printer. Since many DOS programs still do not support PostScript, AppleShare PC provides an Epson LQ-2500 emulation—if the application can print to an Epson, it can print via AppleShare.

A competitor to AppleShare is Dayna's DaynaNET, which also runs over LocalTalk hardware. Priced from $595 in a four-user pack to $3,995 for 100 users, it is a specially adapted version of Novell NetWare employing an IBM PC AT compatible as server. DOS workstations may be added too, although you will need to bridge to a NetBIOS-compatible LAN if you also want to run multiuser DOS software. A feature called Stamper supports the use of DOS files on Mac computers by letting users "stamp" files with a Macintosh desktop icon.

LocalTalk's pulse can be quickened with Tops' ***FlashBox*** ($189), which improves transmission speed to 770K bits/sec. Dayna's $189 ***DaynaTALK*** goes further, claiming up to 850K bits/sec; ***DaynaTALK for the PC*** ($289) comes with a PC LocalTalk card and runs at 1.7M bits/sec.

CHOOSING WORKSTATIONS

Although you can set up a basic multiuser LAN by cabling up whatever workstations you already have, there are some points to consider when adding new machines. PC-compatible workstations need 640K bytes of RAM, since LAN software drivers steal memory from users' precious DOS workspace. And when you get to the workgroup level, any dedicated server should be at least a fast AT compatible.

The new breed of low-profile machines is ideal—though if you're buying a machine with just three expansion slots, make sure it has serial, parallel, and VGA ports built in. Since you'll be giving up one slot to a LAN adapter, you need to make sure there's room for future expansion. Similarly, if you are buying new machines for an AppleTalk network, make sure they're Macintosh SEs or other Macs offering at least one slot.

DEPARTMENTAL SYSTEMS

Faster multiuser performance via dedicated servers

If you already have a small workgroup LAN running multiuser applications, the first step in expanding it to support more workstations is upgrading the system software. Novell's $1,595 ELS NetWare Level II lets up to eight DOS (or OS/2) PCs and Macintoshes share the same NetWare server. It comes with a coupon for a free copy of *NetWare For Macintosh*, a $200, server-based application that gives NetWare its Macintosh connectivity. To connected Macs, the server appears just as if it were an AppleShare server—fully compatible with Macintosh multiuser software—yet also allows file exchange with DOS machines and access to network resources such as printers. A 100-user version, Advanced NetWare, is $2,995; 3Com's competing 3+Share sells for $2,995 in a version supporting unlimited users.

You will eventually need a faster server too. Although 80286 computers may be employed, if you're starting from scratch we highly recommend a machine based on the 80386. Now available in prices to fit all budgets, these PCs boast better speed and more sophisticated memory management. They're better at running OS/2 and most LAN operating systems.

TAKING THE BUS

ISA or Micro Channel

Compaq computers enjoy a reputation for speed and freedom from compatibility problems. The **DESKPRO 386/20e** is a small-footprint machine with room for four internal storage devices; it costs $6,099 when equipped with a 40M byte hard disk. Powerful enough to improve the performance of your LAN, the DESKPRO 386/20e includes the same Flexible Advanced Systems Architecture and 82385 cache controller as on Compaq's more expensive machines. Serial and parallel ports, plus a mouse interface and Compaq's integrated 16-bit VGA are all built onto the motherboard. Compaq also offers the **DESKPRO 386/25e**, which crams 25 MHz processing speed into the same size package. It's priced at $7,699 in a 60M byte version.

IBM, of course, offers a wide range of Micro Channel machines suitable to be either servers or workstations. Although fewer LAN adapter cards are available for Micro Channel than for the classic AT bus, the number is growing—and Micro Channel's compactness and auto-configuration brings some real advantages. IBM's range includes the compact **PS/2 Model 70**. If you want a 120M byte configuration, it costs $8,995 in a 25 MHz configuration and $6,395 in a 20 MHz version.

IBM has recently bucked the industry trend that says a company's most expandable PC must also be its most expensive. The tower-style **PS/**

2 Model 65SX has the same SCSI disk adapter, seven expansion slots, and room for four internal hard disk drives, as IBM's top-of-the-line systems. However, because it uses an 80386SX processor, it costs just $5,995 in a 120M byte configuration.

AST seems to be dedicated to helping you start small and upgrade later, In fact, its modular **CUPID-32** systems feature what must be the industry's highest degree of upgradability. You can start with an 80386SX processor, and later drop a 80386/33 or 80486 CPU card into the same system. Some AST models also feature modular expansion buses. You can start with an industry-standard ISA bus (like that used in the original PC AT). Later, you can change buses, installing an enhanced EISA bus (see below for details about the benefits EISA will give LAN users).

Among its many other systems, NEC offers the **PowerMate SX Plus**, with the features to shine either as a server or a workstation, including 2M bytes of RAM, and built-in VGA and 800 x 600 "Super VGA" graphics support. It features four full-size 8/16-bit slots, and a fifth slot dedicated to high-speed memory expansion. There are three internal, half-height bays for storage devices: two 5¼-inch, and one 3½-inch.

The PowerMate SX Plus's hard disk options are the same as on NEC's more expensive systems—a 42M byte drive with a average access time rated at a rapid 28 milliseconds; a 100M byte drive with a 23-millisecond access time and an Enhanced Small Device Interface (ESDI) controller; and a 140M byte ESDI drive with an 18-millisecond access time. List prices for the PowerMate SX Plus range from $3,499 for a 42M byte machine to $4,399 for a 100M byte one.

Epson's complete range of PC compatibles is topped by the **Equity 386-20**, a 20 MHz 80386-based system. Priced at just $5,599 with a 90M byte hard disk, it is particularly suited for use as a budget LAN file server because of its nine expansion slots and room for five disk drives. The 90M byte drive features an 18-millisecond access time and uses an Enhanced Small Device Interface (ESDI) controller, which permits extra-rapid movement of data from the disk to the CPU.

ETHERNET OR TOKEN-RING

At this departmental level, Ethernet cards remain a popular choice, especially those offering 16-bit bus connectors, on-board buffers, and coprocessors, all of which enhance performance. Besides the Western Digital card mentioned before, they include AST's $595 **Ethernet Card**, which can run without a wait state in AST's own computers, 3Com's $895 **Etherlink Plus**, which can save workstation RAM by downloading LAN software into its own memory, and Novell's $495 **NE-2000**. Ethernet cards are available for the Micro Channel as well: 3Com's $595 **EtherLink/MC**, Novell's $495 *NE/2*, and Western Digital's $499 **EtherCard Plus/A**.

IBM's Token-Ring network is favored especially by those with a range of IBM hardware because it can connect directly to bigger computers: for example, the front-end processor (FEP) on a mainframe. An IBM **Token-Ring Adapter II**, which sends data at 4M bits/sec, costs $650; its Micro Channel equivalent, the **Token-Ring Adapter/A**, costs $750. You also need a $693 MAU (Multistation Access Unit) for every eight PCs.

Many, if not most, Token-Ring users choose to upgrade from the IBM system software, installing either NetWare or 3+Share. It's possible to use third-party Token-Ring hardware too, such as 3Com's **TokenLink** and **TokenLink Plus** adapters ($595 and $945, respectively). The TokenLink Plus has an 80186 coprocessor and a massive 256K buffer to improve performance. Western Digital offers its $399 **TokenHub**, a four-port multistation access unit, together with the $499 **TokenCard WS**, a 4M bits/sec adapter for work-stations. The $599 **TokenCard**, intended for a file server, includes a 128K byte buffer. Thomas-Conrad's **Token-Ring Adapter/AT** has both 128K bytes of on-board RAM and a 16-bit data path; it costs $595.

Because a single server becomes overloaded when you have from twenty to forty users, adding more workstations in corporate LANs usually means interlinking many different departmental servers with high-speed "spines." Accordingly, IBM has upgraded its Token-Ring to use high speed adapters that can run at 16M bits/sec. They're the $895 **Token-Ring Adapter 16/4** and **Token-Ring Adapter/A 16/4** Apple boards.

Apple offers the $1,250 **TokenTalk NB** board, a 4M bits/sec Token-Ring adaptor for the Macintosh II, IIc and IIcx family of machines. The advanced TokenTalk NB has its own 68000 microprocessor and 512K bytes of RAM, making it a computer in its own right. The board handles all communications processing so the Mac can get on with other jobs; it comes with ***SMB File Transfer Utility*** software, which puts files into MS-DOS formats so you can trade them with an IBM PC LAN server.

All Macintoshes except the basic Plus have a slot that can accept an Ethernet adapter. For the Macintosh SE, offerings include 3Com's $595 **Etherlink/SE** or Novell's $495 **NAE/1000**. For the Macintosh II, IIc and IIcx, you can choose from Apple's $699 **EtherTalk NB card**, 3Com's $595 **Etherlink/NB**, or Novell's **NAE/2000** ($595).

These Ethernet boards replace the Mac's built-in LocalTalk hardware, and may be used with AppleShare, DaynaNET, or Tops software. They give you the option of connecting Macintoshes via Ethernet to a file server running 3+Share or NetWare for the Macintosh software. Novell's server software is compatible with all Macintosh multiuser applications, while 3Com's server gives you the option of connecting even older Macs that only have LocalTalk ports.

Thanks to the Mac's standard SCSI port, users can in fact install to an Ethernet by using an external box that plugs into that port (such a device is presently the only way to attach a **Mac Portable** to Ethernet, though, of course, the Portable does have a LocalTalk connector. SCSI Ethernet adapters are not as fast as internal boards, but they get the job done. Choices include the Adaptec **Nodem**, the Compatible Systems **Ether+**, the Nuvotech **NuvoLink SC**, and the Dove **FastnetSCSI**.

Companies that have invested heavily in twisted-pair wiring to carry LocalTalk signals can convert their existing cables to Ethernet, thanks to the emerging 10BASE-T standard, now being adopted by many manufacturers. It uses a star topology and enables twisted-pair cable to carry Ethernet signals at 10M bits/sec. Products are available, or forthcoming, from David Systems, Cabletron, and Farallon. Indeed, DOS-only sites can use 10BASE-T-type setups too, thanks to new products from Hewlett-Packard and others. Hewlett-Packard's **EtherTwist** system permits connecting twisted-pair wiring to machines using either the company's $445 **EtherTwist PC interface card**, or its $595 **Micro Channel interface card**. A twelve-port **EtherTwist hub** sells for $1899. You can add other companies' Ethernet cards—such as those available for the Apple Macintosh—to an EtherTwist setup using a $159 adapter that goes between the cable and the card. 3Com and Synoptics offer equivalent products, though different manufacturers' boards can't necessarily be interconnected. You should check with your dealer to make sure the setup you're considering actually is feasible.

CORPORATE BACKBONES

Multiple systems running multiuser and distributed applications

There is no simple dividing line between a departmental LAN and a larger, all-encompassing system. When you have dozens or hundreds of users on a system, however, it is necessary to make sure that all the links in the chain are as solid as possible.

Novell's SFT NetWare ($4,695) includes many security features. A "hot fix" feature locates disk faults on a server hard disk, records their locations, and then avoids using the bad locations. You can also mirror all data to a second disk, using either one or two controllers for complete security. Novell also offers NetWare 386, a $7,995 version rewritten specially to run up to three times faster on 80386 computers. NetWare 386 features much easier installation and enhanced print services. It includes the same security features as SFT NetWare, plus several new security options. For high performance, file servers can employ Novell's **NE/2-32**, a $995 Ethernet card with a 32-bit Micro Channel connector.

ADDING BACKUP AND STORAGE

Every server at this level should have a tape backup device, set to archive server data at least at the end of each day. Irwin produces a wide range of tape drives, including mini-cartridge models ideal for backing up a Macintosh. Its **Model 6000** is a 250M bit drive, available in either internal or external configurations. You can purchase the drive in a $2,004 **Network Priority Pack** bundle that combines three tape cartridges with Fresh Technology's ***MAP Assist*** software. MAP Assist permits centralized backup of all LAN workstation hard disks, without moving the tape drive from computer to computer.

Another leading tape drive manufacturer is Maynard, offering what must be one of the industry's widest lines. The company's **MaynStream 2200HS** employs 8mm video cassettes to store up to 2.2G bytes of data, with a transfer rate of up to 13.7M bytes/minute! The $7,495 drive is not cheap, but its SCSI interface and carrying handle mean you can move it from machine to machine, including PC to Mac. Maynard supplies software that can back up a NetWare 386 LAN even while it is up and running, temporarily skipping any open files while preserving correct user access levels.

A similar 8mm-based unit hails from Mountain. The $7,495 **FileSafe 2100** claims a sustained data transfer rate of 14.4M bytes/minute, with a 1.5 M bytes/sec burst mode. ***FileTalk***, Mountain's LAN utility, can operate in the background, saving data from a file server as well from as all workstation hard disks.

Aside from tape backup, a LAN server is as certain as death and taxes to need added storage as the number of users on your LAN grows. Plus offers a modular system based on its **Impulse** hard disk drives—which, individually, are units with built-in 64K byte RAM caches and effective 12-ms (millisecond) access times. The Impulses come in 42M and 84M byte configurations, and are available in a **320Lan Cluster** which includes four 84M bit drives, an external expansion unit, and a drive array controller. Plus, pointing out that the multi-drive architecture eliminates bottlenecks, claims this is "the highest-performance LAN subsystem on the market." Device drivers for NetWare, 3Com's 3+Open, and Microsoft's OS/2 LAN Manager are included.

Plus' special system apart, you'll probably add disk storage to your server via a controller based on either ESDI (Enhanced Small Device Interface) or SCSI (Small Computer System Interface). These controllers run about five times faster than the ST-506 system used in the original AT, so they don't bog down when connected to really large disks. Also, they permit you to attach multiple drives to your machine—from four to seven per controller—which often becomes essential on a LAN server. SCSI has a slight edge in multiple drive installations, because it allows disks to perform concurrent I/O without help from the computer.

CMS, a veteran hard disk manufacturer, has adopted SCSI for its series of drives. Sold in either 325M byte or 650M byte sizes, these drives are available as internal systems, or in external cabinets with a standard SCSI connector. They offer an average access time of 16.5 ms , and a sparkling "burst mode" transfer rate of up to 10M bytes/sec. The **Prevails** are rated for a 150,000-hour MTBF (Mean Time Before Failure), which equates to 17 years of operation.

A sample member of the range is **CMS' E65050**, an external 650M byte system that costs $6695. Along with many other hard drives from third-party vendors, the Prevails are available already COMPSURFed (specially formatted for use with Novell NetWare).

Core offers a vast range of hard drives in both SCSI and ESDI versions. The company's top model, the **20-MHz HC-650**, has a 150,000-hour MTBF, a five year warranty, and a 17-millisecond access time—it's even available with NetWare 2.1x preinstalled. Micro Channel users will benefit from the companion **20 MHz Bus Master Controller**. This transfers data at a steady 2M bytes/sec., and, more important, frees the computer's main CPU up to do about 20 percent more work. You can install several of these controllers to perform duplexing (saving your data on two separate disks). Core's **LAN 650/DUP** gives you the ideal drives to duplex to.

Storage Dimensions produces ESDI and SCSI systems for PC, PS/2 and Mac, as well the **LANstor** series (all COMPSURFed at the factory). The $2,799 **MacinStor MAC 175-ZFP** is designed to fit neatly under the **Mac Plus**, **SE**, and **SE/30**. With 175M bits of storage, it's rated for an 18-ms average access time and a data transfer rate of about 2M bytes/sec. Also shown is the **LAN2-320S** ($5,070), an external system containing dual power supplies. It comes with certified Novell drivers, and a 320M byte drive with 17-ms average seek time.

Another way of adding storage, or moving software from server to server, is with Iomega's **Bernoulli Drives**. Bernoulli Drives blend hard- and floppy-disk technology, using 44M bit disk cartridges resembling giant floppies. A Bernoulli disk rotates at high speed, "flying" in contact to the drive's read/write head (if anything goes wrong, the medium just falls away harmlessly). The disks themselves cost just $125 each, can take a shock up to 1,000 Gs (equivalent to an eight-foot drop), and weigh just ounces.

The latest Bernoulli Drives connect to either PC or Mac using SCSI interfaces, and feature average access times of under 22 ms: the $2,795 **Dual 44** can copy cartridges easily and can even "boot" your computer, acting as a hard disk substitute. LAN backup can be accomplished in under three minutes per 44M bytes. With Iomega's ***Bernoulli for NetWare*** software, you can back up a LAN server and even run NetWare from the Bernoulli .

SPEEDIER SERVERS

Many benchmarks suggest that server speed is the main factor in network performance. Instead of buying a PC off the shelf and turning it into a server, you might choose to select hardware specifically designed for the role. 3Com's **3S/501** ($12,750) is an 80386 system with 2M bits of RAM, a 150M bit hard disk, and a 250M byte tape drive for backup. It comes with both Ethernet and LocalTalk interfaces, and offers a special disk controller and "dual-ported" memory for faster processing.

However, it has to be said that off-the-shelf 80386 PCs leave little to be desired as LAN servers. Compaq's **DESKPRO 386/33** ($14,999 with a 320M byte hard disk) has a high-performance disk controller and RAM cache; its seven ISA (Industry Standard Architecture) expansion slots carefully maintain timing compatible with every XT/AT expansion board. The DESKPRO 386/33 line ranges from the **84 MB Model 84** ($10,499) to the **Model 650**, which has a 15 MHz ESDI controller and 650M byte hard disk ($17,999).

AST's **Premium/386/33** costs $10,245 in a 320M byte configuration, and can hold up to 32M bytes of high-speed RAM on two special expansion slots. NEC also produces a 33 MHz 80386 system, called the **PowerMate 386/33E**. This machine uses the EISA expansion bus, EISA (Extended Industry Standard Architecture) means a computer can both accept standard PC expansion cards (8- and 16-bit), and hold 32-bit adapters with greatly enhanced capabilities.

THE EISA ADVANTAGE

The EISA bus offers a "burst" mode that lets data move three times faster than in previous machines. It also supports "bus masters"—expansion boards that have their own processors and can take control, moving data around without any help from a PC's CPU. Consider the case of a machine configured with a network adapter, several hard disks (with their own controllers), modems, mainframe connections, and maybe a fax board thrown in. Responsiveness of a heavily laden system will be much faster if some, or all, of the adapters are EISA boards. EISA also can automatically configure a system and prevent conflicts between boards (ordinarily common on LAN servers).

EISA expansion slots are compatible with old 8- and 16-bit expansion slots, so you're free to keep using the old PC-compatible terminal emulation, data acquisition, or LAN interface boards you already have. However, EISA cards will give you a data transfer rate up to 15 times faster—up to 33M bytes per second.

Compaq's EISA-based **SYSTEMPRO** has been making waves since units first started to ship. The idea of building an ultra-fast PC compatible wasn't brand new. Nor was the idea of building a dedicated LAN server, configured to work fast even when shared by multiple users. But Compaq had the revolutionary idea of combining both in one machine. Its SYSTEMPRO is a floor-standing tower system with space for eleven mass storage devices and eleven full-size expansion slots.

The SYSTEMPRO ships with a 33 MHz 80386 CPU-on-a-card, mounted in one of two special processor slots. You can add a second 80386 today. Later this year, Compaq will ship a 33 MHz 80486 card, complete with a 128K byte RAM cache. Buyers will be able to add this card into existing SYSTEMPROs, or even build units with two 80486s from scratch. The 80386 processor card supports both Weitek 3167-33 and Intel 80387-33 math coprocessors, which may be installed simultaneously. It has an Intel 82385 cache controller and 64K bytes of cache RAM. The SYSTEMPRO costs $15,999, including 240M bytes of disk storage. A second 80386 processor board costs $3,499.

The machine acts just like a docile PC compatible when required. But a multiprocessor-aware operating system will unlock the SYSTEMPRO's full power. The first to arrive has been SCO UNIX with MPX (multiprocessor extensions), designed to use the two processors symmetrically. However, OS/2 LAN Manager from Microsoft will use one processor to manage file transport while the other runs OS/2 applications. NetWare 386 and Banyan's VINES will also support the SYSTEMPRO's multiple processors.

The SYSTEMPRO's outstanding I/O performance is what really tips the scales. The SYSTEMPRO's 32-bit **EISA Intelligent Drive Array Controller** can control up to eight 420M byte disk drives. By reading and writing data to more than one disk simultaneously—"data stripping"—the controller makes performance actually become faster as you add more drives. Should a drive fail while the unique data guarding feature is working, the controller first beeps to notify you, then identifies the failed drive, and finally restores data to a replacement.

NEC's **PowerMate 386/33E** system is an EISA computer that comes with NEC's **EISA Peripheral Controller**, an EISA bus master that can handle up to seven SCSI hard disk drives. It uses a 68000 processor, and avoids bottlenecks by giving disk transfers access to system memory directly. The controller supports concurrent high-speed hard disk activity by queueing requests for data. The PowerMate includes five EISA slots, two 8/16-bit slots, and five bays for 5¼-inch storage devices. It costs $8,499 for a system with 2M bits of RAM and a 100M bit hard disk.

EISA BOARDS

Manufacturers have announced a flood of EISA-specific boards. Some of the first to reach the market include a 32-bit Token-Ring card, sold by Compaq as the 32-bit **DualSpeed Token-Ring Controller** and by Proteon as the **Pro/NET-4/16 EISA Interface**. Operable at 16 or 4M bits/sec, this features its own custom bus mastering circuitry and a 128K byte RAM cache. Data transfers from the LAN adapter card to the host CPU's system memory at up to 33M bytes/sec. You can use the cards alongside all other token-ring boards, via either shielded or unshielded twisted-pair cabling.

Novell's **NE3200 interface card**—incorporating a 80186 processor and the Intel **82355 Bus Master Interface Controller**—is the EISA way to boost performance for Ethernet LANs. It supports both thick and thin coaxial cables, and operates at 10 M bits/sec. Another way to connect EISA machines to an Ethernet is with Computone's **ALC**. This modular board—with an integral 80386SX to help move data—offers an Ethernet feature module, but other available modules include asynchronous, synchronous, fax, and scanner interfaces.

ARCnets too can go EISA, with Standard Microsystems' **ARCnet EISA 3200 board.** This actually includes four Arcnet ports on one board, transmitting data in parallel without even working up a sweat. Boasting the EISA 33M bytes/sec transfer of data from the board to system memory, it works at the standard ARCnet data rate externally. Finally, Codenoll's **CodeNet 8300** links EISA machines to fiber-optic LANs, which will some day run at over 100M bits/sec via the emerging FDDI standard.

80486 SYSTEMS

It might seem like overkill to use an 80486 system as a file server. However, if you want the very highest performance, this is the way to get it: The 80486 processor is fully software-compatible with the 80386, 80286, and 8086. However, it can process more information in fewer clock cycles, and it includes both a cache controller with 8K bytes of static RAM and an 80387-compatible math coprocessor. At comparable clock speeds, the '486 offers up to three times the performance of the 80386. Compaq's **DESKPRO 486/25** is built around a 25 MHz 80486.

Compaq has boosted performance even more on the DESKPRO 486/25 by including an additional 128K byte RAM cache and "second-level" cache controller. A **25 MHz Weitek 4167** math coprocessor may be installed too. The DESKPRO 486/25 offers seven spaces for mass storage devices and seven EISA expansion slots. The $13,999 **Model 120** comes with a 120M byte hard disk featuring an integrated controller (which leaves all the expansion slots free); other versions feature 320M byte or 650M byte ESDI-based drives. Since this is an EISA system, you could also install Compaq's Intelligent Drive Array Controller.

NEC's combination of the EISA bus and the 80486 processor is called the **PowerMate 486/25E**. It can be expanded up to 16M bytes of memory using a special high speed memory slot, and 64M bytes of RAM via EISA slots. It comes with the same NEC EISA Peripheral Controller previously mentioned, providing extremely rapid disk performance. Prices are $11,999 with 2M bit of RAM and a 118M bit hard disk; with a 300M bit hard disk, $13,999.

AST offers one of the least-expensive name-brand 80486 computers. Called the **Premium 486/25**, it sells for just $9,995 complete with a 110M byte hard disk. If the six expansion slots of this typical desktop system don't sound like enough, you'll want to know about the Hewlett-Packard **Vectra 486 PC**. The Vectra is a tower-standing system that combines the 80486 processor with the EISA bus. Its combination of eight EISA slots, six mass storage shelves, and a 64M byte RAM limit provides expandability no other 80486 system can match today. You could install two full-height hard disk drives, two floppy disk drives, a tape backup device, and a CD-ROM unit. The Vectra 486 PC's stable 360-watt power supply is ready with a connector for each of the six devices.

You can put virtually any PC hard disk subsystem in the Vectra 486 PC. HP offers a variety of drives, all with average access times under 17 milliseconds. The HP drives in the 108-670M byte range use the company's 20 MHz **Enhanced Small Device Interface (ESDI)** board (twice as fast as the original ESDI controllers).

Vectra 486 PC prices range from $10,499 for a floppy-disk only unit, to $19,499 for one with the 670M byte hard disk drive.

DISKLESS WORKSTATIONS

Although they're somewhat controversial, diskless workstations are popular with many DP managers. Scaled-down 80286 PCs without floppy disk drives, they can offer cost savings. A more important attribute, though, its that they prevent users from removing data without permission, and bar the introduction of unauthorized software (a computer virus could, after all, spread over a LAN from machine to machine).

The recently introduced COMPAQ **DESKPRO 386N** and **DESKPRO 286N** (based on a 16 MHz 80386SX and 12 MHz 80286) operate quietly, thanks to a special variable-speed fan. They have a small footprint and are less than four inches high, yet incorporate built-in VGA graphics and mouse support, plus two ISA expansion slots. Both machines come in a diskless configuration, though, actually, even if you order the available 20-120M byte hard disks and 5¼-inch or 3½-inch floppy disk drives, they won't compromise LAN security. Thanks to exclusive features built into the system, the drives can be temporarily disabled by a manager when the DESKPRO is used by, say, a temporary employee. Prices start at $1,699 for a diskless DESKPRO 286N, and range to $3,199 for a 40M byte DESKPRO 386N.

3Com's diskless **3Station/2E** ($2,195) builds in VGA graphics and an Ethernet adapter. It has 1M byte of RAM, with room for an additional 3

M bytes more, and since the 3Station doesn't need to set memory aside to address expansion boards, it delivers 128K of extra DOS workspace for users. AST's **Bravo/286 Model 1** ($995 without floppy disk drive) has an integral hard disk controller, so the security-conscious can configure workstations with local hard disk drives but still omit the floppy.

OS/2 SOFTWARE

A relatively new type of LAN system software is that which runs under OS/2. A server running OS/2 is freed from the DOS 640K limit, and allows multiple programs to communicate using both NetBIOS and OS/2's "named pipes" function. There are few LAN applications that require OS/2 today, but developers are busy creating distributed programs that will run faster and more efficiently with it. For example, programs such as databases can be divided into a "front end," with which the user asks for data, and a "back end," where a server works to fulfill the request.

IBM's ***OS/2 Lan Server*** 1.2 costs $1,040 and requires the server to have 4M bytes of RAM; workstations may be running either DOS, augmented by a $245 ***PC Lan*** program, or OS/2 Extended Edition ($830). 3Com's version, 3+Open, costs $3,495 for unlimited-user server software, and can be used with network adapters from IBM, Sytek, Ungermann-Bass, and 3Com. 3+ Open Internet ($995) is an option for bridging Token-Ring and Ethernet networks.

Apple's $399 ***AppleTalk Internet Router*** allows a Macintosh equipped with LocalTalk, EtherTalk and TokenTalk interfaces to merge Token-Ring, Ethernet and LocalTalk networks so they function like a single AppleTalk network. This allows a company to incorporate pre-existing departmental networks into a single, high-performance system. All users can share files and printers, no matter where they are.

MAINFRAME GATEWAYS

Peripheral-sharing is at its most important, ironically, in a giant "cost-no-object" LAN. To connect to a mainframe—the ultimate peripheral—with standalone PCs, you might need a 3270 adapter for each machine and a host of modems and leased phone lines. In contrast, a LAN permits workstations to share a single adapter, connecting to the mainframe concurrently over a single line.

Every major LAN software vendor offers a mainframe gateway: Novell's range is called **PCOX/GW**, 3Com's line is **Maxxess**, and IBM's the **PC 3270 Gateway**. Third-party vendors include DCA, with its **Irmalan** package (priced at $1,995 for a package that connects five workstations to a mainframe). Apple Macintosh IIs may use Apple's $1,495 combination of ***MacDFT*** software and a coprocessor-equipped **Coax-Twinax Card**.

MODEM GATEWAYS

LAN modem gateways are also popular. Though 2,400 bps modems have become cheap, it is a major undertaking to add modem phone lines to many office telephone systems. With a gateway, you save time and money; just two fancy 9,600 bps modems could be shared by a dozen different users. Novell's **NACS** costs $2,390 for a four-port server board and software. IBM's offering is the $1,260 **LAN ACS**, which runs over the **ARTIC**, an up-to-32-port board for the PC or Micro Channel bus (priced around $1,500 in a basic version). The ARTIC features its own on-board communications coprocessors to boost performance.

Fax servers are a possible option in many network servers. The most innovative we've seen is Castelle's **FaxPress LAN** facsimile server, a gray box that cables up directly to any NetWare LAN— Ethernet, ARCnet, or Token-Ring—without requiring a dedicated PC. Attach the FaxPress to a phone line and a laser printer, and it can receive faxes unattended, printing them with the highest possible quality. Even better, the FaxPress lets users send faxes from any LAN workstation—from within every application. It contains 2.5M bytes of RAM and a PCL interpreter. Outgoing faxes may be prepared easily, and you can dress them up with all the graphics and soft fonts you like. Essentially, it's the equivalent of printing directly to a remote fax machine.

References & Resources

- *A comprehensive glossary*
- *Recommended reading*
- *Acknowledgements*

References & Resources

Glossary

A

Access method Way to determine which workstation or personal computer will be next to use the LAN. A set of rules used by LAN hardware to direct traffic on the network. It is the main method used to distinguish various LAN hardware types, e.g. Ethernet, Token-Ring and ARCnet use different access methods. The access method, how a LAN governs users' physical (electrical) access to the cable, significantly affects the LAN's features and performance. Examples of access methods are token passing (ARCnet and Token-Ring) and Carrier Sense Multiple Access with Collision Detection, or CSMA/CD (Ethernet).

Address A set of numbers that uniquely identifies something: a workstation on a LAN, a location in computer memory, a packet of data travelling through a network. Similar to the address of a house.

Algorithm A "recipe" for making a computer do something. A sequence of steps followed by a computer to accomplish a task.

Analog signal An electrical signal that varies over a continuous range of voltage or electrical current values, as opposed to a digital signal, which varies discretely between two values, usually one and zero. An analog signal changes continuously as it is sent. Digital signals change between two values and never have the values in between. Most voice transmission is analog (though this is changing). It is easiest to think of analog signals as sine waves of various sizes. Because the phone system uses analog signals most of the time, modems are needed to change the digital signals used by computers into the analog signals used by the phone system. Compare with digital signal.

ANSI American National Standards Institute. A voluntary organization that helps set standards and also represents the U.S. in some international standards bodies.

AppleTalk Apple Computer's proprietary LAN for Iinking Macintosh computers and peripherals. AppleTalk is a CSMA/CD network that runs at 115K bits per second and will accommodate up to 32 devices. Not to be confused with LocalTalk, the hardware part (cables, connectors, etc.) of AppleTalk.

Application A software program that carries out some useful task. Database managers, spreadsheets, communications packages, graphics programs, and word processors are all applications. Application is also used more generically to encompass a task. For example, a widget maker needs to take orders over the phone and transmit these orders to a warehouse where the widgets are shipped. This whole procedure might be called an order entry and inventory control application. The software used to accomplish the task is called application software. Application software should be distinguished from system software, the software used by the computer itself to accomplish tasks for application software. Network operating systems are also considered part of system software. DOS, 0S/2, NetWare, MVS, 3+ and UNIX are all examples of system software.

Architecture The manner in which hardware or software is structured. Architecture typically describes how the system or program is constructed, how its components fit together, and the protocols and interfaces used for communication and cooperation among modules or components of the system. Network architecture defines the functions and description of data formats and procedures used for communication between nodes or workstations.

ARCnet Attached Resource Computer Network. One of the earliest and one of the most popular LANs ever invented. A 2.5M-bits-per-second LAN that uses a modified token-passing protocol. Developed by Datapoint, Arcnet interface cards are now manufactured by many vendors, including Standard Microsystems and Pure Data, Ltd. The advantages of ARCnet are ease of installation and use, well-documented technology, a star-wired topology and the use of coaxial cable. Some ARCnet vendors offer twisted-pair cable, too.

Audit trail A record of events taking place. On networks this is used to keep track of what goes on, who uses what resources at what time, etc. An important tool for network management.

B

Background task A secondary job usually performed while the user is performing a primary task. For example, many network servers will carry out the duties of the network (like controlling who is talking to whom, or giving someone access to the files on disk) in the background, while at the same time the user is running his own application (like word processing). Background also refers to tasks suspended while a user works on something else. A terminate-and-stay-resident program like ***SideKick*** or ***SuperKey*** is said to be in the background before the user hits a key sequence to bring it to the foreground.

Back-end Referring to the part of a database server that performs data storage, management and security functions. Opposite of the front end, the part of a database server that interfaces with the user, formats data for presentation and creates reports. The back-end is often called the server. The front end is often called the client.

Backup First the semantics. "Back up" is the verb, as in, "I back up the hard disk so I don't lose anything." "Backing up" is an alternative form of this case. "Back-up" is the adjective, as in, "l just bought a back-up disk." "Backup" is the noun, as in, "Tape backup is very important on a LAN." A back-up copy of a file is a second copy, stored on tape, floppy disk or hard disk. Backup insures that if the original copy is destroyed or damaged, the file can be restored, at least partially. Most LAN managers recommend backing up important files on a daily basis, and the entire system on a monthly basis.

Back-up server A program or device that copies files so at least two up-to-date copies always exist.

Baseband Local area networks, as a whole, fall into two categories—broadband and baseband. The simpler, cheaper and less sophisticated of the two is baseband. In baseband LANs, the entire bandwidth (capacity) of the LAN cable is used to transmit a single digital signal. In broadband networks, the capacity of the cable is divided into many channels, which can transmit many simultaneous signals. While a baseband channel can only transmit one signal and that signal is usually digital, a broadband LAN can transmit video, voice and data simultaneously. The electronics of a baseband LAN are simpler. The digital signals from the sending devices are put directly onto the cable without modulation of any kind. Only one signal is transmitted at a time. Multiple "simultaneous" transmissions can be achieved by a technique called time division multiplexing (See Multiplexing.) In contrast, broadband networks (which typically run on coaxial cable) need more complex electronics to decipher and pick off the various signals they transmit. Attached devices on a broadband network require modems to transmit. Attached devices to baseband networks do not. (See **Broadband**.)

Batch command The name of a batch file. The command used to run a batch file, which is just a list of commands.

Batch file A text file with the extension .BAT that contains DOS commands. When you type the name of the file, DOS carries out the commands in the file in the order they appear in the file. Many computer programs are installed on your hard disk or loaded using batch files, as are many LAN operating systems. Batch files simplify life. If you use batch files wisely, you can save yourself typing things over and over again. It also means you don't have to remember all the commands to do something, just the first one. Batch files can be used to load other programs or to change the parameters of your computer. Anything that can be done from DOS (and some things that can't) can be done from a batch file.

Batch processing A type of data processing where related transactions are grouped, transmitted, and processed together by the same computer at the same time. A type of processing where time is not critical and no user input is needed while the processing (i.e. the "crunching") takes place. An example of batch processing is the corporate payroll. All the employees' weekly times are processed at one time. The other type of data processing is called real time. An example might be the entering of sales orders by clerks, who answer 800 lines and take orders for product. A LAN can handle both types of data processing.

Binary A numbering system that allows only two values, zero and one. Binary is the way most computers store information, in combination of ones and zeros: Voltage on or voltage off. (See also **Bit**.)

Bit A binary unit of information that can have either of two values, zero or one. The most basic way of storing and transmitting information. Contraction of BInary digiT.

Block A collection of transmitted information which is seen as a discrete entity. Usually has its own address, control, routing and error checking information. See also packet and packet switching.

Bridge Equipment which connects different LANs, allowing communication between devices on separate LANs. As in "to bridge" several LANs. Bridges are protocol-independent, but hardware-specific. They will connect LANs with different hardware and different protocols. An example would be a device that connects an Ethernet network to a Starlan network. With this bridge it is possible to send signals between the two networks, and only these two networks. This differs from gateways and routers. Routers connect LANs with the same protocols but different hardware. The best example are the file servers that accommodate different hardware LANs. Gateways connect two LANs with different protocols by translating between them, enabling them to talk to each other. The bridge does no translation. Bridges are best used to keep networks small by connecting many of them, rather than making a large one. This reduces the traffic faced by individual computers and improves network performance.

Broadband There are typically two methods LANs use to convey information—baseband and broadband. The simpler, cheaper and least sophisticated of the two is baseband. In baseband LANs, the digital signals from the sending devices are put directly onto the cable without modulation of any kind. Only one signal is transmitted at a time. Broadband is more complex, more expensive and more sophisticated. You can usually carry several signals simultaneously on a broadband LAN—perhaps several data channels, maybe a video channel. The channels on a broadband network are typically kept separate with a technique called frequency division multiplexing (see multiplexing). Each channel is made to occupy (modulated to) a different frequency slot on the cable. At the receiving end it is demodulated down to its original frequency. This technique is how 50 channels of TV occupy one coaxial cable on cable TV (CATV). They all come in a different frequency. When you change channels, you change the frequency on which you are receiving. On broadband LANs, most equipment can't change frequency like a TV. Instead, each device is assigned a channel. Those devices talking on the same channel can communicate, in effect making up one network. Those on other channels make up other networks. In this way, a broadband LAN can carry many networks—voice, video and data.

Broadcast message A message from one user sent to all users. Just like a TV station signal. On LANs, all workstations and devices receive the message.

HOOK UP WITH LAN MAGAZINE

Return attached card to get your FREE ISSUE!

LAN
THE LOCAL AREA NETWORK MAGAZINE

yes!

Send a FREE issue of LAN and enter my trial subscription. If I like it, I'll pay the special discount rate of $19.97 per year (for 11 additional issues, 12 in all), – saving more than 52% off the cover price! If I don't wish to subscribe, I'll write cancel on your first invoice. The FREE issue is mine to keep.

Name ______________________________

Company ______________________________

Address ______________________________

City, State, Zip ______________________________

Cover price is $3.50 per issue. Please allow up to six weeks for delivery of first issue. Foreign orders must be prepaid in U.S. funds. Canadian/Mexican orders add $6 per year for surface mail. All other foreign add $15 per year for surface mail or $40 per year for air mail.

B00888

LAN
THE LOCAL AREA NETWORK MAGAZINE

yes!

Send a FREE issue of LAN and enter my trial subscription. If I like it, I'll pay the special discount rate of $19.97 per year (for 11 additional issues, 12 in all), – saving more than 52% off the cover price! If I don't wish to subscribe, I'll write cancel on your first invoice. The FREE issue is mine to keep.

Name ______________________________

Company ______________________________

Address ______________________________

City, State, Zip ______________________________

Cover price is $3.50 per issue. Please allow up to six weeks for delivery of first issue. Foreign orders must be prepaid in U.S. funds. Canadian/Mexican orders add $6 per year for surface mail. All other foreign add $15 per year for surface mail or $40 per year for air mail.

B00888

LAN
THE LOCAL AREA NETWORK MAGAZINE

yes!

Send a FREE issue of LAN and enter my trial subscription. If I like it, I'll pay the special discount rate of $19.97 per year (for 11 additional issues, 12 in all), – saving more than 52% off the cover price! If I don't wish to subscribe, I'll write cancel on your first invoice. The FREE issue is mine to keep.

Name ______________________________

Company ______________________________

Address ______________________________

City, State, Zip ______________________________

Cover price is $3.50 per issue. Please allow up to six weeks for delivery of first issue. Foreign orders must be prepaid in U.S. funds. Canadian/Mexican orders add $6 per year for surface mail. All other foreign add $15 per year for surface mail or $40 per year for air mail.

B00888

NO POSTAGE
NECESSARY
IF MAILED
IN THE
UNITED STATES

BUSINESS REPLY MAIL
FIRST CLASS PERMIT NO. 7183 NASHVILLE, TN

POSTAGE WILL BE PAID BY

LAN
THE LOCAL AREA NETWORK MAGAZINE

MILLER FREEMAN PUBLICATIONS
P.O. BOX 41094
NASHVILLE, TN 37204-9845

NO POSTAGE
NECESSARY
IF MAILED
IN THE
UNITED STATES

BUSINESS REPLY MAIL
FIRST CLASS PERMIT NO. 7183 NASHVILLE, TN

POSTAGE WILL BE PAID BY

LAN
THE LOCAL AREA NETWORK MAGAZINE

MILLER FREEMAN PUBLICATIONS
P.O. BOX 41094
NASHVILLE, TN 37204-9845

NO POSTAGE
NECESSARY
IF MAILED
IN THE
UNITED STATES

BUSINESS REPLY MAIL
FIRST CLASS PERMIT NO. 7183 NASHVILLE, TN

POSTAGE WILL BE PAID BY

LAN
THE LOCAL AREA NETWORK MAGAZINE

MILLER FREEMAN PUBLICATIONS
P.O. BOX 41094
NASHVILLE, TN 37204-9845

HOOK UP WITH LAN MAGAZINE

Return attached card to get your FREE ISSUE!

Buffer A software program, storage space in RAM or a separate device used to compensate for differences in the speed of data transmission. A printer buffer is the simplest example. The computer can send data to be printed many times faster than the printer can print it. There are two alternatives. Slow the computer down (the typical alternative). Or, put a buffer between the computer and the printer. Have the computer dump to the buffer. And the printer take from the buffer as it's ready. Exactly like a water dam.

Bulletin board system A fancy name for an electronic message system typically running on a PC. Call up, leave messages, read messages. The system is like a physical bulletin board. (That's where the name comes from.) Some people call bulletin board systems electronic mail systems.

Bus network A one-cable LAN, in which all workstations are connected to a single cable (also called "a transmission medium"). On a bus network all workstations hear all transmissions on the cable. Each workstation then selects those transmissions addressed to it based on address information contained in the transmission. The simplest and now the most common LAN topology. It is possible to connect bus networks together, using a bridge.

Byte A group of 8 (sometimes 7) bits. Often used to represent a character. Bytes are also units of storage and transmission. A hard disk's capacity is measured by the number of bytes it will hold.

C

Cabling Just what it sounds like: the medium that connects nodes on a LAN. Cabling can be twisted-pair, coaxial, twinaxial or fiber optic. The advantages and disadvantages vary. (See also **Twisted-pair**, **Coaxial**, **Twinaxial** and **Fiber optic**.)

CAD Computer-Aided Design. A CAD program might be as simple as having computerized drafting tools. It might be as complex as having layouts of integrated circuits, speciality designs which can be pulled up and included into your own design. CAD may also allow for the simulation and testing of various products and inventions before they are actually manufactured. CAD is one of the applications typically run on sophisticated LANs. The typical CAD user has a powerful workstation with a large color monitor, lots of computer memory and a large hard disk storage system.

Chat A common name for a type of messaging done over a network. Chatting involves short, usually one-line messages sent from one node to another. Usually, a chatting facility is RAM-resident, meaning it can be "popped up" inside an application program. Users are usually notified of an incoming chat by a beep and a message at the bottom of their screens.

Client/Server model This term refers to an architecture for LAN applications programs. Under this architecture, the software is split into two parts: client and server. The server component provides things for the client part. The client part interacts with the user. The two parts run on different machines. Usually the server part is a more powerful machine than the client part. The most common client/server application is the database server. This is a database management system (DBMS) where the functions are split into a "front-end" that interacts with the user (client) to enter data, ask questions of the data and write reports and a "back-end" that stores the data, controls access to data, protects data and makes necessary changes to the data. The main advantages of the client server model are: less network traffic, much better performance and greater flexibility in the application and availability of data.

Coaxial cable A type of electrical cable in which a solid piece of metal wire is surrounded by insulation and then surrounded by a tubular piece of metal whose axis of curvature coincides with the center of the piece of wire, hence the term coaxial. Coaxial cables have wide bandwidth and can carry many data, voice and video conversations simultaneously. CATV runs on coaxial cable. So do some LANs. One problem with coaxial-based LANs is the difficulty of connecting to and removing workstations from the LAN. Coaxial cable is a cumbersome, thick medium, suited to more permanent installations such as CATV installations in households. Nevertheless, improvements in connectorization have made coaxial cable easier to use. It remains very popular.

Collision The result of two workstations trying to use a shared transmission medium (cable) simultaneously. The electrical signals, which carry the information the workstations are sending, bump into each other. This ruins both signals. This means the workstations both have to re-transmit their information. In most systems, a built-in delay will make sure the collision does not occur again. The whole process takes only fractions of a second. Collisions do, however, slow a LAN down since they cause data to be sent again.

Collision detection The process of detecting that simultaneous (and therefore damaging) transmission has taken place. Typically, each transmitting workstation that detects the collision will wait some period of time and try again. Collision detection is an essential part of the CSMA/CD access method. Workstations can tell that a collision has taken place if they do not receive their own transmission within a certain amount of time (fractions of a second). Another form of collision detection is simply that no acknowledgement is recieved.

Common file system A combination of hardware and software that provides all users of a network with access to the same information. (See **File server**.)

Communications server Also called an asynchronous server or asynchronous gateway. A communications server is a type of gateway that translates the packetized signals of a LAN to asynchronous signals, usually used on telephone lines or on direct connections to DEC and other type minicomputers and mainframes. It handles different asynchronous protocols and allows nodes on a LAN to share modems or host connections. Usually, one machine on a LAN will act as a gateway, sharing its serial ports for connection to modems or minicomputers. All devices on the LAN can use this machine to get to the modems and the minicomputer.

CPU Central Processing Unit. That part of a computer in which mathematical operations are performed. The heart of the computer. It manipulates the 1s and 0s to give the information you can use.

Crosstalk The introduction of signals from one communication channel into another. Often happens when cables cross each other. Also the name of a popular asynchronous communications software program made by DCA/Crosstalk Communications, Alpharetta, GA.

D

Database Data stored in computer-readable form, and usually indexed or sorted in a logical order. Users can use the index or logical arrangement to find the item of data they need. Used to store names, addresses, order entry data and so on. A typical data base is inventory. Databases in a central file server are one of the most common LAN applications.

Database server Software that doles out database data to PCs on a LAN the way a file server doles out files. A database server uses the Client/Server model architecture. Part of the program, called the server, runs on a central server machine that usually stores the data. Another part of the program, called the client, runs on one or more PCs. The server part controls the data, protecting it, granting access to multiple users, updating and deleting records and communicating with other servers holding data. The two parts of the program talk to each other over the network. The client will ask for records or add them. The server will search the database for records or add the new ones. The advantages of this are a reduction in network traffic, an increase in efficiency, a reduction of response time, greater data security and more memory at the PC since it doesn't have to load all the program into memory, only the client part.

Data integrity A measure of how consistent and accurate computer data is. Data integrity can be threatened by hardware problems, power failures and disk crashes, but most often it is threatened by application software. In a database system, data integrity can be threatened if two users are allowed to update the same item or record of data at the same time. Record locking, where only a single user at a time is allowed access to a given data record, is a method of insuring data integrity.

DBMS Short for Database Management System. A program or collection of programs that creates and maintains a database, and allows users to retrieve information from that database. Many DBMSs also have report writers and application generators in addition to the standard package.

Destination address That part of a message which indicates for whom the message is intended. Usually a collection of characters or bits. Just like putting a destination address on an envelope.

Digital signal A signal that is either zero (off) or one volt (or one "something"), rather than as a continuum of voltages. Think of a digital signal as a collection of ones and zeros flowing down the cable. It is the opposite of an analog signal which has many values along a continuum. (See **Analog signal**.)

DIP switch Abbreviation for Dual In-line Package. A little "on-off, yes-no," switch typically mounted on a printed circuit board and used to configure various options for the device. For example, a DIP switch might be used to set the address of an Arcnet card or to turn the automatic line feed on for a printer. DIP switches are used on many LAN interface cards to set the interrupt request line and the DMA channel used by the card.

Disk A storage medium for digital data. Can be hard or floppy. Disks store information as magnetic pulses, which are created by short bursts of voltage. Different sections of the disk are electronically magnetized or charged in specific patterns that represent the information being stored, be it letters, numbers or symbols.

Disk server A device equipped with disks and a program that permits users to create and store files on the disks. Each user has access to their own section of the disk. It gives users disk space which they would not normally have at their own personal computers. Some sort of connection between the disk server and PC is needed, like a LAN. Compare with file server, which allows users to share files.

Diskless PC Just what it says: a PC without a disk drive. Used on a LAN, a diskless PC runs by booting DOS or another operating system from the file server. It does this via a read-only memory chip on its network interface card called a remote boot ROM. When the machine is turned on, programs in this boot ROM are executed. They go out over the network to the file server and look for the operating system to be loaded into the diskless PC memory. The file server acts as the disk for the diskless PC. Diskless PCs are sometimes cheaper than PCs with disks, they're more compact and they offer better security, since users can't make off with floppy disks of important and sensitive data.

Distributed data processing The processing of information in separate locations equipped with independent computers. The computers are connected by a network, even though the processing is geographically dispersed. Often a more efficient use of computer processing power since each CPU can be devoted to a certain task. A LAN is the perfect example of distributed processing. Compare with parallel processing.

Distributed database A database that allows users on multiple nodes to access data as though the files were stored locally. A distributed database will require database server operation on each of the different machines holding data. These need to communicate what they have to each other plus make it available to multiple users.

DOS Disk Operating System A program or set of programs that instruct a disk-based computing system to schedule/supervise work, manage computer resources, and operate/control peripheral devices, including disk drives, keyboards, screens and printers. Comes in different types from different vendors.

Dumb terminal A workstation that doesn't have a computer in it and therefore can't do much with the data you feed it. Typically just a keyboard and a screen. The **DEC VT100** is the world's most popular dumb data terminal.

E

Echo The return of transmitted data. Echo means what you send and what is received at the other end is bounced back to you and is what you see or your screen. The idea of "echo" is that the sender can be sure the data has reached its destination because it is being sent back by the receiving device which had to receive it to send it back. The above is an explanation of full duplex echo. There's also half duplex echo where you see what you type, not necessarily what is received at the other end. This is called local echo.

EIA Electronics Industries Association. U.S. trade organization that issues its own standards and contributes to ANSI.

Electronic mail A messaging system operating over some sort of communications medium, often a LAN. Most E-Mail systems allow users to write lengthy messages and send them to a choice of other users on the system. Many E-Mail systems are dial-up services, like MCI Mail or CompuServe. Others are applications running under a network operating system on a LAN.

Ethernet A CSMA/CD, 10M-bit-per-second network developed at Xerox's Palo Alto Research Center, Palo Alto, CA. One of the most popular baseband LANs in use. DEC and Intel participated with Xerox to make Ethernet a network standard that provides computers with network access on a transmit-at-will basis. If two transmissions collide they wait and try again until they get through. Ethernet sends data at a raw speed of 10M bits per second. It runs on either coaxial cable or twisted pair wiring.

F

Fiber optic cable A data transmission medium consisting of glass fibers. Light-emitting diodes send light through the fiber to a detector which then converts the light back into electrical signals. Fiber optic cable will be the predominant medium for LANs in the future. Right now, it's as cheap as copper cable, though fewer installers are familiar with it. Fiber optic cable offers immense bandwith, absolute protection from eavesdropping, electromagnetic interference and radioactivity. When the bomb drops, fiber optic LANs will still work, if they're running unattended.

File An ordered collection of data, stored on a disk or tape. Files are of various sizes and can contain any type of information.

File locking A method of insuring data integrity. With a file locking system, only one user can update a file at a time. Other users are locked out, unable to access the file. (Compare with **Record locking**.)

File server A computer containing files, which are shared by everyone connected to a LAN. In some LANs the device is a PC. In other LANs, this device is a special computer with a huge disk drive and specialized software. In still other LANs, any PC can be a file server, depending on the software it runs. File servers can offer all types of resources, from simple data storage, to gateways and protocol conversion. A file server usually has software rules for allowing LAN users to get into and out of the files and databases it stores. There are also software rules for the other devices, like serial and gateway ports, that a file server shares.

Flag A program-readable symbol that indicates data are available, that space is available to store data, or that some operation has been completed. Also used in packet transmission to indicate the beginning and end of the packet. It refers to a group of bits or bytes which provides some instruction to computer devices.

G

Gateway A computer system and its software that permit two networks using different protocols to communicate with each other. Common gateways hook PC-based LANS into IBM mainframes (SNA gateways) or to X.25 packet-switched public network systems (X.25 gateways).

Graphics-based interface An interface that allows the user to select a menu item by using a mouse to select a graphic icon. (See Presentation Manager and Windows.)

H

Handshake A preliminary procedure, usually part of a communications protocol, to establish a connection. Sometimes, during the handshake, two computers will exchange the conditions under which they will communicate. Other times, they just alert each other of the impending communication—like saying "hello" and shaking hands when you meet someone.

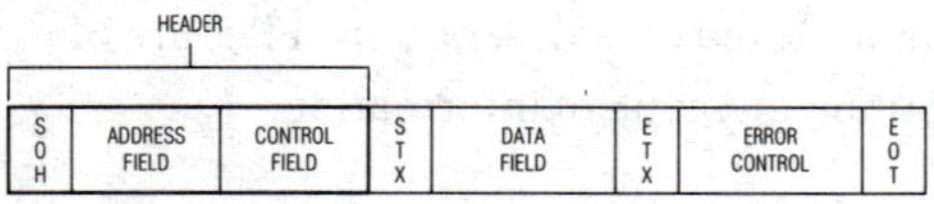

Header:
SOH = start of header; STX = start of text; ETX = end of text; EOT = end of transmission.

Hardware Computers, printers, disks, interface cards and other hard things. Think of hardware as the paper and pencil while software is the message being written.

Header That part of a message, at the beginning, which contains destination, address, source address, message numbering, and possibly other information. It helps direct the message along its journey.

Host A computer system that provides computer service for a number of users. Usually a mainframe.

Hub The center of a star topology network or cabling system. File servers often act as the hub of a LAN. They house the network software and direct communications within the network. They may also act as the gateway to another LAN.

Hybrid network A LAN with a mixture of topologies and access methods. For example, a network that includes both a Token-Ring and a CSMA/CD bus.

I

IBM LAN Server IBM's network operating system based on OS/2. It is the program that provides the traditional services of a network operating system for workstations that can run either DOS or OS/2. It runs under OS/2 on a server PC and provides file and print sharing, communications, messaging and other services.

IBM 0S/2 Extended Edition IBM's proprietary extension to OS/2, which among other things allows a workstation to work in conjunction with IBM minicomputers and mainframes. Extended Edition also has a database management system included.

Interface A demarcation between two devices, where the electrical signals, connectors, timing and handshaking meet. Often the procedures, codes and protocols that enable the two devices to interact are included or carried out by the interface. An example is an RS-232-C port. Some of its 25 pins are used to send different information and makes sure devices can talk to each other. The pins carry different messages, like "request to send," "acknowledgement" and others.

Interface card A printed circuit board fitting in the expansion chassis of a computer to make the physical connection between computer and LAN cable. The interface card is responsible for getting raw bits from the computer onto the network and vice versa. This requires translation from parallel to serial form and back, buffering, packet creation, encoding/decoding, cable access and transmission and reception.

Intelligent terminal A terminal which can be programmed. A PC.

J

Job Task to be done by a computer.

K

K A standard quantity measurement of computer storage. A K is loosely defined as one thousand bytes. In fact, it is 1,024 bytes, which is the equivalent of two raised to the tenth.

L

LAN (See **Local area network**.)

LAN Manager A network operating system from Microsoft (Redmond, WA) for servers running OS/2.

LAN manager A person who manages a LAN. Duties can include adding new users, installing new hardware and software, diagnosing network problems, helping users, performing backup and setting up a security system. Unlike MIS managers, LAN managers are rarely formally trained in LAN management. They learn by doing.

LAN Server IBM's network operating system based on OS/2. It is the program that provides the traditional services of a network operating system for PCs based on OS/2. It runs in a server PC and provides file and print sharing, communications, messaging and other services.

Local Area Network A data communications network spanning a limited geographical area, a few miles at most. It provides communication between computers and peripherals.

Locking Preventing several people getting to and changing the same data simultaneously. Locks may be permanent and prevent access completely, or they may be "advisory"—a user is warned the data is being used by another user. Locks prevent the destruction of data that can occur if two people access a file or record at the same time. (See also **File locking** and **Record locking**.)

Log-in The process of identifying and authenticating oneself to a computer system. Used to control access to computer systems or networks.

M

Mainframe A large computer normally supplied complete with peripherals and software by a single large vendor, often with a closed architecture. Mainframes almost always use dumb terminals, connected in star configurations.

Minicomputer A small or medium computer accessed by dumb terminals. A minicomputer is bigger and usually more powerful than a PC.

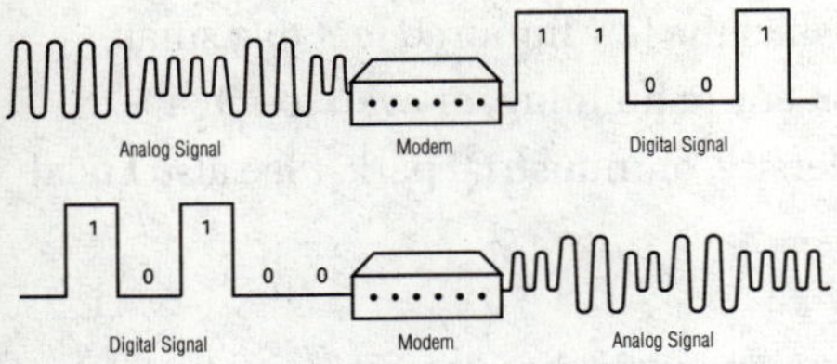

Modem

Modem A device that converts digital data from a transmitting device into a signal suitable for transmission over a telephone (analog) channel. At the other end, another modem reconverts the analog signal to digital data for use by the computer. The word modem comes from MOdulator/DEModulator.

MS-DOS The Microsoft Disk Operating System, the standard operating system for computers equipped with the Intel 8086, 8088 and 80286 (or equivalent) microprocessors. PC-DOS is IBM's version of MS-DOS.

Multitasking The simultaneous performing of two or more tasks by a computer. Multitasking allows a user to recalculate a spreadsheet while writing an essay. OS/2 allows multitasking by providing a time-slice method in which many programs share the processor.

Multiuser The ability of a computer to support multiple users while providing a full range of capability to each one.

N

NetBIOS Network Basic Input/Output System from IBM. Part of the original IBM PC network program. Like the BIOS of an individual computer, NetBIOS is an interface that applications use to gain access to computer resources, only this time they are on a network instead of in just one machine. It is the most popular network applications programming interface in PC networking. Hundreds of applications use it.

NetWare The most popular network operating system, produced by Novell, of Orem, UT, and supported by almost every hardware and software manufacturer. Available in a variety of versions, including NetWare 386, which uses special functions of the 80386 processor for more rapid operation. NetWare for the Macintosh, a component now included with every copy of NetWare, allows DOS PCs and Macintosh computers to be interconnected.

Network Networks are common in our lives. Think about trains and phones. Networks tie things together. Computer networks connect all types of computers and computer-related things together—terminals, printers, modems, door entry sensors, temperature monitors, etc. Local area networks exist within a limited geographic area—like the few hundred feet of a small office, or they can span an entire building, or even touch a "campus," such as a university, or industrial park. (See also **Local Area Network**.)

Network access control Electronic circuitry that determines which workstation may transmit next or when a particular workstation may transmit

Network architecture The structures and protocols of a computer network. (See **Architecture**.)

Network interface controller Electronic circuitry that connects a workstation to a network. Usually a card that fits into one of the expansion slots inside a personal computer. It works with the network software and computer operating system to transmit and receive messages on the network. Also called network interface card.

Network operating system The software used to connect devices, share resources, transfer files and perform network activity. Usually, there are two parts to a network operating system: server and workstation (requester). The workstation (requester) part puts the PC on the network. It reroutes things over the network when needed. The server part runs on a PC called, appropriately enough, the server. The server software makes disks, software and ports available to other PCs on the network. They access these resources using the requester. In some networks, workstations and servers can be the same machine so all users can share some of their resources as well as access those of other users.

Network topology The geography of a network. For example, whether it is mesh, star, bus or ring. The layout.

Nodes Points in a network where service is provided, service is used, or communications channels are interconnected. Nodes are sometimes used interchangeably with workstations.

Noise Random electrical signals, generated by circuit components or by natural disturbances, that mess up transmitted data by introducing errors. Noise can come from lightning, crossed cables, electrical motors.

Non-proprietary LAN A LAN that can connect the equipment of many vendors.

O

Operating system The software of a computer that controls the execution of programs, typically handling the functions of input/output control, resource scheduling, and data management.

OS/2 The second-generation operating system co-developed by Microsoft and IBM to exploit the power and speed of personal computers based on the Intel 80286, 80386, and 80486 microprocessors. Key features include support of multitasking and programs larger than 640K bytes, sophisticated memory management capabilities, a graphical user interface and process-to-process communications facilities. OS/2's multitasking forms the basis for distributed applications on LANs.

OS/2 Extended Edition IBM's proprietary extension to OS/2, which among other things allows a workstation to work in conjunction with IBM minicomputers and mainframes. Extended Edition also has a database management system included.

P

Packet A group of bits, including address, data and control elements, that are switched and transmitted together. Think of a packet as one sentence or one group of numbers being sent at a time. Frame and packet are often used interchangeably. (See also **Packet switching.**)

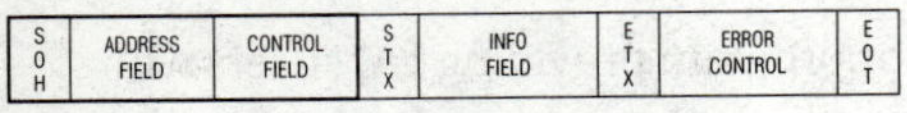

Packet

Packet buffer Memory space set aside for storing a packet awaiting transmission or for storing a received packet. The memory may be located in the network interface controller or in the computer to which the controller is connected. (See **Buffer**.)

Packet switching A data transmission method, using packets, whereby a channel is occupied only for the duration of transmission of the packet. The packet switch sends the different packets from different data conversations along the best route available in any particular order. At the other end, the packets are reassembled to form the original message which is then sent to the receiving computer. Because packets need not be sent in a particular order, and because they can go any route as long as they reach their destination, packet switching networks can choose the most efficient route and send the most efficient number of packets down that route before switching to another route to send more packets. The other advantage of packet switching is the unified format that every message is molded into.

PC-NET IBM's DOS-based networking systems software product, developed with Microsoft. Officially known as the IBM PC LAN Program.

Peer-to-peer A description of communications between two equal devices. Most easily understood in comparison to terminal-host communications. Under the latter a mainframe does all the processing and the communicating devices, including PCs, act like terminals, just doing input and output. With peer-to-peer communications both computers perform processing of data at both ends, not just input and output.

Port A place where data can enter or leave the network or computer. Examples are the serial and parallel "ports" on the back of most PCs. A port is also a fancy name for a plug or receptacle, like those on the back of most PCs.

Presentation Manager Software jointly developed by Microsoft and IBM that extends the OS/2 operating system to include a graphical user interface. Users can view text in multiple styles and graphics side-by-side in applications especially written for Presentation Manager (such as 1-2-3/G from Lotus). Since every copy of OS/2 now comes with Presentation Manager, the majority of OS/2 applications use its services. (See also **Windows**.)

Printer server A computer and/or program providing LAN users with access to a centralized printer. A person using the LAN will send a message to the printer server computer. This computer will then assign it a piece of memory or disk space to store its file while it waits to be printed. With a printer server, users can send to the printer any time. Their print jobs are usually handled in the order they are received. But "big bosses" can be given priorities and can be bumped to the top of the queue. Print servers allow fewer printers to satisfy more users. Print servers are also especially useful for expensive, laser or high speed printers, because they spread the cost of these expensive machines over many users, thus making expensive printers more affordable.

Proprietary LAN A LAN that runs the equipment of only one vendor. A proprietary LAN cannot join IBM PCs to DEC minicomputers. DEC and Wang both make proprietary LANs. Some people say such LANs are more "bug-free." They also tend to be more expensive. They also tend to tie you to one vendor, although some makers are now coming out with bridges which connect proprietary LANs to non-proprietary LANs.

Protocol A set of rules for communicating between computers. These govern format, timing, sequencing, and error control. Think of protocol as the rules for communicating. Without these rules, the computer won't make sense of the stream of incoming bits. There can be sets of protocols in some networks, with each protocol handling rules for a subset of the entire task of communication. This set of protocols is often referred to as a suite of protocols or protocol suite. Protocol stack is another term used to describe a set of protocols.

Q

Queue Just what it sounds like. A line of tasks, such as computer jobs or messages, waiting for service—for processing, printing, storing, etc. A task waiting in a queue can be assigned a "priority," so that important tasks can jump ahead.

R

RAM Random Access Memory. A chip or collection of chips where data can be entered, read and erased. The basic idea of RAM is to speed your computer up. Your CPU could use your floppy as RAM, accessing your floppy every time it needed information. But this would be excruciatingly slow. RAM is the fastest memory device. The fast speed of RAM is good. However, RAM loses its contents when you lose or turn off power. This is bad. Life is a tradeoff. (Compare with read-only memory and EPROM.)

Record locking The most common and most sophisticated means for multiuser LAN application to maintain data integrity. In a record locking system, users are prevented from working on the same data record at the same time. That way, users don't overwrite other users' changes and data integrity is maintained. But though it doesn't allow users into the same record at the same time, record locking does allow multiple users to work on the same file simultaneously. So multiuser access is maximized. (Compare with **File locking**, which only allows a single user to work on a file at a time.)

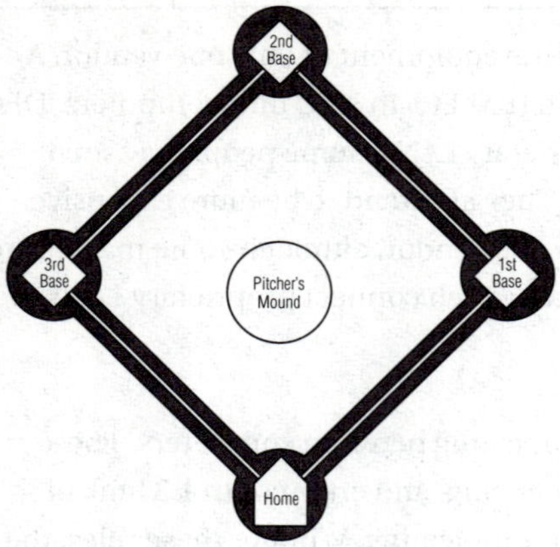

Routing strategies:
The second baseman must get the ball to home to tag the runner. He can't throw directly to home, but he knows how to get there. If the coach taught him to take the shortest route, he would throw to the pitcher, who would throw to the catcher. This is like a router using a high speed line over a slow one. If, however, he were taught to take the least number of hops, he would have to decide if he should throw the ball to the first baseman, third baseman, or the pitcher, who would in turn throw it to the catcher. A second baseman in the major leagues would check which players were busy, and adjust the path accordingly.

Remote station Any piece of equipment attached to a LAN by a telephone company supplied link. Technically, that includes all devices that aren't servers. Usually it refers to a workstation at a distant location, linked to the main LAN by a modem. (See **Modems**.)

Ring A LAN topology (organization) where each workstation is connected to at least two other workstations. This forms a loop (or a ring). Data is sent from workstation to workstation around the loop in the same direction. Each PC acts as a repeater by resending messages to other PCs. Rings have a predictable response time, determined by the number of PCs. The more PCs, the slower the LAN. Network control is distributed in a ring network. Loss of one PC may disable the entire network, however. But many ring LANs have a way of recovering very fast should one PC die. Another PC may jump in and take over the control functions. Or you can simply remove a PC physically from the ring, therefore automatically joining the two on either side together. This is how the IBM Token-Ring works.

Routing The process of choosing the best path through the LAN. Routing lets PCs which are not directly connected communicate by passing messages along to adjacent PCs. Sort of like forwarding mail. Telephone switches and some data switches have a software/hardware feature called least-cost routing whereby they route calls over the least costly phone lines—WATS, tie lines, MCI, etc. Routing is a difficult science in data networks because there are so many factors to take care of, especially when moving through networks of networks.

S

Server A computer providing a service to LAN users, such as shared access to a file system, a printer, a modem or an electronic mail system. Usually a combination of hardware and software. Think of it as the butler of the network, distributing information and resources to requesting users. Servers can be PCs, minicomputers, mainframes, or specialized computers designed to do nothing but dole out services to multiple users. (See **File server**, **Print server**.)

Server-based application Distributed application in which the main portion of software resides on a server machine. This machine satisfies requests from other machines running the second portion of software. The two portions of the software communicate over the network, using some type of protocol. The advantages include reduced network traffic, greater flexibility and higher performance. Each part of the application can be specialized for the job its doing. Examples are database and communications servers.

Server-client model Model of distributed processing where one machine, running one portion of an application's software, provides services to one or many computers running a second portion of software. Has many advantages in a network environment. (See **Server-based application**.)

Shielding The process of protecting a cable (consisting of one or more plastic-coated conductors) with a grounded metal surrounding so that electrical signals from outside the cable cannot interfere with transmission inside the cable. Shielding will also lessen the chance that the information movement along the cable will interfere with other signals on other, adjacent cables. LANs should always be installed with the best quality shielded cable. They will run far better.

Software The set of instructions for carrying out various applications and tasks. Examples are programs like WordStar, Lotus 1-2-3 and dBASE III. (See also **Hardware**; compare with firmware.)

Source address The part of a message which indicates who sent the message. Often included in the header of a packet. The top left hand address on the envelope.

SPOOL Simultaneous Peripheral Operation On Line. A program or piece of hardware that controls a buffer of data going to some output device, most commonly a printer or a tape drive. A spool allows users to send data to a device, say a printer, even while that device is busy. The spool will control the feeding of data to the printer by using a buffer or by creating a temporary file in which to store the data to be printed. (See **Buffer**, compare with **Queue**.)

SQL Structured Query Language. A database query language originally from IBM for its mainframe databases. It is a tool used to get information into and out of a database. It is now being used by many database vendors as a standard way to manipulate data. This will mean many database programs can interact and exchange data. It also helps database servers and distributed databases since it can be used on a network as a way to communicate between database programs.

T

Terminal A point in a network at which data can either enter or leave. Examples are modems, personal computers, dumb terminals, and telephones.

Token A unique combination of bits. When a LAN workstation receives a token, it has now been given permission to transmit. (See **Token passing**.)

Token bus A LAN with bus topology that uses token passing as its access method. ARCnet and MAP LANs are the most popular of these types of networks.

Token passing An access method. A token is passed from workstation to workstation thereby passing permission to send a message. When you have the token, you can send. You then attach your message to the token which "carries" it around the LAN. Every station in between you and whom you want to send to, "sees" the message, but only the receiving workstation accepts it (because that's whom it's addressed to). When the receiving station gets the message, it releases the token to be used by the next station. The entire process of generating and passing tokens around the LAN takes fractions of a second.

Token-Ring Type of network hardware in which individual PCs are given access to the network by a token that passes from PC to PC in a ring. The IEEE standard for Token-Ring (802.5) has a raw data speed of 4M bits per second. Versions that work at 16M bits per second are also available.

Toplogy Description of the physical connections of a network. Or the description of the possible logical connections between nodes, indicating which pairs of nodes are able to communicate. Think of it as a map of the "road" between all the things attached to a LAN. Examples are bus, ring, star and tree.

Tree A LAN topology in which there is only one route between any two of the nodes on the network. The pattern of connections resembles a tree.

Twisted-pair Two insulated wires wrapped around (i.e. twisted around) each other. The pair of wires may be surrounded by a shield, a jacket or additional insulation, or similar pairs of wires. Twisted-pair wiring is most often used to connect telephones, terminals and computers to PBXs. Twisted-pair wiring has a misleading usefulness—its ubiquity (namely, it is in every building under the sun). However, it suffers several disadvantages. PBX wiring is often too thin. PBX wiring has often been spliced many times. PBX wiring goes to the wrong place. Namely, it "homes" back to the central PBX cabinet. Existing PBX wiring is not good for wiring LANs, for example. And finally, worst of all, most twisted-pair wire is not shielded. This makes it susceptible to electromagnetic interference. However, twisted-pair wiring is easier to install, less expensive and easier to change than coaxial cable, though its bandwidth (information carrying capacity) is usually smaller.

U

UNIX Computer operating system originally developed by AT&T. Also works on some personal computers. Considered to be very flexible and very powerful.

V

Virtual device A device provided to a computer—and any applications you run on that computer—via a network operating system. Virtual devices mimic actual physical devices, and include disks, serial ports, and printer ports. For example, a PC connected to a LAN might seem to the user as though it has a hard disk drive, when actually that drive only exsists as a virtual device—an area set aside on the hard disk of the LAN's disk server. Similarly, applications may "think" they are printing to a local printer, when actually output is being sent over the LAN to a print server. Virtual devices essentially act as a "front," hiding the LAN from users and applications software that might not otherwise be able to access it easily.

W

Wide area network A data communications network designed to serve an area of hundreds or thousands of miles. Public and private packet switching networks and the nationwide telephone network are good examples of wide area networks.

Windows Software from Microsoft (Bellvue, WA) that extends the DOS operating system to include a graphical user interface. Users can view text in multiple styles and graphics side-by-side in applications especially written for Windows (such as Word for Windows, Excel, and Pagemaker). Windows applications are now increasingly written specifically for LANs—they can, for example, display a LAN's topology on screen as a graphic, simplifying the chore of LAN administration. (See also Presentation Manager.) The term "windows" may also be used generically to describe any technique where a computer's screen is split in order to display output from several programs, or components of a single program, simultaneously.

Workstation Input/output device at which an operator works. Usually a personal computer, sometimes a terminal. A device which you can send data to or receive data from a computer.

WYSIWYG An acronym (pronounced "wizzy-wig") for What You See Is What You Get. Refers to the ability of software to display graphics on the monitor that look substantially the same as printer output.

Recommended Reading

BOOKS

LANs Explained, A Guide to Local Area Networks, by W. Scott Currie, Halsted Press, a division of John Wiley & Sons, New York, 1988.

Local Area Networks, An Introduction to the Technology, by John E. McNamara, Digital Press, Burlington, MA, 1985.

Understanding Local Area Networks, by Stan Schatt, Howard W. Sams & Company, Indianapolis, IN, 1987.

MAGAZINES

ComputerLand Magazine, published bi-monthly by ComputerLand Corporation, P.O. Box 9012, Pleasanton, CA, 94566

LAN Magazine, published monthly by Miller Freeman Publications, 500 Howard Street, San Francisco, CA, 94105.

LAN Technology, published monthly by M & T Publishing, Inc., 501 Galveston Drive, Redwood City, CA, 94063.

Acknowledgements

The publisher and editor of this ComputerLand Guide to Local Area Networks would like to thank the staff of *ComputerLand Magazine* and *LAN Magazine* for their assistance in putting together this book and for their generosity in providing us access to the valuable material they've published over the years. We urge all readers of this guide to subscribe and read regularly these two magazines for continuing, up-to-date information and guidance in the rapidly changing world of Local Area Networks.

Sources and specific author credits for the material in this book:

What is a LAN? (page 4) — From "The LAN Tutorial" by Aaron Brenner, *LAN Magazine*, August/88; and "A Guide to Networks" by David Gancher, ComputerLand Corporation, 1989.

Why Buy a LAN? (page 4) — From "Local Area Networks" by Steve Steinke, *Computerland Magazine*, January/February 1987: "The LAN Tutorial" by Aaron Brenner, *LAN Magazine*, August/88; and "A Guide to Networks" by David Gancher, ComputerLand Corporation, 1989.

Can a LAN Work in My Operation? (page 7) — From "Local Area Networks" by David Fogle, *ComputerLand Magazine*, March/April 1988.

How to Choose the Right LAN for Your Particular Business (page 11) — By David Fogle.

File Servers (page 19) — From "The LAN Tutorial" by Aaron Brenner, *LAN Magazine*, March/89

Print Servers (page 22) — From "The LAN Tutorial" by Aaron Brenner, *LAN Magazine*, July/89.

Server Hard Disks and Optical Disks (page 26) — From "Driving LANs" by Shyamala Reddy, *LAN Magazine*, May/89.

Fax Servers (page 28) — From "Files By Fax" by David Greenfield, *LAN Magazine*, April/89.

Workstations (page 32) — By David Fogle.

Cabling (page 35) — From "The LAN Tutorial" by Aaron Brenner, *LAN Magazine*, February/89.

Bridges (page 40) — From "The LAN Tutorial" by Aaron Brenner, *LAN Magazine*, June/89.

Network Operating Systems (page 47) — From "The LAN Tutorial" by Aaron Brenner, January/89.

Connecting PCs to Macs (page 52) — From "NetWare for Mac" by Gary Baker, *LAN Magazine*, June/89.

Introduction to Applications (page 60) — From "Guide to Local Area Network Software" by Jonathan Angel, *ComputerLand Magazine*, July/August 1989.

LAN Applications (page 61) — From "The LAN Tutorial," *LAN Magazine*, April/89.

Word Processors, Communications, Accounting, Spreadsheets, Desktop Publishing, Integrated Software, Groupware (pages 64 to 86) — From "Guide to Local Area Network Software" by Jonathan Angel, *ComputerLand Magazine*, July/August 1989.

Electronic Mail (page 65) — From "The Mail Minefield" by Gary Baker, *LAN Magazine*, April/89.

Database (page 74) — From "Instant Information" by Ed Tittel, *LAN Magazine*, November/88; and "The DBMS Design" by Aaron Brenner, *LAN Magazine*, November /89.

Printing (page 80) — From "Fit to Print" by Shyamala Reddy, *LAN Magazine*, June/89.

LAN Management Software (page 88) — From LAN Management by Jim Carr, *LAN Magazine*, December/89.

Protocol Analyzers (page 95) — From "The LAN Shrink" by Shyamala Reddy, *LAN Magazine*, December/89.

Backup (page 101) — From "The LAN Tutorial", *LAN Magazine*, December/89.

LAN Security (page 105) — From "The LAN Tutorial" by Aaron Brenner, *LAN Magazine*, August/89; and "Sensible Paranoia" and "For Your Eyes Only" by David Greenfield, *LAN Magazine*, April/89.

What Makes a Network Work (page 113) — By Doug Thompson.

Glossary (page 150) — From The Local Area Network Glossary, by *LAN Magazine*/89.

All other introductory and editorial text written by Alan Rinzler, who also thanks David Gancher, David Fogle, and Jonathan Angel for their technical support and invaluable assistance overall.